DATE DUE

Samuel Johnson, Biographer

SAMUEL JOHNSON, BIOGRAPHER

Robert Folkenflik

CORNELL UNIVERSITY PRESS
Ithaca and London

Cornell University Press gratefully acknowledges a grant
from the Andrew W. Mellon Foundation that aided
in bringing this book to publication.

First published 1978 by Cornell University Press.
Published in the United Kingdom by Cornell University Press Ltd.,
2-4 Brook Street, London WIY IAA.

International Standard Book Number 0-8014-0968-3
Library of Congress Catalog Card Number 78-58050
Printed in the United States of America
*Librarians: Library of Congress cataloging information
appears on the last page of the book.*

For Vivian

Contents

Preface

Johnson once said he could write "the Life of a Broomstick," or so Boswell quotes a source he does not identify.[1] Whether this variation on Swift's famous "Meditation upon a Broomstick" is an authentic Johnsonian dictum or was simply foisted upon him by a contemporary is of less importance than the recognition of Johnson as a highly skilled professional biographer.

The time has come for a longer look at Johnson as a biographer. Although there are many articles on the subject, several theses devoted to the sources of his biographies and the making of some individual lives, and good chapters in recent books by Lawrence Lipking, Paul Fussell, Donald Greene, and Leopold Damrosch (this last appearing too late for me to take into account), there is no book in English devoted to the whole of his biographical production. Bergen Evans' Harvard doctoral thesis, "Dr. Johnson as a Biographer" (1932), comes closest, but it is essentially a source study and remains unpublished. Frede Warburg's published Hamburg dissertation, *Samuel Johnson als Biograph* (1927), a modest sixty-page work, has never been translated, and it suffers from a superficial approach. With the great resurgence of interest in Johnson as critic and moralist in recent years, a reassessment of the literature he loved most and wrote best would seem to be overdue.

In the course of my study I have come to believe that

1. *Boswell's Life of Johnson*, ed. G. B. Hill (Oxford: Clarendon Presss, 1905), II, 389.

9

Johnson's achievement as a biographer, particularly as a literary biographer, has often been misinterpreted. Although almost all of the historians of biography have honored Johnson as a great biographer, or at least a great theorist, they have not recognized the sophistication with which he approaches the writing of a literary life. This is so perhaps because the broad outline of literary biography which they trace begins at a primitive time when the writings of an author figured in an account of his life merely as *res gestae* and ends with the nineteenth or twentieth century, when interest in the connections between life and art fully blossomed. And, wedded as most of these historians are to some conception of "true" biography, they take this relentless movement toward ever greater unity of artist and work as a norm; anyone who lags behind his age in yoking the man and his writings together does not fare well. That is to say, the historian of biography generally subscribes to some form of expressive theory concerning the relationship of art and the artist—as, for that matter, do most modern literary biographers. In any history of biography which traces such a development, Johnson's achievement as a biographer, for reasons that will become apparent, is sure to be downgraded or distorted. In order to see that achievement whole and in relation to the biographies and biographical theory of his day, I have attempted to focus on the *Lives of the Poets*, and, to a lesser degree, on his earlier biographies in the context of the totality of his thought, and to show how his conception of man determines their nature. For although Johnson's biographies are related in a general sense to Christian and classical biography, they are far more profoundly influenced by Christian and classical conceptions of man that had not been central to biographical writings before his own appeared. Johnson is best known as a literary biographer, but I have thought it right to speak of him as a biographer generally with special emphasis on literary biography. Since he thought of his subjects first as men and then as writers, an exclusive focus would distort his conception of biography.

This study, then, does not impose an a priori conception of biography upon its subject. I have continually asked myself what Johnson was trying to do in any given situation, and anything of

value here will have come from the attempt to take him more
fully on his own terms. I shall have much to say about the many
critics from his time to ours who have attacked him for not being
William Mason, James Boswell, or any number of undistin-
guished eighteenth-century panegyrists.

Since my purpose is to show the principles and the sensibility
which underlie Johnsonian biography and the nature of the
biographies themselves, I have thought it unnecessary to correct
Johnson on matters of fact unless the mistake is relevant to the
point under consideration or misleading to the reader. On the
question of Johnson's accuracy there has been much sharp criticism, taking its impetus, in many cases, from Boswell's petulant
detail of Johnson's failure to correct certain particulars that
Boswell himself had supplied. The most thorough student of
Johnson's biographies and their sources has come to the conclusion that "three fourths of the errors in the *Lives of the Poets* are
to be found in the sources from which he drew his materials, and
the number of places in which he corrected erroneous sources
amounts to a creditable list."[2] More important is the Crocean
distinction—not without dangers, but nonetheless true—that
one can write a weak chronicle and good history. Johnson writes
good biographies even at times when his grasp of the facts that
form the chronicle, the day-by-day unfolding of the events of a
life, is uncertain.

Chapter 1 sketches the eighteenth-century interest in biography and particularly Johnson's interest, as displayed in his aid
to others, his numerous abortive biographical projects, and the
variety of his actual productions. Chapter 2 considers Johnson's
biographical program in the context of his conception of man,
and his opposition to the historians and panegyrical biographers

2. Bergen Evans, "Dr. Johnson as a Biographer" (Ph.D. diss., Harvard, 1932),
I, 200. But see James Lyons Battersby, Jr., "Samuel Johnson's *Life of Addison*:
Sources, Composition, and Structure" (Ph.D. diss., Cornell, 1965), pp. 205–22,
and George Lorant Lam, "Johnson's *Lives of the Poets*: Their Origin, Test and
History, with Remarks on Sources and Comment on His *Life of Cowley*" (Ph.D.
diss., Cornell, 1938), p. 439. These studies present less sympathetic views. I have
found Johnson to be both the corrector and the perpetrator of mistakes. Though
he was not as painstakingly accurate as his friend Edmond Malone, he would
seem to have been a far more conscientious scholar than all but a fraction of the
biographers of his time.

of his day. It concentrates on his belief in the uniformity of mankind as well as in the characteristics of the individual, and shows the importance of the private side of man's existence for Johnsonian biography. Chapter 3 tries to find the common traits of those men treated with greatest approbation in his biographies. In Chapter 4 the emphasis is on Johnson as moral interpreter and artist. With Chapter 5 there is a shift from biography as the life of any man to literary biography. The forms of Johnson's early biographies are considered with respect to the form of the *Lives of the Poets*. Chapters 6 and 7 deal with exclusively literary questions and are complementary. The former examines Johnson's reasons for separating life and art and shows the importance of this separation in the *Lives of the Poets*. The latter determines that he is interested nevertheless in certain connections between life and art and examines his way of envisaging the experience, sincerity, and originality of the poet. Chapter 8 attributes the differences between Johnson's style in the *Rambler* and the *Lives* to his idea of biographical style and explores his use of a plainer basic style, varied by a repertory of stylistic means, that can easily accommodate factual material without sacrificing the possibilities of expressiveness. Chapter 9 considers in detail a work that is arguably Johnson's greatest and unquestionably the one that best fulfills his own conditions for biographical excellence.

I hope that my choice of topics covers a range of the inevitable and the original; if I have consciously slighted any, I have at least done so with the knowledge that they are the chestnuts of Johnsonian scholarship—his inaccuracy, pomposity, prejudices, and so on—which have been emphasized out of all proportion to their significance and have often blocked the way to a fuller appreciation of Johnson's achievement.

Johnson has long been attacked for prejudices; I have emphasized his principles. He has long been accused of shirking research; I have emphasized his conscious artistry. I must admit at the same time that a great proportion of my commentary is based on biographies written over a four-year period toward the end of Johnson's long life, and that he certainly had varying degrees of interest in his fifty subjects and varying amounts of material to work with. We have, however—to paraphrase Boswell—seen too much of lazy Sam and prejudiced Sam. This book presents a very different Johnson.

I owe a long-standing debt of gratitude to Samuel Holt Monk, whose graduate courses at the University of Minnesota first directed me toward the study of eighteenth-century literature. David Novarr, Douglas Archibald, and Scott Elledge of Cornell University read an earlier version of this book. Professor Elledge volunteered to read my manuscript in its new incarnation. I would not have put him in double jeopardy in this way, but I am grateful once again.

Parts of Chapters 2 and 7 were read in 1972 as papers at the annual meeting of the American Society for Eighteenth-Century Studies at UCLA in March and of the Johnson Society of the Central Region at the University of Toronto in May. I am grateful to William Cameron, chairman of the Biography Section of the ASECS, for help and to George Falle, president of the Johnson Society, for hospitality. When the former paper was accepted for publication as "Johnson's Art of Anecdote" in volume III of *Studies in Eighteenth-Century Culture*, Harold Pagliaro, the editor, made useful comments. The essay is reprinted by permission of The Press of Case Western Reserve University (Cleveland, 1973; copyright © 1973 by The Press of Case Western Reserve University).

For various kinds of aid and conversation I want to thank M. H. Abrams, W. J. Bate, James L. Clifford, Donald D. Eddy, George Ford, Donald J. Greene, Geoffrey H. Hartman, Frederick W. Hilles, William R. Keast, Herman W. Liebert, Jacob Perlstein, Joseph H. Summers, and the students in my graduate and undergraduate courses in eighteenth-century literature who participated in the shaping of some parts of this book. I am especially indebted to Paul K. Alkon and Carey McIntosh, who read the whole manuscript.

I am also grateful to the staffs of the New York Public Library, the Pierpont Morgan Library, and the libraries of Cornell University, Columbia University, Yale University, Harvard Univer-

14 Preface

sity, and the University of Rochester. Mary Hyde generously permitted me to use her unparalleled private collection of Johnsonian materials.

While I was at work on the manuscript for this book, Cornell awarded me a Class of 1916 Fellowship, and the University of Rochester provided a Summer Research Fellowship and typing aid. An opportune fellowship from the National Endowment for the Humanities enabled me to spend 1973-74 in London reading history and completing my study. Bernhard Kendler and his courteous and efficient colleagues at Cornell University Press were all most helpful. George H. Ford, my chairman for a number of years, supported my various applications. For assistance in London I am indebted to the staffs of the British Library (especially the Keeper of Manuscripts, who has kindly allowed me to publish Johnson's Memorandum on the Life of Pope—Add. Ms. 5994), the Institute of Historical Research, and the libraries of the University of London.

My greatest debt, for help from start to finish, is to my wife, who often felt about my time spent with Johnson the way Margaret Montgomerie Boswell felt about her husband's.

ROBERT FOLKENFLIK

Laguna Beach, California

Abbreviations

WORKS OF JOHNSON AND BOSWELL

I have tried to limit the abbreviations used in this book to the most important and frequently cited standard works.

Hebrides   James Boswell. *Journal of a Tour to the Hebrides with Samuel Johnson, LL.D.* Ed. Frederick A. Pottle and Charles H. Bennett. New York: The Literary Guild, 1936.

Letters   *The Letters of Samuel Johnson: With Mrs. Thrale's Genuine Letters to Him.* Ed. R. W. Chapman. 3 vols. Oxford: Clarendon Press, 1952.

Life   James Boswell. *Boswell's Life of Johnson.* Ed. George Birkbeck Hill and L. F. Powell. 6 vols. Oxford: Clarendon Press, 1934-50.

Lives (I, II, III)   Samuel Johnson. *Lives of the English Poets.* Ed. G. B. Hill. 3 vols. Oxford: Clarendon Press, 1905. Usually appearing in the text by volume and page only. This edition is based on the 1783 *Lives* and includes a number of variant readings.

Rasselas   Samuel Johnson. *The History of Rasselas, Prince of Abissinia: A Tale.* Ed. R. W. Chapman. Oxford: Clarendon Press, 1927.

Savage   Samuel Johnson. *Life of Savage.* Ed. Clarence Tracy. Oxford: Clarendon Press, 1971.

Works   Samuel Johnson. *Works.* [Ed. F. P. Walesby]. 11 vols. Oxford: Talboys and Wheeler, 1825.

Yale   Samuel Johnson. *The Yale Edition of the Works of Samuel Johnson.* New Haven: Yale University Press, 1958-.

I. *Diaries, Prayers, and Annals.* Ed. E. L. McAdam, Jr., with Donald and Mary Hyde. © 1958 by Yale University Press, Inc.

II. *"The Idler" and "The Adventurer."* Ed. W. J. Bate, John M. Bullitt, and L. F. Powell. Copyright © 1963 by Yale University.

III, IV, V. *"The Rambler."* Ed. W. J. Bate and Albrecht B. Strauss. Copyright © 1969 by Yale University.

VI. *Poems*. Ed. E. L. McAdam, Jr., with George Milne. Copyright
© 1964 by Yale University.
VII, VIII. *Johnson on Shakespeare*. Ed. Arthur Sherbo. Copyright
© 1968 by Yale University.
IX. *A Journey to the Western Islands of Scotland*. Ed. Mary Lascelles.
Copyright © 1971 by Yale University.
X. *Political Writings*. Ed. Donald J. Greene. Copyright © 1977 by
Yale University.

PERIODICALS

BNYPL	*Bulletin of the New York Public Library*
ECS	*Eighteenth-Century Studies*
JBS	*The Journal of British Studies*
MLN	*Modern Language Notes*
MP	*Modern Philology*
N&Q	*Notes and Queries*
PQ	*Philological Quarterly*
RES	*Review of English Studies*
SEL	*Studies in English Literature*
SP	*Studies in Philology*
UTQ	*University of Toronto Quarterly*

Samuel Johnson, Biographer

In biography there can be no question that he excelled, beyond all who have attempted that species of composition; upon which, indeed, he set the highest value.

Boswell on Johnson

CHAPTER 1

Introduction: Johnson and Eighteenth-Century Biography

"The proper study of mankind is man." Pope's gnomic line, which Samuel Johnson frequently quoted with approval, might easily be taken as a motto for the eighteenth century. But, as Imlac admonished Rasselas, anyone whose "business is with man" must take into account a great deal. And in that age, though the study of man took many forms, perhaps none was as valued for its presentation of human reality as biography.

By careful selection it is not too difficult to prove that any age was interested in anything; but if we limit our inquiry to the members of the Johnson circle and those just outside its circumference, we will not find before or after as impressive a group of biographers. Even Bloomsbury cannot boast a pair of biographers to match Johnson and Boswell (or a third like Goldsmith). Several of Johnson's own biographers are familiar: Boswell, whose European reputation was founded in part on his "Memoirs of Pascal Paoli"; Sir John Hawkins, who had also written a short life of Izaak Walton; Mrs. Thrale, Johnson's anecdotist; Arthur Murphy, who wrote the lives of Fielding, Garrick, and Tacitus. Some less well-known friends wrote less well-known biographies: Thomas Tyers, William Shaw, William Cooke. But it did not take Johnson's death to make biographers of a number of his friends. Anna Williams, the blind poet who lived in Johnson's house for most of the thirty years they were acquainted, had translated Père la Bléterie's *Life of the Emperor Julian* (1745) several years before they met Dr. Thomas Lawrence, one of Johnson's physicians and an old friend, wrote a Latin life of Frank Nicholls and an English one of William Harvey. Thomas Davies, the actor-turned-bookseller who introduced Boswell to Johnson, wrote a biography of their friend David Garrick. Goldsmith wrote and translated several biographies, one of which, *The Life of Richard Nash, Esq.*, is among the great biographies of the age. Bishop Percy, who had contributed to the *Biographia Britannica*, struggled valiantly to write a biography of Goldsmith, but finally at the turn of the century gave his materials and the pages he had written to some London booksellers to be edited.[1] Sir Joshua Reynolds wrote biographical sketches. Edmond Malone helped Boswell with the *Life of Johnson* and later wrote a short biography of Reynolds and an important scholarly *Life of Dryden*, perhaps the immediate ancestor of modern academic biography. Dr. Charles Burney wrote two biographies, and his daughter Fanny wrote an early nineteenth-century biography of him. The first work of Sir William Jones, as befitted that great polylingual orientalist, was a translation of a Persian life of Nadir Shah into French.[2] Such friends as John Hoole, John Hawkesworth, Samuel Derrick, Thomas Birch, Robert Shiels, and William Oldys all wrote biographies.

Johnson, who was ready to help in almost any literary endeavor, turned over his "Life of Ascham" to James Bennet to publish as his own and wrote the "Life of Zachary Pearce" for Pearce's chaplain John Derby. He would suggest a biographical design to a friend and then give aid and advice in the writing. At the death of Samuel Foote, the comedian and playwright, he said, "Murphy ought to write his life, at least to give the world a Footeana. . . . I would really have his life written with diligence" (*Letters*, II, 231). And on the death of Bennet Langton's Uncle

---

1. For Tyers, Shaw, and Cooke see Robert E. Kelley and O. M. Brack, Jr., *Samuel Johnson's Early Biographers* (Iowa City: University of Iowa Press, 1971). See Katherine Balderston, *The History and Sources of Percy's Memoir of Goldsmith* (Cambridge: Cambridge University Press, 1926), for an account of the peregrinations of this biography.

2. Mentioned by Scott Elledge in *Eighteenth-Century Critical Essays* (Ithaca: Cornell University Press, 1961), II, 1174.

Peregrine, he told Langton why his uncle deserved commemoration, urging the usefulness of such an account to society and
the necessity of gathering his materials quickly:

We must now endeavour to preserve what is left us, his example of Piety,
and economy. I hope you make what enquiries you can, and write down
what is told you. The little things which distinguish domestick characters
are soon forgotten, if you delay to enquire you will have no information,
if you neglect to write, information will be in vain.
His art of life certainly deserves to be known and studied. He lived in
plenty and elegance upon an income which to many would appear
indigent and to most, scanty. How he lived therefore every man has an
interest in knowing. [*Letters*, I, 186]

Johnson clearly thought the writing of biography as a com-
memorative act was valuable to the biographer as well as his
readers.[3] Langton followed this advice, and Boswell printed his
short account of his uncle in a long note in the *Life of Johnson*
(*Life*, II, 18–19n.).

Johnson was not always this successful. Sir John Hawkins says
that he and Johnson tried to persuade Samuel Dyer to write a
life of Erasmus, but Dyer settled for the less strenuous task of
revising a translation of Plutarch's *Lives*.[4] In 1760, Johnson
helped Hawkins himself, who was writing a life of Izaak Walton
which was frequently reprinted and which Johnson praised
many years later as "very diligently collected, and very elegantly
composed."[5]

In a letter to an unknown Oxford correspondent, perhaps
Thomas Warton, Johnson suggested the writing of a life of
Richard I or of Edward the Confessor (*Letters*, I, 103). These are
not offhand suggestions; he considered that he had a proprie-
tary right to such projects and cautioned his correspondent to
keep them secret. He was a professional writer and would either
use them himself or reassign them to others. Thomas Davies
acknowledged in the "Advertisement" to his *Life of Garrick*

3. As did Plutarch. See the beginning of his "Timoleon."
4. *The Life of Samuel Johnson, LL.D.,* 2d ed. (London, 1787), pp. 227–28.
5. *Letters*, I, 405. The fullest account of this work is in Bertram H. Davis, "The
Rival *Angler* Editors: Moses Browne and John Hawkins," *English Writers of the
Eighteenth Century* (New York: Columbia University Press, 1971), pp. 90–108.

(1780) that Johnson had provided "several diverting anecdotes" and an account of Garrick's early life.[6] In his *Life of Swift* (III, 1) Johnson mentions that he had given John Hawkesworth the plan by which Hawkesworth wrote his *Life of Swift*. The "plan" was in all probability the notion that Delany's and Orrery's biographies were essentially complementary. W. R. Keast has shown that Robert Shiels, who wrote "Cibber's" *Lives of the Poets*, one of the sources of Johnson's *Lives*, was indebted to Johnson for many passages and abridged Johnson's lives of Savage and Roscommon with relatively few verbal changes.[7] And Johnson recounted sending Samuel Derrick to Dryden's relatives in search of materials for Derrick's "Life of John Dryden, Esq." (*Hebrides*, p. 204). In the many letters Johnson sent to John Nichols asking for books or miscellaneous information while he was undertaking the *Lives of the Poets*, he suggests that Nichols should write a supplement to Anthony à Wood's *Athenae Oxonienses*; that he should collect more information on Jortin, Markland, and Thirlby (a later letter supplied some anecdotes about Thirlby to get him started); and, in a touching phrase, that "perhaps we may talk a life over."[8] But Johnson's encouragement of others was only one side of a sustained interest in biography which manifested itself in a multitude of biographical schemes.

2

Johnson's defense of moral knowledge over scientific knowledge in the *Life of Milton* puts second only to religion "an acquaintance with the history of mankind, and with those examples which may be said to embody truth and prove by events the reasonableness of opinions" (I, 100). In reading through Johnson's works and the vast corpus of Johnsoniana, one en-

6. *Memoirs of the Life of David Garrick, Esq.* (London, 1780), I, A4 ʳ⁻ᵛ. Davies, in a passage regretting that he had no further help from Johnson, implies that the writing in the biography is all his own.

7. "Johnson and 'Cibber's' *Lives of the Poets*, 1753," in *Restoration and Eighteenth-Century Literature: Essays in Honor of Alan Dugald McKillop*, ed. Carroll Camden (Chicago: University of Chicago Press, 1963), pp. 89–101, and see also James L. Battersby, "Johnson and Shiels: Biographers of Addison," *SEL*, 9 (1969), 521–53.

8. *Letters*, II, 511, 514; III, 238. And see Frederick W. Hilles, "Johnson's Correspondence with Nichols: Some Facts and a Query," *PQ*, 48 (1969), 226–33.

counters a large number of unfulfilled biographical projects and a frequently expressed interest in writing particular lives. The majority of these unwritten lives, like the majority of those he wrote, would have been literary biographies. Very early in his career he published proposals for an edition of Politian's poems, which would have included a *vita Politiani* (*Life*, I, 90). The great English writers were, of course, high on his list. He intended to write the life of Chaucer, and Sir John Hawkins claims that he "had bound himself to write the life of Shakespeare" for Coxeter.[9] His comments on Rowe's "Life of Shakespeare," which he affixed to his own edition, indicate that the materials were too scanty. He also planned an edition of Bacon with his life (*Life*, III, 194). George III suggested that Johnson should write the literary biography of England (*Life*, II, 40), and in particular a life of Spenser, but in the case of Spenser neither the king nor the booksellers, who later made the same suggestion, were successful. Johnson was willing, but "Warton had left little or nothing for him to do."[10] He had at one time intended to edit Walton's *Lives* and to write a life of Walton (*Letters*, I, 404; *Life*, II, 520). But when Dr. George Horne asked for help with an edition he was planning, Johnson accidentally put him off the project by claiming, erroneously, that Lord Hailes was already at work on one (*Life*, II, 279). He told Mrs. Garrick that he would be "the editor of [Garrick's] works, and the historian of his life" if she wished it.[11] And for a time he had possession of Bishop Percy's materials for a life of Goldsmith.[12] These last two projects were certainly motivated by the wish to commemorate his dead friends. All we have now are the brief encomiums in his lives of Smith and Parnell.

9. *Life*, IV, 381n.; Hawkins, *The Life of Samuel Johnson, LL.D.*, 2d ed., p. 440.

10. *Life*, IV, 410, 491n.; the quotation is from Thomas Tyers, *A Biographical Sketch of Dr. Samuel Johnson*, ed. Gerald D. Meyer (Los Angeles: Augustan Reprint Society, 1952), p. 20, and see *European Magazine*, 1 (1782).

11. Arthur Murphy, "An Essay on the Life and Genius of Samuel Johnson, LL.D.," *Works*, I, lxvii.

12. J. M. Osborn, "Edmond Malone and Dr. Johnson," in *Johnson, Boswell, and Their Circle: Essays Presented to Lawrence Fitzroy Powell in Honour of his Eighty-Fourth Birthday*, ed. Mary M. Lascelles, James L. Clifford, J. D. Fleeman, and John P. Hardy (Oxford: Clarendon Press, 1965) p. 4: Balderston, *Percy's Memoir of Goldsmith*, pp. 20–23.

Not all of his projected lives were of literary men. In the 1740's he wanted very much to write a life of King Alfred. Years later he thought of writing a life of Cromwell, which he expected would be of interest because Cromwell had risen from lowly origins to become the ruler of the English nation. Cajoling General Oglethorpe into writing an autobiography, he said that he would write his life himself if he were given the materials (*Life*, I, 177; IV, 235; II, 351). And after a discussion about Johnson's schoolfellow Joseph Simpson, a well-off barrister whose marriage to a prostitute and heavy drinking turned him into a charity case, "but still with a dignity of deportment," Johnson "seemed willing to write Joe's life, and wished to have materials collected."[13] Perhaps the most unexpected of his projects was a biography of Ignatius Sancho, a former slave (if we may trust a hand-written note in a copy of Sancho's Shandean *Letters* bearing the bookplate of Joseph Jekyll, his biographer: "Previous to the publication in 1782 Dr. Johnson had promised to write the Life of Ignatius Sancho, which afterwards he neglected to do").[14] Appropriately, one of his large projects was "Lives of Illustrious Persons, as well of the active as the learned" (*Life*, IV, 382n.). That this collection, in which he intended to imitate Plutarch (yet another project was the translation of Plutarch's *Lives*), would have leaned toward the learned we can have little doubt.

Other projected biographical collections, by themselves or as parts of larger works, were the "Lives of the Painters," the "Lives of the Philosophers," the "History of the Revival of Learning in Europe . . . with the lives of the most eminent patrons and the most eminent early professors of all kinds of learning in different countries."[15] Such projects, like the *Lives of the Poets*, hark back to the Greek and Roman interest in a series of lives

13. James Boswell, *The Ominous Years: 1774–1776*, ed. Charles Ryskamp and Frederick A. Pottle (New York: McGraw Hill, 1963), pp. 323, 324.

14. Quoted by Paul Edwards in his introduction to *Letters of the Late Ignatius Sancho, an African* (London: Dawsons, 1968), p. vi.

15. George Monck Berkeley claimed that Johnson asked his family's permission to write a life of the great Bishop Berkeley. The circumstances look suspicious. See A. A. Luce, *The Life of George Berkeley, Bishop of Cloyne* (London: Thomas Nelson and Sons, 1949), for an account. For the lives of the painters see Tyers, *A Biographical Sketch*, p. 15; for the other projects, *Life*, IV, 381–382n.

grouped by profession as an attempt to deal with types as well as individuals.[16] His uncompiled "Collection of Letters from English Authours" would have included "some account of the writers" (*Life*, IV, 382n.). Johnson believed that "an edition of a posthumous work appears imperfect and neglected without some account of the author ("Life of Browne," *Works*, VI, 475). On his deathbed Johnson agreed to write the life of John Scott, a Quaker poet and essayist. Whether he would have carried out this plan one cannot say, for he died within a few months. His friend John Hoole later wrote the life and told this story in a preface.[17] It is not surprising that Johnson was "asked to undertake the new edition of the *Biographia Britannica*," the major English eighteenth-century biographical encyclopedia; nor, with all these biographical schemes in his head, is it suprising that he came to regret having turned down the offer (*Life*, III, 174).

There was, however, a limit to the number of possible biographies he would entertain. When a bumptious young nobleman enthusiastically pressed the idea that Johnson, who had just finished the *Lives of the Poets*, might now begin the lives of the prose writers, his only answer was "Sit down, Sir!"[18] Yet according to a contemporary he was willing at about that time to contemplate writing the lives of the English lawyers.[19]

Johnson's actual career as a biographer was almost coterminous with his career as a professional writer. We have no idea of the nature of his essays for the *Birmingham Journal*, in 1732–33, but from October 1738, when he wrote the "Life of Father Paul Sarpi," a sketch of under twenty-five hundred words, as his first article for the *Gentleman's Magazine*, until 1784, the year of his death, when he revised the "Life of Edward Cave" for inclusion

16. See Arnaldo Momigliano, *The Development of Greek Biography* (Cambridge, Mass.: Harvard University Press, 1971), p. 13.

17. See John Scott, *Critical Essays* (London, 1785) and *Letters*, III, 225. The project is recounted in Herman W. Liebert's *Johnson's Last Literary Project* (New Haven: Privately printed, 1948).

18. Hester Lynch Thrale Piozzi, *Anecdotes of the Late Samuel Johnson, LL.D.*, 2d ed. (London, 1786), p. 295.

19. See Constance Russell's short account of her ancestor Sir Henry Russell in "Sizars and the Woolsack," *N & Q*, 146 (1924), 399–400.

in the *Biographia Britannica*, there was no decade in which he did
not write at least one biography. A word or two about the *Gentleman's Magazine*: This periodical, perhaps the first modern
magazine, was probably as much for gentlemen in its day as
Playboy is for playboys. It was evidently directed at the busy and
upwardly mobile (or at least aspiring) merchant, as the
subtitle—*Traders Monthly Intelligencer*—appearing in an advertisement for the forthcoming publication suggests. Billed as "a
Collection of all Matters of Information and Amusement," it was
a kind of *Reader's Digest*, with excerpts from current newspapers,
original essays, and poetry. So, from the beginning of his career
Johnson was in the position of writing for an audience we would
now call middle-class and at once purveying culture and information to them.[20] Through the late thirties and early forties he
wrote lives of recently dead scholars, patriotic lives of the admi-
rals Blake and Drake, various short lives of medical figures for
Robert James's *Medicinal Dictionary* (1743), and, in 1744, the
book on which his fame as a biographer for all but the last few
years of his life was to rest, *An Account of the Life of Mr. Richard
Savage, Son of the Earl Rivers*. After this time he wrote two more
lives for the *Gentleman's Magazine*, the "Life of Roscommon"
(1748) and the "Life of Cave," the magazine's founder and
editor (1754). His other periodical biographies were the "Life of
Francis Cheynel," a zealous Puritan divine, in the *Student* (1751)
and the "Memoirs of the King of Prussia" in the *Literary
Magazine* (1756). In 1742 his "Life of Sydenham" had appeared
as the preface to John Swan's edition of the *Works of Sydenham*,
and in the following decades he wrote prefatory biographies of
Sir Thomas Browne (1756), Roger Ascham (1761), and Zachary
Pearce (1777).[21] This biographical activity was capped by the
appearance of the *Prefaces, Biographical and Critical, to the Works of
the English Poets* (1779–81), later to be known (though never so

20. For the *Gentleman's Magazine* see C[arl] Lennart Carlson, *The First
Magazine: A History of the Gentleman's Magazine* (Providence: Brown University
Press, 1938); the advertisement, found in the *Universal Spectator*, January 30,
1731, is quoted on p. 30.

21. The biography of Browne prefaced the *Christian Morals*; that of Ascham, *The
Works of Ascham*, ostensibly edited by James Bennet; that of Pearce, Pearce's
Commentary on the Four Apostles, edited by John Derby.

designated by Johnson) as the *Lives of the Poets*. And on these biographies, so various and so much of a piece, we shall focus.

Since I believe that the consistency of Johnson's thought permits the selection of evidence from all of his writings, I must deal with the most serious attack on this position. In "The Moral and Philosophical Basis of Johnson and Boswell's Idea of Biography," Anthony J. Tillinghast asserts that there was a change in Johnson's basic attitude with respect to the relative merits of biography and autobiography between 1751 and 1759.[22] He bases his opinion on Johnson's praise of biography in *Rambler* No. 60 and preference of autobiography to biography in *Idler* No. 84. But the *Rambler* essay is really praising biographical literature in general; Johnson rarely makes a distinction between the two kinds, and the word "autobiography" did not yet exist. His attitude is consistent, and Tillinghast has evidently overlooked Johnson's statement in favor of the memoir-writer in his "Review of the *Account of the Conduct of the Dutchess of Marlborough*" (1742): "Authors of this kind have, at least, an incontestable superiority over those whose passions are the same, and whose knowledge is less. It is evident that those who write in their own defence, discover often more impartiality, and less contempt of evidence, than the advocates which faction or interest have raised in their favour."[23] These are the same grounds for his preference in *Idler* No. 84. His theoretical position on the principles of biography remains, as far as I can tell, unchanged throughout his forty-five years as a professional biographer.

Johnson's *Lives*, coming late in his career, has often been taken as a book of wisdom, and of this view there should be no complaint.[24] His whole life was excellent preparation for the

---

22. In *Johnsonian Studies*, ed. Magdi Wahba (Cairo: Privately printed, 1962), pp. 115-31.

23. *Works*, VI, 5. The *Supplement* to the *OED* finally pushes the first use of "autobiography" back into the eighteenth century, when it appeared in a 1797 review of Isaac D'Israeli in the *Monthly Review*. The first user, previously unidentified as far as I know, was William Taylor of Norwich.

24. For a few examples see Walter Raleigh, "Johnson's Lives of the Poets," in *Six Essays on Johnson* (Oxford: Clarendon Press, 1910); Ian Watt, "Dr. Johnson and the Literature of Experience," in *Johnsonian Studies*, ed. Wahba, 15-22.

writing of literary biography: the bookseller's son who attended Oxford and became a man of all literary trades; the journalist, reporter, and reviewer; the Harleian bibliographer; the *Dictionary* compiler; the editor of Shakespeare—all played their part. He wrote poetry, essays, fiction, and a drama. His daily life was literature. He was a friend of Savage and Collins, an acquaintance of Thomson, and Mallet, was early brought to the attention of Pope and Swift, and had many friends in common with his subjects. But beyond his personal knowledge of those whose lives he wrote, the breadth of his literary experience, his sheer scope, enabled him to touch on the lives of his subjects in a variety of ways. In the *Lives of the Poets* we are even more apt to be impressed with his accumulated wisdom than with his ability to draw on specific knowledge.

CHAPTER 2

"Trifles with Dignity": The Task of Johnsonian Biography

The objections of Samuel Johnson's contemporary Robert Potter to the *Lives of the Poets* can be seen as an attack on Johnson's conception of biography: the emphasis on private and domestic affairs, the use of minute particulars and anecdotes, and the concern for the uniform nature of man:

We are sorry to see the masculine spirit of Dr. Johnson descending to . . . "anile garrulity." In reading the life of any eminent person we wish to be informed of the qualities which gave him the superiority over other men: when we are poorly put off with paltry circumstances, which are common to him with common men, we receive neither instruction nor pleasure. We know that the greatest men are subject to the infirmities of human nature equally with the meanest; why then are these infirmities recorded? Can it be of any importance to us to be told how many pair of stockings the author of the Essay on Man wore? Achilles and Thersites eat, and drank, and slept; in these things the Hero was not distinguished from the buffoon: are we made the wiser or the better by being informed that the translator of Homer stewed his Lampreys in a silver dish?[1]

While following the well-established "doctrine of dignity," this criticism anticipates the age of hero worship and its ethic of biographical suppression: it leads to a division of mankind into men and supermen and an oversimplification of each. Johnson's belief in the uniform nature of man forces us to understand the differences between the hero and the buffoon with respect to

1. *An Inquiry into some Passages in Dr. Johnson's "Lives of the Poets": Particularly His Observations on Lyric Poetry and the Odes of Gray* (London, 1783), p. 4.

their common humanity, and permits us to recognize the complexity of the individual.

In an age that saw the beginnings of realism in the novel, Johnson spoke for biographical realism. He explicitly opposes his own methods to the idealization of panegyrists and historians. His work rests on the assumption that men are essentially similar and that the business of the biographer is to relate those facts which are common to human experience.

Ultimately, the differences between Johnson and the historians can be seen as a conflict about the nature of man and the constituent qualities of human dignity. On the continent Lessing, in a review of Voltaire's *Essay on Manners* (1753), assessed the relative merits of biography and history: "Either one considers man in particular or in general. Of the first approach one can hardly say it is the noblest pursuit of man. What is it to know man in particular? It is to know fools and scoundrels. . . .The case is quite different with the study of man in general. Here he exhibits greatness and his divine origin."[2] And Voltaire's own comments on biography were equally stringent. The "all-too-human" was, for him, beneath the notice of history.[3] In England, the best historians felt much the same way. Hume, a year after Lessing's review, unwillingly described James I, rod in hand, instructing his ignorant favorite Robert Carr, and remarked: "History charges herself willingly with a relation of the great crimes, or the great virtues of mankind; but she appears to fall from her dignity, when necessitated to dwell on such frivolous events and ignoble personages."[4]

Although Johnson would undoubtedly agree that such events are undignified, his conception of human nature would not permit him to ignore them. Man's frailty and his foibles are intrinsically a part of his nature; to leave them out because they do not display greatness is to misrepresent the nature of man, and, therefore, to make one's narrative useless. Johnson's objec-

2. Quoted by Ernst Cassirer in *The Philosophy of the Enlightenment*, trans. Fritz C. A. Koelln and James P. Pettigrove (1932; rpt. Boston: Beacon Press, 1964), p. 216.
3. Cassirer, *Enlightenment*, p. 216.
4. David Hume, *The History of Great Britain* (Edinburgh, 1754), I, 48.

tions to the historians' reasoning stress the deceptiveness of biography and history that focus exclusively on man as hero: "He that recounts the life of another, commonly dwells most upon conspicuous events, lessens the familiarity of his tale to increase its dignity, shews his favourite at a distance decorated and magnified like the ancient actors in their tragick dress, and endeavours to hide the man that he may produce a hero" (*Idler* No. 84, *Yale*, II, 262). Since the purpose of biography is to provide morally useful examples, the depiction of a subject as essentially different in kind from other men (and for Johnson any man who appeared to have no foibles and only a public existence was certainly different in kind) would severely limit its application. If the subject is perfect, the reader may admire him, but he will hardly attempt to imitate him.

An image in one of the *Idler* essays seems to embody Johnson's stance as a biographer: "In the ancient celebrations of victory a slave was placed on the triumphal car, by the side of the general, who reminded him by a short sentence, that he was a man" (*Idler* No. 51, *Yale*, II, 160). Throughout his biographies he never ceases to remind his readers that the eminent man who is his subject is essentially the same as other men. When, for example, Sir Thomas Browne, whom Johnson admired, claims that his life is a "piece of poetry," Johnson brings him back to earth from his *altitudo*. Although he grants that life itself is in some ways "miraculous" because as finite beings we cannot comprehend its beginnings, he feels that Browne has in mind something "by which he imagined himself distinguished from the rest of mankind," and he goes on to consider the circumstances of Browne's life. Browne had much the same education as other men; he led the secure, uniform life of a scholar; he "traversed no unknown seas, or Arabian deserts":

What it was that would, if it was related, sound so poetical and fabulous, we are left to guess; I believe without hope of guessing rightly. The wonders, probably, were transacted in his own mind; self-love, cooperating with an imagination vigorous and fertile as that of Browne, will find or make objects of astonishment in every man's life; and, perhaps, there is no human being, however hid in the crowd from the observation of his fellow-mortals, who, if he has leisure and disposition to recollect his own thoughts and actions, will not conclude his life in some sort a miracle, and imagine himself distinguished from all the rest of his species by many discriminations of nature or of fortune. ["Life of Browne," *Works*, VI, 480]

In a sense Imlac's advice to the astronomer might have been Johnson's to Browne: "keep this thought always prevalent, that you are only one atom of the mass of humanity . . ." (*Rasselas*, ch. 46, pp. 206–7).

Moreover, to remind us that the hero is a man is to remind us that he is mortal. Every biography is a *memento mori*. Mrs. Thrale seems to have learned that the *Lives of the Poets* are lessons in human mortality. Writing to Johnson about the illness of John Perkins, her late husband's manager and now part-owner of his brewery, she remarks: "how shocking it is, that if the Ship does with hard fighting weather the Storm, it is at last almost sure to sink in the Harbour. But so all the Poets Lives say, and tho' Perkins has very little poet's Stuff in him I trow—Yet he will die, just like the best of them" (*Letters*, II, 442). She had evidently noticed in Johnson's *Lives* the frequency with which death comes at the most inopportune moment. No sooner does preferment or security arrive than death discloses the vanity of human wishes. Thomson "was now at ease, but was not long to enjoy it; for, by taking cold on the watch between London and Kew, he caught a disorder, which, with some careless exasperation, ended in a fever that put an end to his life, August 27, 1748" (III, 294). The death of Ambrose Philips falls into the same pattern: "Having purchased an annuity of four hundred pounds, he now certainly hoped to pass some years of life in plenty and tranquillity; but his hope deceived him: he was struck with a palsy, and died June 18, 1749, in his seventy-eighth year" (III, 323). Johnson could easily have pointed out that Philips lived somewhat beyond the biblical threescore years and ten and therefore received an extra portion of life, but this is not the way he interprets mortality. Death's unexpected appearance is also behind the anecdote to which Potter so strenuously objects. The lampreys in the silver pot, symbols of luxury and the happy indulgence in sensual pleasure, putatively cause Pope's death.

The details are well chosen to remind us of man's frailty.[5]

Paul Fussell has suggested that the long Latin epitaphs found in some of Johnson's short lives may be intended to satirize the poets by contrasting their inflated pretensions with their actual achievements.[6] What is even more remarkable, however, is Johnson's contrivance, in the midst of the *Life of Dryden*, of an ironic epitaph for Elkanah Settle. After presenting Dryden and Settle as equal antagonists at one point in their careers, Johnson combines a general comment on the fall of reputations with the pathos and black humor of Settle's later life in an extraordinary thumbnail biography:

Such are the revolutions of fame, or such is the prevalence of fashion, that the man whose works have not yet been thought to deserve the care of collecting them; who died forgotten in an hospital; and whose latter years were spent in contriving shows for fairs, and carrying an elegy or epithalamium, of which the beginning and end were occasionally varied, but the intermediate parts were always the same, to every where there was a funeral or a wedding, might with truth have had inscribed upon his stone
"Here lies the Rival and Antagonist of Dryden." [I, 375]

In the "Memoirs of the King of Prussia," Johnson's only life of a living man, the conclusion is, I believe, meant to be taken ironically: "The lives of princes, like the histories of nations, have their periods. We shall here suspend our narrative of the king of Prussia, who was now at the height of human greatness, giving laws to his enemies, and courted by all the powers of Europe" (*Works*, VI, 474). Most of the scholars who have written anything about this biography assume that Johnson intended to continue his narrative, for the word "suspend" seems hardly to admit of any other construction. I suggest rather than the first sentence signals the ironic nature of the "suspension." Johnson's paragraph is addressed to those who are aware of human mortality. They will realize that, unlike a narrative, life, which exists in continuous time, cannot be suspended and that the

5. For a view of this anecdote in the context of heroism, see Chapter 3.
6. *Samuel Johnson and the Life of Writing* (New York: Harcourt, Brace, Jovanovich, 1971), p. 273.

picture of Frederick "at the height of human greatness" is therefore a false one. We leave the king to his successes with the
knowledge that soon he, like Charles XII, will merely point a
moral or adorn a tale. Johnson's conclusion shows the vanity of
human wishes at its most delusive.

A satisfactory gloss on this passage is provided by one of his
footnotes to *Hamlet*. Admonishing those who attack the dead, he
asks them "to remember, amidst our triumphs... , that we
likewise are men; that *debemur morti*, and as Swift observed to
Burnet, shall soon be among the dead ourselves" (*Yale*, VIII,
985). It is altogether characteristic of Johnson that he should
arrange the *Lives of the Poets* chronologically by date of death, not
birth.[7]

2

The distinction between the dignity of history and the usefulness of biography had been expounded by Bacon in the *Advancement of Learning*, and employed by Dryden in his *Life of
Plutarch*; it had become one of the commonplaces of
eighteenth-century historical writing. Johnson asserts that it is a
false distinction, and that those lives which are most fit to be
imitated by the majority of mankind are the real examples of
human dignity:

It is frequently objected to relations of particular lives, that they are not
distinguished by any striking or wonderful vicissitudes. The scholar
who passed his life among his books, the merchant who conducted only
his own affairs, the priest, whose sphere of action was not extended
beyond that of his duty, are considered as no proper objects of publick
regard, however they might have excelled in their several stations,
whatever might have been their learning, integrity, and piety. But this
notion arises from false measures of excellence and dignity, and must
be eradicated by considering, that in the esteem of uncorrupted reason,
what is of most use is of most value.[8]

Johnson's biographical practice and his attack on history are
motivated by a broader conception of human dignity than that

7. See Harlan W. Hamilton, "The Relevance of Johnson's 'Lives of the Poets,'"
English Studies Today 11 (Bern, 1966), 341.
8. *Rambler* No. 60, *Yale*, III, 320–21. The views expressed in *Rambler* No. 60
were not dominant even in this age of domestic heroes. Johnson's friend John

of the historians and of the biographers who imitated them. It is interesting to note that the epigraph to *Rambler* No. 60 turns Horace's praise of poetry over philosophy to a preference for biography over philosophy:

> *Quid sit pulchrum, quid turpe, quid utile, quid non,*
> *Plenius et melius Chrysippo et Crantore decit.*

To a large extent the Christian ethic behind so much of his work gives his biographies their breadth. He finds value in many of those incidents in a man's life which do not display an exalted purpose or issue in great deeds. In speaking, for instance, of Milton's books for schoolboys, the *Artis Logicae* and the grammar, he says: "To that multiplicity of attainments and extent of comprehension that entitle this great author to our veneration may be added a kind of humble dignity, which did not disdain the meanest services to literature" (I, 147).[9] "Humble dignity" is a Christian paradox. It stresses at once man's littleness and his ability to act for the good of his society in significant though unheroic ways. Throughout Johnson's biographies the men he praises most, like Boerhaave or Watts, carry out their tasks, whether great or small, with a sense of their own humbleness (*Works*, VI, 281; III, 308).

The stance he takes is not patronizing. He is entirely willing to apply such thinking to his own productions. When Joseph Fowke said that Johnson was far superior to the other biographers of his time, Johnson replied, "I believe that is true. The dogs don't know how to write trifles with dignity" (*Life*, IV, 34n.) Such a mixture of pride and humility is most characteristic of Johnson. In his King of Brobdingnag mood he is apt to remind us that there is "nothing too little for so little a creature as man," and it was probably in such a mood that he announced

---

Hawkesworth, writing two years later in the *Adventurer*, can say: "Biography would always engage the passions, if it could sufficiently gratify curiosity: but there have been few among the whole human species whose lives would furnish a single adventure" (*Adventurer*, No. 4, in *The British Essayists*, ed. Lionel Thomas Berguer [London, 1823], XXIII, 18).

9. And see *Rambler* No. 137, *Yale*, IV, 362. Interestingly, Johnson praises a member of a later generation of the family, Milton's granddaughter, for her "humble virtue" in his "Prologue to *Comus*."

to Boswell that he had been hired to write "little Lives, and little Prefaces, to a little edition of the English poets" (*Letters*, II, 170). The little edition ran to fifty-six octavo volumes. His prefaces, originally published in ten octavo volumes, would be the equivalent, as Paul Fussell has noted, of six modern novels. In the advertisement to the *Prefaces, Biographical and Critical, to the Works of the English Poets* he confesses, in one of literary history's greatest understatements, that "I have been led beyond my intentions."

Perhaps the clearest expression of his idea of "humble dignity" is to be found, not in one of his biographies, but in his biographical poem "On the Death of Mr. Robert Levet." In this poem the use of oxymorons ("Obscurely wise, and coarsely kind") enables Johnson to avoid pure panegyric, and he praises Levet by alluding to the Biblical parable of the talents (Matthew 20:14-30). The key to the parable is that even the single talent must be employed, and this is the key to the Johnsonian redefinition of dignity. In the *Life of Savage* his praise of Abel Dagge, the Keeper of Bristol Newgate Gaol, takes the form of an epitaph as it attempts to sum up the man in a phrase of oxymoronic force: "Virtue is undoubtedly most laudable in that State which makes it most difficult; and therefore the Humanity of a Gaoler, certainly deserves this publick Attestation; and the Man whose Heart has not been hardened by such an Employment, may be justly proposed as a Pattern of Benevolence. If an Inscription was once engraved to the *honest Toll-gatherer*, less Honours ought not to be paid *to the tender Gaoler*" (*Savage*, pp. 126-27).

His ability to find this dignity in even the lowliest of men is indicated by his preference in actual epitaphs. In his "Essay on Epitaphs," Johnson quotes the epitaph on Epictetus ("Epictetus, who lies here, was a slave and a cripple, poor as the beggar in the proverb, and the favourite of heaven"), and says:

In this distich is comprised the noblest panegyrick, and the most important instruction. We may learn from it, that virtue is impracticable in no condition, since Epictetus could recommend himself to the regard of heaven, amidst the temptations of poverty and slavery; slavery, which has always been found so destructive to virtue, that in many languages a slave and a thief are expressed by the same word. And we may be, likewise, admonished by it, not to lay any stress on a man's outward circumstances, in making an estimate of his real value, since Epictetus the beggar, the cripple, and the slave, was the favourite of heaven. [*Works*, V, 266]

Mock-doctor, jail keeper, crippled slave: Johnson can commemorate these people without irony because their lives demonstrate that "virtue is impracticable in no condition." He reverses the poetics of the tragic hero, whose *hamartia* rouses pity and fear because his fall proves we can all fall, and gives us the man at the bottom of the heap, whose goodness can inspire us to emulation, for his virtue proves that we can all be virtuous. Despite the fact that the epitaph is Greek and Epictetus a Stoic, Johnson's praise is Christian—a far from surprising conjunction in the eighteenth century.

Another aspect of his redefinition of dignity is observable in his praise of Pope's epitaph on Mrs. Corbet:

I have always considered this as the most valuable of Pope's epitaphs; the subject of it is a character not discriminated by any shining or eminent peculiarities, yet that which really makes, though not the splendour, the felicity of life, and that which every wise man will choose for his final and lasting companion in the languor of age, in the quiet of privacy, when he departs weary and disgusted from the ostentatious, the volatile, and the vain. Of such a character, which the dull overlook and the gay despise, it was fit that the value should be made known, and the dignity established. Domestick virtue, as it is exerted without great occasions or conspicuous consequences in an even unnoted tenor, required the genius of Pope to display it in such a manner as might attract regard, and enforce reverence. [III, 262]

This quotidian dignity is of great importance to Johnson. His emphasis on the constantly repeated tasks of life, on the "minute," the "invisible" things which added together account for a major portion of existence, should not appear strange to twentieth-century readers, who have been told that Sisyphus is the archetypal man. His attempt to show more fully the nature of man and the terms of his existence led him to reject much of the history writing of his time as irrelevant or misleading.

One critic has claimed that Johnson's praise of Pope's epitaph on Mrs. Corbet is inspired by his discerning in her "traits appli-

cable to his own wife."[10] But the traits Johnson commends here
are so thoroughly a part of his thought, and, on the basis of our
knowledge of his life,[11] so tenuously a part of his marriage, that
it is more likely that Johnson imaged his life with Tetty in terms
similar to this tribute to Mrs. Corbet than that the passage is
simply a reflection of his married life.

One of the fruits of Johnson's insistence on the importance of
domestic life is his tribute to Pope: "The filial piety of Pope was
in the hightest degree amiable and exemplary; his parents had
the happiness of living till he was at the summit of poetical
reputation, . . . and found no diminution of his respect or tenderness. Whatever was his pride, to them he was obedient; and
whatever was his irritability, to them he was gentle. Life has,
among its soothing and quiet comforts, few things better to give
than such a son" (III, 154). In this passage Pope's flaws are used
to set off his domestic virtues. Too many later biographers and
editors, influenced by the picture of Pope as *un politique aux choux
et aux raves*, portrayed him as a filial hypocrite who set a statue of
his mother at the center of his garden in order to enhance his
own image. Whereas the nineteenth-century biographers, like
the historians who followed the doctrine of dignity in the
eighteenth century, find the essence of a man in his career and
public doings, Johnson believes that a man reveals himself most
fully in his private and domestic affairs. Indeed, in the *Life of
Addison* he explicitly couches the difference between history and
biography in terms of public vs. private: history "may be formed
from permanent monuments and records" but biography "can
only be written from personal knowledge" (II, 116). Thus his
interpretation of this aspect of the poet's character is not determined by his previous knowledge of Pope's attitude toward the
world at large. And the theme of the parents living to enjoy their
son's success appears with some frequency (e.g., *Watts*, III, 304).

Johnson is interested in the domestic and private side of man's
life because all men share this kind of existence. He thought that

10. Edward A. Bloom, *Samuel Johnson in Grub Street* (Providence: Brown University Press, 1957), pp. 125–26.
11. See James L. Clifford, *Young Sam Johnson* (New York: McGraw-Hill, 1955),
passim.

the presentation of domestic life would naturally evoke a response in the reader because "what is nearest us, touches us most" (*Letters*, I, 240). Rowe's *Jane Shore*, "consisting chiefly of domestick scenes and private distress, lays hold upon the heart" (II, 69). And for the same reason his *Fair Penitent* is "easily received by the Imagination, and assimilated to common life" (II, 67). Johnson also praised Butler's *Hudibras* because of its domestic images, but he recognized that "many qualities contribute to domestick happiness, upon which poetry has no colours to bestow" (I, 209, 254). Clearly, biography was the place to show them, and to display the misery that resulted when they were lacking. Johnson tells of Fenton's insistence that a sister who had made an unfortunate marriage be invited to a family dinner; and he quotes the letter that Lyttelton's father sent his son when the book that marked the poet's renunciation of atheism was published. When he does write of a prince, Charles Frederick of Prussia, better known as Frederick the Great, he focuses in the first part of his biography on the tensions between the prince and his father (*Works*, VI, 435–43). He emphasizes the king's brusque and brutal temper, his suppression of the prince's attempts to flee the country, and his obliging his son to marry a fat Brunswick princess. This permits Johnson to see the prince's policies on ascending to the throne as personal reactions to his father's cruelty. The private life is Johnson's key to the public behavior.

Biographical literature may present us with "a more exact knowledge" of public figures "because we see them in their private apartments, in their careless hours, and observe those actions in which they indulged their own inclinations, without any regard to censure or applause."[12] It is not surprising that Johnson agreed with Reynolds, who said that "the real character of a man is to be found out by his amusements" (*Life*, IV, 316), and he thought that conversation, not speeches, best displayed the powers of a man's mind (*Life*, IV, 179). We can therefore understand why he claimed that "nobody can write the life of a man, but those who have eat and drunk and lived in social intercourse

12. "Review of the *Account of the Conduct of the Dutchess of Marlborough*," *Works*, VI, 6.

with him" (*Life*, II, 166; *Lives*, II, 116), and why he believed that
"more knowledge may be gained of a man's real character, by a
short conversation with one of his servants, than from a formal
and studied narrative, begun with his pedigree, and ended with
his funeral."[13] In his portrait of Pope, which was in part based
on a conversation with a servant, Johnson mentioned Pope's fur
doublet, canvas bodice, and flannel waistcoat, the three pair of
stockings with which he filled out the shape of his skinny legs
and the velvet cap which covered his balding head. This passage
was one of the centers of Robert Potter's displeasure. Ironically,
Potter focused his ire on the most functional of all the references
to clothes to be found in the *Lives* (or, for that matter, in any of
the late seventeenth- and eighteenth-century historical literature
with which I am familiar). Pope's infirmities necessitated some of
this apparel—without the bodice he could not even stand
erect—and the daily routine of having it put on led, in Johnson's
opinion, to Pope's petulance and self-indulgence. Pope's vanity,
despite his deformity, is conveyed by the cap and stockings.

Such knowledge did not appear petty to Johnson. He told
Boswell that "the true strong and sound mind can embrace
equally great things and small" (*Life*, III, 334), and his writings
amply show that he possessed such a mind himself. Johnson's
dictum that there is "nothing too little for so little a creature as
man," we ought to remember, was a direct response to Boswell's
wondering aloud whether he should use such minute particulars
in his journal. The narrative section of a Johnsonian biography
usually employs a great number of details, and the "character,"
which contains a generalized account of the moral and intellectual qualities of the man, often includes a highly par-

13. *Rambler* No. 60, *Yale*, III, 322. Johnson may have put this belief into
practice in his *Life of Pope*, in which he describes Pope's "petty peculiarities" on
the basis of an account given by "a female domestick of the Earl of Oxford, who
knew him perhaps after the middle of life" (*Lives*, III, 197). Although the immediate source for the remarks of this unnamed servant is not apparent from
the text, Bergen Evans, who first compared Johnson's account with the original
article in the *Gentleman's Magazine*, conjectures that Johnson spoke to the woman
himself in order to get some of the information which does not appear in the
article ("Dr. Johnson as a Biographer" [Ph.D. diss., Harvard, 1932], I, 187). Here
Johnson would seem to be anticipating the Boswellian cross-examination in
order to elicit knowledge about Pope's private life.

ticularized "portrait." Boswell, himself a lover of biographical details, thought that Johnson's biographies were notable for "the minute selection of characteristical circumstances" *(Life,* I, 256).

Scholars have often been guided in their evaluation of Johnson's use of general and particular by the well-known comments in Chapter 10 of *Rasselas,* a practice that happily seems to be on the wane. Here Imlac maintains that "the business of a poet... is to examine, not the individual, but the species; to remark general properties and large appearances: he does not number the streaks of the tulip, or describe the different shades in the verdure of the forest. He is to exhibit in his portraits of nature such prominent and striking features, as recall the original to every mind; and must neglect the minuter discriminations... for those characteristicks which are alike obvious to vigilance and carelessness" *(Rasselas,* p. 50). Whether or not this statement describes the ideal poet—and Rasselas doubts that any real poet could live up to such lofty requirements—it is certainly not the desired practice of the biographer. "A blade of grass is always a blade of grass" and a tulip a tulip, but men, though essentially alike, are significantly different.[14] Johnson defends the detail primarily because it helps to define the individual. In the "Life of Browne" he refers to "those minute peculiarities which discriminate every man from all others" *(Works,* VI, 494), and in the *Life of Addison* he regrets the loss of "the delicate features of the mind, the nice discrimination of character, and the minute peculiarities of conduct" (II, 116). Hence for Johnson the very heart of biography is the well-chosen particular.

Details are also necessary if any action is to serve effectively as an example for future actions. Johnson sees the circumstantial account as a rebuff to that unconscious conspiracy of the ignorant and lazy, who are always "ready to satisfy themselves, and intimidate the industry of others, by calling that impossible which is only difficult" ("Boerhaave," *Works,* VI, 285).

In his own biographies Johnson has frequent cause to criticize the highly generalized biographies of his subjects written by his

14. Hester Lynch Piozzi, *Anecdotes of the Late Samuel Johnson, LL.D.,* 2d ed. (London, 1786), p. 100.

predecessors, and to regret his inability to go beyond their presentation. Of Edward Grant's Latin life of Roger Ascham, Johnson remarks: "Graunt [*sic*] either avoided the labour of minute inquiry, or thought domestick occurrences unworthy of his notice; or, preferring the character of an orator to that of an historian, selected only such particulars as he could best express or most happily embellish. His narrative is, therefore, scanty, and I know not by what materials it can now be amplified" *(Works,* VI, 503–4). This is a complaint Johnson voiced throughout his career as a biographer. In the "Life of Boerhaave," one of his earliest biographies, he excludes the mention of some facts about Boerhaave which he knows only through hearsay, and implores, "with the greatest earnestness, such as have been conversant with this great man, that they will not so far neglect the common interest of mankind, as to suffer any of these circumstances to be lost to posterity" (*Works*, VI, 285). The urgency of his request may be explained by a footnote to the *Life of Savage* which asserts that "it is a Loss to Mankind, when any good Action is forgotten" (*Savage*, p. 17n.). And of Cowley Johnson complains that Sprat "has given the character, not the life of Cowley; for he writes with so little detail that scarcely any thing is distinctly known, but all is shown confused and enlarged through the mist of panegyrick" (I, 1). The "character" is permitted to be general; a life must make use of details. Johnson recognizes that Sprat was writing in a dangerous age, but the effects of his caution are destructive to biography nonetheless: "Such are the remarks and memorials which I have been able to add to the narrative of Dr. Sprat, who, writing when the feuds of the civil war were yet recent and the minds of either party easily irritated, was obliged to pass over many transactions in general expressions, and to leave curiosity often unsatisfied. What he did not tell cannot, however, now be known" (I, 18).

Minute particulars seemed to need defense throughout the eighteenth century, even though the effects of the Lockean Revolution were beginning to be felt. In *Tom Jones* Fielding claims that "there are many little circumstances too often omitted by injudicious historians, from which events of the utmost importance arise."[15] And Richardson's characters defend the minuteness of their letters and journals on psychological grounds. The novel thus complemented the theory and practice of Johnson and prepared the way for the more elaborate particularization of Boswell, both of whom were attacked for their details and whose enduring success has had much to do with this element of their work.

3

In Johnson's biographies such particulars most commonly appear in the anecdote, a genre of which the eighteenth-century historian disapproved for much the same reason that he was apt to attack biography itself. "It is," said Voltaire of the anecdote, "derogatory to the dignity of history, whose motto should be 'tell posterity nothing but what is worthy of posterity.' "[16] Indeed, Voltaire is in a sense quite right. The anecdote occupies the very lowest place in the hierarchy of historical genres. As defined in the fourth edition of the *Dictionary*, it is "a minute passage of private life," and heroic history has no place for it.[17]

The frequency of Johnson's remarks on anecdotes suggests that he rarely missed a chance to praise them. When Boswell mentioned his intention to write about Corsica, Johnson said: "Give us as many anecdotes as you can" (*Life*, II, 11). After reading the completed book, he found "An Account of Corsica" ordinary but praised the "Journal," which was packed with anecdotes and specific details. His wide reading included such collections of anecdotes as the French *Ménagiana* (*Life*, II, 241), and he thought "Horry Walpole ... had got together a great many curious things and told them in an elegant manner" (*Life*, IV, 314). He was also ready to recommend anecdotes to his readers. In a review of Joseph Warton's *Essay on the Writings and Genius of Pope*, he says: "The facts, which he mentions, though

15. Ed. Frank Kermode (New York: New American Library, 1963), p. 188.
16. Quoted by J. B. Black, *The Art of History: A Study of Four Great Historians of the Eighteenth Century* (London: Methuen 1926), p. 54.
17. I owe this reference to Clarence Tracy, "Johnson and the Art of Anecdote," *UTQ*, 15 (1945), 90.

they are seldom anecdotes, in a rigorous sense, are often such as are very little known, and such as will delight more readers than naked criticism" *(Works,* VI, 38). It is not surprising that a man who was interested in biography and was curious especially about its private and domestic aspects should find the anecdote congenial to his tastes.

Though he knew that a collection of small disjointed incidents does not constitute a great work, Johnson confessed: "I love anecdotes. I fancy mankind may come in time to write all aphoristically, except in narrative; grow weary of preparation and connexion and illustration and all those arts by which a big book is made. If a man is to wait till he weaves anecdotes into a system, we may be long in getting them, and get but few in comparison of what we might get" *(Hebrides,* p. 22). Distinguished by a familiar, almost conversational tone, in keeping with the intimacy of its subject matter, the anecdote would naturally appeal to Johnson. Like the seventeenth-century character, the anecdote, which became popular in England only after the middle of the eighteenth century,[18] tends toward satire. Its characteristic lightness of touch makes it an apt vehicle for commenting on man's folly. By its very nature likely to be antiheroic, it deals more often with the frustration of action, or with the embarrassing and unsavory, than with success. Johnson often used the word "anecdote" in the sense, found in the first edition of his *Dictionary,* of "something yet unpublished; secret history." "Secret history," if not necessarily scabrous, frequently turned out to be at odds with the image of a man projected by his public acts. This is the kind of knowledge one might gain from a short conversation with a man's servant, and, as the famous aphorism has it, "No man is a hero to his valet." Such a genre could have no place in the monument to human dignity which was the ideal of so much neoclassical history. Made to order for the display of the vanity of human wishes, the anecdote is part of the redefinition of reality which is the task of Johnsonian biography.

18. Donald A. Stauffer, *The Art of Biography in Eighteenth-Century England* (Princeton: Princeton University Press, 1941), p. 486.

The greatest obstacle to the understanding and evaluation of Johnson's art of anecdote is judging it by Boswellian standards. In what has been called an "excellent essay dealing with the ineffectiveness of Johnson's use of anecdotes to delineate personality,"[19] the most influential critic of Johnson's biographical anecdotes, Clarence Tracy, says that "too often they seem to have been dragged in more out of respect to the paper value of minute facts than with any understanding of their biographical possibilities." Tracy's harsh judgment of Johnson rests on a Boswellian norm: "It is clear that, for all his theoretical emphasis on minute facts and the evanescent aspects of personality, Johnson made no more than a feeble effort himself in his various biographies to perceive the man entire and in action in the Boswellian manner"[20] The biographies of Johnson and Boswell are very different in intention, form, and tone, as well as in scope. They are exemplars of separate biographical traditions: the concise prefatory biography and the amply documented life-and-times; and they are the products of totally different minds. The differences between them suggest the necessity of seeing what Johnson himself was trying to do.

In Johnson's biographies a certain number of anecdotes do not seem to make an immediately apparent contribution to the delineation of the subject. The isolation of such anecdotes is due, however, to more than a theoretical commitment to "minute facts." Johnson's love of anecdotes fuses aesthetics and morality.[21] The delineation of the subject was for Johnson only one function of the anecdote in his work. His didactic intentions are one of the sources of his isolated anecdotes. In his praise of anecdotes and private details in *Rambler* No. 60 Johnson emphasizes the personal usefulness to the reader of the detail as

19. Robert E. Kelley, "Studies in Eighteenth-Century Autobiography and Biography: A Selected Bibliography," in *Essays in Eighteenth-Century Biography*, ed. Philip B. Daghlian (Bloomington: Indiana University Press, 1968), p. 108.
20. "Johnson and the Art of Anecdote," pp. 90, 92–93.
21. Historically, we can distinguish different kinds of anecdotes, but my intentions take another direction in this inquiry. For such distinctions see Elizabeth Hazelton Haight, *The Roman Use of Anecdotes* (New York: Longmans, Green, 1940).

well as its function in giving a picture of the whole man:

There are many invisible circumstances which, whether we read as en-
quirers after natural or moral knowledge, whether we intend to enlarge
our science, or increase our virtue, are more important than public
occurrences.

... Thus the story of Melancthon affords a striking lecture on the
value of time, by informing us, that when he made an appointment, he
expected not only the hour, but the minute to be fixed, that the day
might not run out in the idleness of suspense; and all the plans and
enterprizes of De Wit are now of less importance to the world, than
that part of his personal character which represents him as "careful of
his health, and negligent of his life." [*Yale*, III, 321–22]

The detail may thus be separable from the narrative in which it
occurs, a nugget of knowledge whose value to the reader does
not always depend on its context in the subject's life. In fact,
Johnson's love of anecdotes and his musing that writers may in
time forego all "preparation and connexion and illustration"
confirm that details have just such an independent value.

Another kind of isolated anecdote occasionally appears in
Johnson's biographies. Tracy mentions Johnson's remark that
he learned of Pope's friend Cromwell only "that he used to ride
a-hunting in a tye wig," and says: "This fact is left to speak for
itself whatever its message may be, for Johnson cannot use it in
creating a picture of the man."[22] But here Johnson's technique is
not that of the novelistic or dramatic biographer, but that of the
philosophical biographer. He presents in passing and with rue-
ful irony an inadequate anecdote as a suggestion of the evanes-
cence of human knowledge and human existence. In the *Life of
Dryden* Johnson presents two anecdotes that he had from
eyewitnesses:

Of the only two men whom I have found to whom he was personally
known, one told me that at the house which he frequented, called Will's
Coffee-house, the appeal upon any literary dispute was made to him,
and the other related that his armed chair, which in the winter had a
settled and prescriptive place by the fire, was in the summer placed in
the balcony; and that he called the two places his winter and his summer

22. "Johnson and the Art of Anecdote," p. 90.

seat. This is all the intelligence which his two survivors afforded me. [I, 408–9]

Boswell would simply have slipped the two accounts into places where they would have added a dash of color and authenticity. Johnson's complaint about his lack of material is thematically part of his biography. This is all he could find out firsthand, not about some wretched poetaster, but about Dryden; and the anecdotes are all the more striking because they both refer to Dryden's literary dictatorship. Here we have a prose analogue to *The Vanity of Human Wishes*. Johnson uses his lack of knowledge to force the reader into a confrontation with the void. For the most part, however, his anecdotes contribute both to the picture of the man and to the edification of the audience.

Johnson often generalizes his anecdotes. Those he singles out for praise in *Rambler* No. 60 are not located firmly in time and place, in the manner of Boswell, but refer rather to traits which remain constant and appear not once but often in a man's lifetime. When Johnson said that "nobody can write the life of a man, but those who have eat and drunk and lived in social intercourse with him," he could hardly have suspected that the dinner table would become the great scene of Boswell's biography of him. His use of anecdotes is dependent on their not giving undue prominence to a minor and perhaps misleading aspect of a man's life. In discussing Swift's friendship with the great, he comments on the Dean's supposed "equality and independence" by saying: "In accounts of this kind a few single incidents are set against the general tenour of behaviour" (III, 21).

Boswell's interest is in the individual scene; he gives a picture of "the general tenour of behaviour" chiefly by accumulating different scenes which contain similar characteristics. Johnson often prefers to generalize, even when he obviously could present a single instance, in order to convey economically the endurance of certain characteristics. For example, he comments on his employer Edward Cave's "chilness of mind" in conversation by generalizing what would appear to be a unique event: "he was watching the minutest accent of those whom he disgusted by seeming inattention; and his visitant was surprised when he

came a second time, by preparations to execute the scheme
which he supposed never to have been heard" (*Works*, VI, 434–
35). The *Life of Savage* contains many such generalized anecdotes:

> He was himself so much ashamed of having been reduced to appear as
> a Player, that he always blotted out his Name from the List, when a Copy
> of his Tragedy was to be shown to his Friends.
> His Conduct with regard to his Pension was very particular. No
> sooner had he changed the Bill, than he vanished from the Sight of all
> his Acquaintances, and lay for some Time out of the Reach of all the
> Enquiries that Friendship or Curiosity could make after him; at length
> he appeared again pennyless as before, but never informed even those
> whom he seemed to regard most, where he had been, nor was his
> Retreat ever discovered.
> ... He could not easily leave off when he had once begun to mention
> himself or his Works, nor ever read his Verses without stealing his Eyes
> from the Page, to discover, in the Faces of his Audience, how they were
> affected with any favourite Passage. [*Savage*, pp. 24, 87, 138]

This method enables Johnson to maintain the concreteness of
his anecdotes and at the same time to give the impression of
recurrence. He believed that many things in life are important
simply because they are frequent.

Particularly interesting in Johnson's generalizing anecdotes is
his ability to epitomize character or social relationships in terms
of duration. His account of Addison's marriage to the Countess
of Warwick may seem by the standards of modern biography to
lack details, but it strongly suggests the nature of their life together and closes with a sentence which has the lapidary quality
of an epigram from the *Greek Anthology*: "The marriage, if un-
contradicted report can be credited, made no addition to his
happiness; it neither found them nor made them equal. She
always remembered her own rank, and thought herself entitled
to treat with very little ceremony the tutor of her son" (II, 110–
11). This interest in the general tenor of life accounts also for his
inclusion in several biographies (such as *Milton* and *Addison*) of
the "familiar day," the typical daily activities of the subject.

In addition to giving the sense of a life lived in time, every
biographer must face the problem of biographic closure, the fact

that the end of a biography is in most cases simply the end of a man's life. In the *Life of Smith* Johnson presents, largely through the addition of telling anecdotes omitted from William Oldisworth's short "character," a lifelike account of a talented hack, "Captain Rag." The mordantly satirical coda of the biographical section comes about through Johnson's combination of an anecdote with the familiar data of death; literary form is wrenched into being by simple factuality:

He eat and drank till he found himself plethorick; and then, resolving to ease himself by evacuation, he wrote to an apothecary in the neighbourhood a prescription of a purge so forcible, that the apothecary thought it his duty to delay it till he had given notice of its danger. Smith, not pleased with the contradiction of a shopman, and boastful of his own knowledge, treated the notice with rude contempt, and swallowed his own medicine, which, in July 1710, brought him to the grave. He was buried at Hartham. [II, 17–18]

The phrase "to swallow one's own medicine" had long been a cliché. Johnson shocks us by putting it to grim literal use. He turns factual narration into the literary language of understatement which is at the heart of so much great eighteenth-century writing.

Boswell's biographical art is essentially comic, but Johnson's, as we have already seen, is frequently satiric. We may take as both a characteristic and a particularly excellent Boswellian scene the dinner at Dilly's, in which Wilkes and Johnson, those mighty opposites, come together in festive amity at the cost of a few jokes at Boswell's expense—a cost he is quite willing to pay, incidentally, for a confrontation he has brought about. Everyone is happy. Boswell as biographer does not choose here between the moralist and the libertine, the supporter of the crown or its enemy. In this celebration of *discordia concors* Boswell himself has yoked the opposites together through all his social arts. In Johnson's *Lives* the moral judgment may be complex, but it is always present, even when delivered through the restraints and obliquities of irony. Boswell generally presents; Johnson frequently exposes.

Tracy, quoting Johnson's description of Savage's "scheme of

life for the country," complains, "But how much of vividness [of
Savage's speech] must have been lost in the indirect discourse."[23]
An examination of this passage should convince us that we have
not loss but gain:

> With these expectations he was so enchanted, that when he was once
> gently reproached by a friend for submitting to live upon a subscrip-
> tion, and advised rather by a resolute exertion of his abilities to support
> himself, he could not bear to debar himself from the happiness which
> was to be found in the calm of a cottage, or lose the opportunity of
> listening without intermission to the melody of the nightingale, which
> he believed was to be heard from every bramble, and which he did not
> fail to mention as a very important part of the happiness of a country
> life. [II, 410]

We have both Savage's words and Johnson's implicit ironic
judgment upon them. The scene is the more ironic for its quiet-
ness. The friend (undoubtedly Johnson himself) reproaches
Savage "gently," the cottage he will retire to is "calm," nightingales will sing "from every bramble." What Savage fails to recognize is that those brambles have thorns and that human beings,
with their quotidian troubles, are not able to do anything, even
listen to birdsong, "without intermission." Much of the rest of
Johnson's biography is given over to a sympathetic though critical account of Savage's altercations and death in the country.
And we hear of nightingales once more. Writing from jail to a
friend (again, probably Johnson), Savage says: "I am now more
conversant with the Nine than ever; and if, instead of a Newgate
bird, I may be allowed to be a bird of the Muses, I assure you,
Sir, I sing very freely in my cage; sometimes indeed in the plain-
tive notes of the nightingale" (II, 423).

Johnson often builds his satiric passages on a slight anecdotal
framework. Of Shenstone's improvidence he says: "In time his
expenses brought clamours about him that overpowered the
lamb's bleat and the linnet's song; and his groves were haunted
by beings very different from fauns and fairies" (III, 352). The
actual bailiffs and tradesmen who hounded Shenstone remain
shadowy figures, but the implication that Shenstone has lost

---

23. "Johnson and the Art of Anecdote," p. 91. Tracy, as Savage's best modern
biographer, has more right to this complaint than another critic might have.

himself in a fanciful world is clear. The Leasowes, as described by Johnson, seem to be a projection into the real world of the dangerous prevalence of the imagination, against which he was always on guard, and it comes as no shock to find that he thinks Shenstone's care for his gardens contributed to his early death.

One more satirical anecdote should make the pattern clear. In the *Life of Prior* Johnson delights in contrasting the pastoral name of the heroine of Prior's lyrics and its implied innocence with the Newgate behavior of her empirical counterpart: "His Chloe probably was sometimes ideal [i.e., imaginary]; but the woman with whom he co-habited was a despicable drab of the lowest species. One of his wenches, perhaps Chloe, while he was absent from his house, stole his plate and ran away" (II, 199–200). The last part of the second sentence sounds like an unrecorded variant from "Tom, Tom, the Piper's Son." Johnson takes Prior's mistress out of a genre that idealizes its characters and puts her into a highly realistic nursery rhyme. The homely monosyllables at the end of the passage forcefully clinch his point. All three of these satiric anecdotes criticize pastoral ideas. Johnson uses the realm of facts to demythologize false notions. Within this literary setting, the "real" calls the "fictional" to account. Johnson's view of life is highly normative, and deviations from that norm often lead to satire.

I have been dealing with isolated Johnsonian anecdotes, but Johnson is also capable of great analytical skill in "preparation and connexion and illustration." The *Life of Addison*, like the lives of Pope, Milton, Savage, Smith, Thomson, and the King of Prussia—to name only a few of the more obvious examples—contains finely integrated anecdotes. If Johnson was unable to make anything of Henry Cromwell's tye wig in the *Life of Pope*, he was perfectly able to place Mandeville's reference to Addison's wig in the context of both men's personalities: "The remark of Mandeville, who, when he had passed an evening in his company, declared that he was a parson in a tye-wig, can detract little from his character; he was always reserved to strangers, and was not incited to uncommon freedom by a character like that of Mandeville" (II, 123). This analysis in turn rests upon a number of anecdotes which show Addison's timidity and reserve. His timidity is apparent in the story of his changing Pope's prologue to *Cato* from "Britons arise, be worth like this approved" to "Britons, attend" for fear that "he should be thought a promoter of Insurrection" (II, 100). It is also apparent in the criticism he deployed to prepare the way for *Cato*, in his packing the house for the first performance of the play, and in his unwillingness to own himself the author of *The Drummer* (II, 99, 100, 106). Johnson uses the testimony of Addison's contemporaries to establish his reserve. He quotes Pope on the charm of Addison's familiar conversation and his stiff dignity before strangers. Johnson later employs Pope's comment as a basis for interpreting both the Mandeville anecdote and Addison's excessive drinking. The private knowledge of Addison's timidity and his high opinion of his own abilities permit the reader to understand why someone as moral as Addison should be apt to drink too much.[24]

The *Life of Thomson* contains a series of anecdotes which do not appear in Murdoch's "Thomson" and leads to a totally different conception of the man. There is Thomson gawking at London and having his pockets picked; Thomson, "whose first want was a pair of shoes"; Thomson, delayed from joining his friends at supper after the premiere of *Agamemnon* because "the sweat of his distress had so disordered his wig, that he could not come till he had been refitted by a barber"; Thomson, whose pronunciation was so awkward that when he was once reading his poetry, Bubb Doddington "was so much provoked by his odd utterance, that he snatched the paper from his hand and told him that he did not understand his verses." O, Jemmy Thomson, Jemmy Thomson, O. But this catalogue is not merely "proof" that Johnson's *Lives* do contain anecdotes, or that he knew and said things which other biographers were ignorant of or suppressed. Surely Johnson's point is that this awkward bumpkin who gets fleeced, sweats over his productions, and reads his own poems so poorly that he is accused of not understanding them is nevertheless an original and important poet. We may tend to think of anecdotes as one step removed from mere gossip (if

24. For a fuller account see James L. Battersby, "Patterns of Significant Action in the 'Life of Addison,'" *Genre*, 2 (1969), 28-42.

that), but Johnson's anecdotes humanize. They help to make his biographies meaningful by making them real.

Johnson's skill at combining the narrative anecdote with his interpretative commentary shows the importance he placed in actual practice on "those arts by which a big book is made." An excellent example is to be found in his treatment of an anecdote of Pope which appears in none of the earlier biographies. We all know the scene in the *Life of Johnson* which Boswell, chagrined at Johnson's refusal to be manipulated into an unsolicited interview with the Earl of Marchmont, offers as an indication of Johnson's dereliction of biographical duty. Following Boswell's self-congratulatory bustle, Johnson says, "If it rained knowledge I'd hold out my hand; but I would not give myself the trouble to go in quest of it." More significant, however, is the use to which Johnson put his information when, his defensive pride assuaged, he finally did meet Marchmont. Johnson begins Marchmont's anecdote of Pope's last sickness in a low key: "While he was yet capable of amusement and conversation, as he was one day sitting in the air with Lord Bolingbroke and Lord Marchmont, he saw his favourite Martha Blount at the bottom of the terrace, and asked Lord Bolingbroke to go and hand her up. Bolingbroke, not liking his errand, crossed his legs and sat still; but Lord Marchmont, who was younger and less captious, waited on the lady, who, when he came to her, asked, 'What, is he not dead yet?' " (III, 189–90). In the context of the *Life* we are reminded of Pope's petulance and his pride, like that of Swift, in being able to treat noblemen on terms of equality; and the action takes on an irony in retrospect when we see Bolingbroke, choked with emotion following Pope's death, unable to complete a sentence eulogizing his friend. But what we certainly do not expect in this atmosphere of petty bickering and lordly *politesse* is Martha Blount's cruel question: "What, is he not dead yet?" The anecdote evidently captured in concrete form something Johnson felt deeply about the instability of human relationships, for it leads in this biography to a masterly short analysis of Pope's friendship with Martha Blount:

She is said to have neglected him, with shameful unkindness, in the latter time of his decay; yet, of the little which he had to leave, she had a very great part. Their acquaintance began early; the life of each was pictured on the other's mind; their conversation therefore was endearing, for when they met, there was an immediate coalition of congenial notions. Perhaps he considered her unwillingness to approach the chamber of sickness as female weakness, or human frailty; perhaps he was conscious to himself of peevishness and impatience, or, though he was offended by her inattention, might yet consider her merit as overbalancing her fault; and, if he had suffered his heart to be alienated from her, he could have found nothing that might fill her place; he could have only shrunk within himself; it was too late to transfer his confidence or fondness. [III, 190]

Through a flashback Johnson gives a generalized account of their long, close relationship. But this quickly fades into multiple conjectures on the effect upon Pope of her coldness, as his sickness progressed. As each conjecture is considered, we move inexorably toward the full pathos of Pope's situation, the certainty that regardless of how Pope chose to interpret her actions or act himself, he could only suffer. One ought also to notice the prose which conveys this analysis. The poignancy begins with the monosyllabic description of Pope's legacy—"Of the little which he had to leave, she had a very great part." (There is irony here, too, for we learn that Pope had to insult Allen in his will in order to placate Martha Blount.) And it is completed by a judicious metaphor. Had Pope given up his friendship with her, "he could have only shrunk within himself." The horror of further shrinkage within that already shrunken body is not dwelt upon, but we are given in full the contraction of human scope as Pope moves toward his death. The cruelest part of Martha Blount's remark is that she was so close to being right.

This nearly unremarked passage surpasses a better-known biographical scene which blends death and human relationships, Lytton Strachey's celebrated tour de force at the end of *Queen Victoria*. There Strachey conjectures that "shadows of the past," images of the dominant personalities whom she knew, appeared to the dying queen.[25] And these images—a shallow stream of consciousness if we think of the novels of the early 1920s—

25. *Queen Victoria* (New York: Harcourt, Brace, 1921), p. 423.

recapitulate the major personages and settings of the biography. Strachey once spoke, with characteristic impishness, of the "foretaste of Stracheyan artistry"[26] to be found in Johnson's *Lives*, but Johnson at his best is capable of fusing morality and art in a manner that Strachey could never reach and hardly aspired to. The tone of Johnson's passage on Pope and Martha Blount, with its blend of sympathy and restraint, is something of which Strachey would be incapable. Johnson's illumination of his subjects through the use of anecdote shows an understanding of the complexity of character and humanity which needs no apology even in the light of the Boswellian aftermath and the Stracheyan revolution.

Johnsonian biography, then, faces the dual task of showing that the subject is a man like other men and of distinguishing the subject from all other men. He paraphrases a similar idea from Cicero in *Rambler* No. 179: "Every man, says Tully, has two characters; one which he partakes with all mankind, and by which he is distinguished from brute animals; another which discriminates him from the rest of his species, and impresses on him a manner and temper peculiar to himself" (*Yale*, V, 177). This program was much broader in scope than that of the biographers of his day, and he thought it best accomplished by focusing on domestic scenes, by using anecdotes and minute particulars, by including the failings as well as the excellencies of his subjects. Johnson believed that in order to profit from the narrative of a man's life, the reader must have a full sense of what it is to be a man.

26. Quoted from a letter in his possession by Frederick W. Hilles, "The Making of *The Life of Pope*," in *New Light on Dr. Johnson*, ed. Frederick W. Hilles (New Haven: Yale University Press, 1959), p. 266. André Maurois also is "struck by the Stracheyesque touch" he finds in the *Lives of the Poets*. With an Olympian disregard of chronology he adds, "In fact, one has but to entitle one half of the work *Eminent Jacobeans* and the other *Eminent Augustans* to make it a wholly modern book" (*Aspects of Biography*, trans. S[idney] C[astle] Roberts [New York: Frederick Ungar, 1966], p. 69).

CHAPTER 3

Johnson's Heroes

Johnson's biographies contain a varied gallery of men. Although he may have had little to do with the selection of many of his subjects, the imagination that shapes these pictures is Johnson's. The heroes and villains of his biographies, the acts he approves and those he condemns, are all dependent upon the nature of his thought.

Johnson was no admirer of the conventional hero of history. The literature of the century was redefining the concept of the hero, and a distinctly antiheroic strain runs through much of his thinking. Johnson, after all, praises England's greatest dramatist by saying "Shakespeare has no heroes: his scenes are occupied only by men." In an *Adventurer* essay on the dangers of judging actions "by the event" he stops to make his purpose clear:

I am far from intending to vindicate the sanguinary projects of heroes and conquerors, and would wish rather to diminish the reputation of their success, than the infamy of their miscarriages: for I cannot conceive why he that has burnt cities, and wasted nations, and filled the world with horror and desolation, should be more kindly regarded by mankind, than he that died in the rudiments of wickeness; why he that accomplished mischief should be glorious, and he that only endeavoured it should be criminal: I would wish Caesar and Catiline, Xerxes and Alexander, Charles and Peter, huddled together in obscurity or detestation.[1]

1. No. 99, *Yale*, II, 433. For the political consequences of such views, see Donald J. Greene's excellent article, "Samuel Johnson and the Great War for Empire," *English Writers of the Eighteenth Century*, ed. John Middendorf (New York: Columbia University Press, 1971), pp. 37–65.

Johnson's attack on conventional heroes is not at odds with his own conception of human heroism. Even those most interested in a heroic ethic in this period attempt to redefine heroism partly through attacks on received notions. At the end of the seventeenth century, in his "Dedication to *Fables*," Dryden breaks into invective to describe an important example of the heroes he dislikes: "Science distinguishes a man of honour from one of those athletic brutes whom, undeservedly, we call heroes. Cursed be the poet, who first honoured with that name a mere Ajax, a man-killing idiot." And just after the end of the eighteenth century Blake can speak of "the silly Greek & Latin slaves of the Sword."

Clearly, one man's hero is another man's villain. And it is in a distinctly antiheroic spirit that Johnson warns of the conventional biographer who "commonly ... shews his favourite at a distance decorated and magnified like the ancient actors in their tragick dress, and endeavours to hide the man that he may produce a hero" (*Idler* No. 84, *Yale*, II, 262). He would retreat from this extremity and try to focus on the similarity between men so that "those whom fortune or nature places at the greatest distance may afford instruction to each other." Thus Johnson, though no democrat, contributes to the development of the democratic hero. His comparison of the prince to a farmer in this essay is sardonic enough to be placed alongside some of Swift's remarks in *A Tale of a Tub:* "The prince feels the same pain when an invader seizes a province, as the farmer when a thief drives away his cow." Johnson has been anticipated here by Dryden, who recognizes that by biography's emphasis on the private over the public, "the pageantry of life is taken away; you see the poor reasonable animal, as naked as ever nature made him; and are made acquainted with his passions and his follies, and find the Demy-God a man."[2]

In assessing Johnson's conception of heroism, we might start with his attitude toward activity in the world. Although his biographies are permeated with his religious values, and the vanity of human wishes is one of his constant themes, he does not

2. "The Life of Plutarch," *Plutarch's Lives* (London, 1683), I, 94.

believe that human accomplishment is necessarily vain. These biographies help to define the range of human possibilities and the proper sphere of achievement. In one of his sermons he says: "There are two circumstances which, either single or united, make any attainments estimable among men. The first is the usefulness of it to society. The other is the capacity or application necessary for acquiring it" ("Sermon XX," *Works*, IX, 475). The first criterion explains his great respect for clergymen, doctors, inventors, and figures who might be collectively grouped as scholars or writers. In the "Life of Boerhaave" he treats the career of one who was kept from becoming an ecclesiastic because he was unjustly accused of subscribing to the views of Spinoza. Instead, Boerhaave became a physician, "a profession, not, indeed, of equal dignity or importance, but which must, undoubtedly, claim the second place among those which are of the greatest benefit to mankind" (*Works*, VI, 278). The "Life of Boerhaave" was Johnson's second biography; his first was that of a priest, Father Paul Sarpi. Among his early subjects were such medical men as Sydenham, Morin, and Browne. His short biographies for James's *Medicinal Dictionary* (1743) must have been congenial work. It is highly appropriate that his most memorable nonsatiric poem should be an elegy for a doctor, Robert Levet. Of the four men who were added to the *Lives of the Poets* at Johnson's request (Pomfret, Watts, Yalden, and Blackmore), three were clergymen and the fourth was a doctor.

The second criterion provides much of the force behind Johnsonian biography. His staunch belief in the exemplary function of narratives of human excellence—and Johnson the biographer is more interested in excellence than Johnson the biographical theorist—is underscored by the value he puts on even the bizarre or ludicrous action, provided it requires ability or application: "Every thing that enlarges the sphere of human powers, that shows man he can do what he thought he could not do, is valuable. The first man who balanced a straw upon his nose; Johnson, who rode upon three horses at a time; in short all such men deserve the applause of mankind, not on account of the use of what they did, but of the dexterity which they displayed" (*Life*,

III, 231). The necessity of striving, of diligence and persistence in the pursuit of an impossible perfection, is a favorite topic.[3] Anyone blinded by the eighteenth-century ideal of prudent mediocrity or focusing only on Johnson's religious dicta will be apt to miss this important facet of his thought.

Although an antiheroic strain runs throughout Johnson's thinking on history and biography, it applies chiefly to social matters. Intellectually, Johnson believes in ambitiousness. In *Adventurer* No. 81 he makes the distinction clear and offers a biographical sketch of the Admirable Crichton by way of illustration. If we should overrate our own abilities with respect to others, there is a danger that we will arrogate to ourselves things that we do not deserve and consequently contribute to the destruction of order, "but to rate our powers high in proportion to things, and imagine ourselves equal to great undertakings, while we leave others in possession of the same abilities, cannot with equal justice provoke censure" (*Yale*, II, 401). He is aware that self-love may distort our estimate, but here no harm is done.

This plea for a reach that may exceed one's grasp, which he represents as a break with common prescriptions, is evident in many of his essays. The fantastic life of Crichton—poet, swordsman, musician, painter, athlete—exemplifies what a man may accomplish if he dares to set his sights high. Polymaths play an important role in the biographies written by a man who believed in freedom of the will and maintained that genius was "a mind of large general powers, accidentally determined to some particular direction" (I, 2). Crichton, however, is so clearly a figure of wish-fulfillment that only Johnson's interest in making his point could overcome his usual skepticism when faced by marvelous feats.

More believable polymaths are also found in Johnson's pages. The modest, humble Herman Boerhaave, the subject of one of Johnson's best early biographies, served successively as professor of physics, botany, and chemistry, finally becoming Chief Physician at St. Augustin's Hospital and Governor of the University of Leyden. His books won him a European reputation, and he was

3. See *Rambler* Nos. 77, 85, 129, 137, 150; *Adventurer* No. 111.

elected to the Académie Française and the Royal Society. Johnson's admiration for Isaac Watts is also immediately apparent; along with Boerhaave, Watts is the nearest to saintliness of any of his subjects (though he applies Cowley's phrase "poet and saint" to Gilbert West). In Watts's character piety predominates; but what clearly impresses Johnson is the combination of Christian piety with varied intellectual attainments. Johnson admits that Watts does not achieve greatness in any single area of literary endeavor, but commends his scope—poet, philosopher, divine, and writer of "a catechism for children in their fourth year" (III, 308). His praise of Watts for "combating Locke" *and* making a child's catechism reminds us of his praise of Milton for writing the *Accidence commenced Grammar*, "a little book which has nothing remarkable, but that its author, who had been lately defending the supreme powers of his country and was then writing *Paradise Lost*, could descend from his elevation to rescue children from the perplexity of grammatical confusion" (I, 132). His respect for broad accomplishment explains why he asserted that the greatest man among the Queen Anne wits was Dr. Arbuthnot (*Life*, I, 425; and see *Lives*, III, 177). And he also was reported to have said that the only man he would rather have been than himself was Hugo Grotius, diplomat, poet, historian, and defender of religion.[4] A clause in his epitaph for Goldsmith, not the famous line but the one before it, *"Qui nullum fere scribendi genus/Non tetigit"* (who almost none of the kinds of writing did not touch), praises his friend's breadth of achievement in words that might well stand on his own tombstone. It is the "comprehensive" mind that deserves the most praise. The epic is the highest of genres because "it requires an assemblage of all the powers which are singly sufficient for other compositions" (I, 170).

These men who do not limit themselves to specialties share another important characteristic of the Johnsonian hero: they recognize their own abilities. "Self-confidence," he says in the *Life of Pope*, "is the first requisite to great undertakings" (III, 89).

---

4. Hester Lynch Thrale, *Thraliana: The Diary of Mrs. Hester Thrale (Later Mrs. Piozzi), 1776–1809*, ed. Katherine C. Balderstone (Oxford: Clarendon Press, 1942), I, 377.

And in the lives of the greatest poets whose biographies he writes, he is certain to discuss this theme. The *Life of Milton* provides the best example of the value and the dangers of self-confidence. Although he scourges Milton's egoism in writing in favor of divorce, his sympathetic account of Milton's literary intentions, as revealed in *The Reason of Church Government*, deals with the same quality of mind in another context: "In this book [Milton] discovers, not with ostentatious exultation, but with calm confidence, his high opinion of his own powers; and promises to undertake something, he yet knows not what, that may be of use and honour to his country" (I, 102). This paragraph, thoroughly Johnsonian in its approbation, should prepare the reader for his praise of *Paradise Lost*. Similar praise of self-confidence can be found in his biographies of Dryden, Addison, and Savage (I, 396; II, 120; *Savage*, p. 102).

Without self-confidence one cannot expect to find genius, which is described in a famous passage from the *Life of Pope* as "a mind active, ambitious, and adventurous, always investigating, always aspiring; in its widest searches still longing to go forward, in its highest flights still wishing to be higher; always imagining something greater than it knows, always endeavouring more than it can do" (III, 217). As he puts it in *Rambler* No. 137, "It is the proper ambition of the heroes in literature to enlarge the boundaries of knowledge by discovering and conquering new regions of the intellectual world."[5]

The failure to strive for greatness leads to mediocre accomplishments. The dull-witted Blackmore had written a series of epic poems, but Johnson thinks it unlikely that he "had ever elevated his view to that ideal perfection which every genius born to excel is condemned always to pursue, and never overtake" (II, 253). Of a piece with these views are some of his comments on the metaphysical poets. The transition from asperities to a more sympathetic judgment is accomplished through his recognition of the essentially ambitious nature of their poetry (I, 21).

A related characteristic which clearly interests him, but obtains

5. *Yale*, IV, 362. And see the account of Shakespeare in "Prologue Spoken by Mr. Garrick."

his approbation only when combined with other qualities that he
desires, is the rise of "worth by poverty depressed." He had
intended to write the life of Cromwell, "saying, that he thought it
must be highly curious to trace his extraordinary rise to the
supreme power" (*Life*, IV, 235). This, we can almost be certain, is
not the central impression which a life of Cromwell by Samuel
Johnson would have made, but the Horatio Alger interest is
hardly accidental. In praising Walton's *Lives*, he found it "won-
derful that Walton who was in a very low situation in life, should
have been familiarly received by so many great men, and that at
a time when the ranks of society were kept more separate than
they are now" (*Life*, II, 263-64). Though Johnson is jealous for
the prerogatives of station and has nothing but contempt for
those who, like Swift, attempt to behave too familiarly with their
superiors, he heartily approves of the self-made man.

His interest is strikingly manifested in a little-known discussion of two great lawyers as possible subjects for biography.
Weighing the claims of Lord Mansfield, he says:

> Born of a noble family, reared with a costly education, and entering the
> world with all Scotland at his heels, what is there to wonder at in his
> elevation? If his nurse had foretold it, you wouldn't have taken her for a
> witch. No, sir. If I were to write the life of an English lawyer it should be
> the life of Lord Hardwicke, a son of the earth, with no education but
> what he gave himself, no friends but of his own making: who still lived
> to preside in the highest Court of the Kingdom with more authority, in
> the Cabinet with more weight, and in the Senate with more dignity,
> than any man who had gone before him. His was indeed an elevation to
> be wondered at. If his nurse had dared to foretell of him that he would
> rise to such a height, sir, she'd have swum for it.[6]

6. Quoted by Sir Arnold McNair, *Dr. Johnson and the Law* (Cambridge: Cambridge University Press, 1948), p. 4, from Philip C. Yorke, *Life and Letters of Lord
Chancellor Hardwicke* (1913), I, 56. Yorke questions the authenticity of the story
because he thinks Johnson would have known better than to call Mansfield's
Scottish birth fortunate. But McNair points out that it was actually an asset; and a
closer reader of Johnson's remarks on the Scots would know that he consistently
considered them in league to advance their own. Another version of this anecdote appears in *Strictures on Eminent Lawyers* (1790). There, in a much less full
and vivid account, it is improbably attributed to Lord Mansfield himself. If the
passage quoted by McNair is apocryphal, it has been concocted by a very skillful
imitator of Johnson. See [Leman Thomas Rede], *Strictures on the Lives and Characters of the Most Eminent Lawyers of the Present Day* (London, 1790), 29-30 n., and cf.
Constance Russell, "Sizars and the Woolsack," *N & Q*, 146 (1924), 399-400, for
Johnson's talk of law with Henry Russell.

In the "Life of Cave" he discusses a man who has "risen to eminence." And he emphasizes what Cave, who as a boy at Rugby was blamed for the pranks committed by those "who were far above him in rank and expectations," accomplished through diligence and literary abilities (*Works*, VI, 429). He also has a grudging respect for that shrewd literary businessman, Alexander Pope, who built a personal fortune from his brilliant poems. One of the less prominent but persistent themes of his biographies is keynoted by reference, as in the *Life of Prior*, to "those that have burst out from an obscure original" (II, 180).

Another important element in Johnson's treatment of his subjects is not apparent in his biographical theory: the tendency to draw on heroic imagery in describing his intellectual heroes. "Those who cannot strike with force, can, however, poison their weapon, and, weak as they are, give mortal wounds, and bring a hero to the grave." Had Johnson said this about what happens in *Hamlet*, we would take his comment as a truism, but applied to the calumnious report that Boerhaave had become a disciple of Spinoza, it gives a metaphorical power to the description (*Works*, VI, 277). If Johnson was wary of the biographer who "endeavours to hide the man that he may produce a hero," he nevertheless frequently enough dignified and elevated his subjects by comparing them to traditional heroes. In the *Lives* he refers to the "heroes in literature" as discoverers and conquerors. Johnson's brilliant adaptation of Suetonius' praise of Augustus as builder of Rome ("*lateritiam invenit, marmoream reliquit,*' he found it brick, and he left it marble") describes Dryden's gift to English poetry (I, 469). And early in the *Life of Milton* Johnson claims, in words that find their echo in his definition of genius in the *Life of Pope*, that "Milton's delight was to sport in the wide regions of possibility; reality was a scene too narrow for his mind. He sent his faculties out upon discovery, into worlds where only imagination can travel" (I, 177-78). Johnson seems to be conscious of the heroic analogy in his biographies. In referring to Dryden's criticism of Shakespeare as "a perpetual model of encomiastick criticism," he says, "The praise lavished by Longinus, on the attestation of the heroes of Marathon by Demosthenes, fades away before it" (I, 412).

The heroic analogy is not always employed for purposes of

elevating the subject, however. Johnson's attitude toward traditional heroes was too ambiguous for that. In the early *Life of Savage* the irony of his comparison clearly cuts both ways: "The Heroes of literary as well as civil History have been very often no less remarkable for what they have suffered, than for what they have achieved." And having said that he would not "wish that Milton had been a rhymer," despite his opinion of blank verse, Johnson adds, "yet, like other heroes, he is to be admired rather than imitated" (I, 194). Indeed, the description of the death of Pope is, as Paul Fussell has noted, distinctly mock-heroic in its overtones: "The death of great men is not always proportioned to the lustre of their lives. Hannibal, says Juvenal, did not perish by a javelin or a sword; the slaughters of Cannae were revenged by a ring. The death of Pope was imputed by some of his friends to a silver saucepan, in which it was his delight to heat potted lampreys" (III, 200). It is worth noting also that this heroic analogue itself is drawn from a satire, in fact from the very portrait on which Johnson's character of Charles XII in *The Vanity of Human Wishes* is modeled.

The excellence of which I have been speaking, however socially useful, is not equivalent to virtue, which always elicits higher praise. Paradoxically, those qualities which gain a man the fame that makes him an interesting subject for biography are not valued most highly in Johnsonian biography. Herman Boerhaave's "knowledge, however uncommon, holds, in his character, but the second place; his virtue was yet much more uncommon than his learning" *(Works,* VI, 290). Sydenham's "skill in physick was not his highest excellence; . . . his whole character was amiable; . . . his chief view was the benefit of mankind, and the chief motive of his actions, the will of God" *(Works,* VI, 412). The virtues Johnson praises may be conveniently divided into social and individual virtues; both types are, in Johnson's works, pre-eminently Christian. Among the social virtues he explicitly singles out for approval in the biographies are charity and compassion, turning one's cheek and forgiving one's enemy. Richard Savage had many bad traits, but Johnson thought that "compassion" was his "distinguishing quality." Savage's gift of half of his only guinea to the woman who had testified against him at his murder trial was "an Action which in some Ages would have made a Saint, and perhaps in others a Hero, and which, without any hyperbolical Encomiums, must be allowed to be an Instance of uncommon Generosity, an Act of complicated Virtue; by which he at once relieved the Poor, corrected the Vicious, and forgave an Enemy; by which he at once remitted the strongest Provocations, and exercised the most ardent Charity" (*Savage*, p. 40). His act is at once rational and passionate; he overcomes the base emotion of revenge, but there is warmth in his charity. Unlike the Stoics, with whom he has, as we shall see, certain affinities, Johnson does not wish to extinguish human passions—a task at once impossible and dehumanizing—but to regulate them and encourage those that concur with virtue.

Charity he looked upon as one of the foremost virtues, and he will often mention specific acts of charity and even name the sums involved. Pope helped Dodsley open a shop and was the principal donor when Savage needed money to go to Bristol. Having detailed these acts in short scope, Johnson adds, "He was accused of loving money, but his love was eagerness to gain, not solicitude to keep it" (III, 214). Swift's charity, on the other hand, was faulty, for although he offered the poor loans without interest, he insisted that they be paid punctually and took those who were tardy to court. This charity with "no provision of patience or pity" can hardly, in Johnson's eyes, be considered charity at all, for it ignores the facts of human frailty. And he finds Congreve culpable for squandering a legacy upon Henrietta, Duchess of Marlborough, who had no need for money, while a branch of his own family was penurious. A large part of the short *Life of Garth* is devoted to the background of the *Dispensary* and praises the charitableness of Garth and of physicians in general in attempting to set up a system for treating the poor without pay.

Yoked to Johnson's insistence on active virtue is an equal insistence on the importance of what he called, in the eighteenth-century sense of the word, "modesty." This term includes our current meaning, but it also means "self-distrust." And self-distrust is the basic attitude toward life which Johnson recommends. Watts, for example, was resentful by nature, "but by his established and habitual practice he was gentle, modest and in-offensive" (III, 307). And his distinction as a writer seems to reside in bringing this cast of mind to his religious writings. As Johnson sees it, until the time of Watts the dissenters had let their zealousness dictate their words, and their writings were "commonly obscured and blunted by coarseness and inelegance of style" (III, 306). Watts's writings, on the other hand, are praiseworthy for "his meekness of opposition and his mildness of censure" (III, 308; see "Boerhaave," *Works*, VI, 200).

One might move from here to the life of another dissenting churchman, which can be taken as the antithesis of this image, much in the manner of Hamlet's "Look here upon this picture, and on this." If Watts is the dissenter as saint, the "Life of Cheynel" presents a nearly demonic Puritan divine. Cheynel suffers from a lack of self-distrust. Like Watts and Boerhaave, he is temperamentally resentful, but Cheynel lets his passion rule him. His actions are always precipitate, and he is totally self-assured. Whereas Watts accepted his position as a dissenter—he might have gone to Oxford or Cambridge on a scholarship had he conformed—Cheynel not only sided with the rebels, but used his position when the Puritans took over Oxford to have the degree that had been denied him for espousing Presbyterian doctrine presented and dated retroactively. When he arrived at Oxford he not only dismissed the old president, Dr. Baily, from his office, but broke down the door in order to evict him. Cheynel's "heat" is remarked throughout the biography, and the personifications used to describe him take on a demonic life of their own. Where one action would be most humane, "Cheynel's fury prompted him to a different conduct" (*Works*, VI, 424). This life, which was originally published in the *Student*, a periodical intended for undergraduates at Oxford and Cambridge, presents a lesson to the reader in one of the early paragraphs: "A temper of this kind is generally inconvenient and offensive in any society, but in a place of education is least to be tolerated."[7] It is noteworthy that Cheynel is close to a traditional kind of hero—the "fighting parson."

7. *Works*, VI, 415. I cannot agree with Edward A. Bloom, who sees as the primary objective of this biography a covert attack on Methodism. See *Samuel Johnson in Grub Street* (Providence: Brown University Press, 1957), p. 114.

The men whom Johnson most admires endure trials and sufferings without complaint and maintain their virtues despite their troubles. They are sustained by their piety, and display, in the words of *The Vanity of Human Wishes*, "Obedient Passions and a Will resign'd." Such men, let us note in defense of Johnson, whose supposed chauvinism and political and religious bigotry have become legendary, include Boerhaave, a foreigner; Watts, a dissenter; and Blackmore, a Whig. The men for whom he has the least sympathy in this context are those who subvert the established order or indulge in social pride (a wishful subversion of order) or self-pity. Cheynel and Milton are the foremost subverters of order among his subjects. Swift, and to some extent Congreve, act in ways unbecoming to their stations in life. Both Pope and Swift behave as though the world were conspiring against them.

The Stoic element in Johnson's thought is firmly grounded in his belief in God. In his biographies Christian Stoicism (*"patientia christiana,"* to use the phrase he borrows from Lipsius) is the proper response to adversity, particularly sickness, and springs from a sense of man's limitations. In one of his earliest productions, the "Life of Boerhaave," he praises Boerhaave's "patience" while bedridden and distinguishes it from that of the Stoics. It is "more rational" because "it was founded ... not on vain reasonings, but on confidence in God" (*Works*, VI, 284). In another early life he discusses the behavior of Dr. Thomas Sydenham, who was subject to attacks of the gout and suffered from kidney stones during the last thirteen years of his life: "These were distempers which even the art of Sydenham could only palliate, without hope of a perfect cure, but which, if he has not been able by his precepts to instruct us to remove, he has, at least, by his example, taught us to bear; for he never betrayed any indecent impatience, or unmanly dejection, under his torments, but supported himself by the reflections of philosophy, and the consolations of religion" (*Works*, VI, 412). The man Johnson admires faces sickness, adversity, and death, as does Roger Ascham, with the "resignation and piety of a true Christian" ("Ascham," *Works*, VI, 518).

Savage, whom one could hardly think of as a Stoic, is credited with "the Virtue of *suffering well*." But the *Life of Savage* is a brilliantly balanced account of vices and virtues, and Johnson immediately qualifies his remark by ironically bringing another Stoic ideal to bear on Savage's behavior: "The two Powers which, in the Opinion of *Epictetus*, constituted a wise Man, are those of *bearing* and *forebearing*, which cannot indeed be affirmed to have been equally possessed by *Savage*; and indeed the Want of one obliged him very *frequently* to practice the other."[8]

Carey McIntosh's article "Johnson's Debate with Stoicism" is full of careful discriminations as to Johnson's acceptance of stoical doctrine, but it misses the limitations of the scope of Stoicism in Johnson's thought. His conclusion, which asserts that "Johnson as moralist is less concerned with 'interpersonal relations' than with individual well-being,"[9] certainly overemphasizes Johnson's religious individualism. For Johnson, who like so many in his day thinks that "man" is synonymous with "social being," salvation is individual, but man must exist in society. And it is his business to help actively his fellow beings. Again, the Stoic *apathia* has nothing in common with the intellectual striving which Johnson desiderates.

The essential unity of the different kinds of actions Johnson admires can be seen, however, by observing the central place in Johnson's thought of man's mortality. Human time is of great importance to him, and the difficulty of achievement in a world of flux was a problem to which he frequently recurred. Hence he most admired men who took cognizance of the human condition by creating for themselves a sense of duration while at the same time recognizing their total dependence on the mercy of God. In this perspective we should notice that the radical difference between his praise of intellectual attainment and his admiration for pious submission begins to evaporate. Early in

8. *Savage*, p. 126. In the second quotation I have made use of the readings present in both the first and last editions.

9. *ELH*, 33 (1966), 336. Donald J. Greene has argued that Christian Stoicism is "a contradiction in terms," but I think that Johnson's use of specific stoic thinkers for Christian ends would seem to warrant the tag ("Johnson as Stoic Hero," *Johnsonian News Letter*, June 24, 1964, p. 8). For a useful account of Johnson's relationship to Stoicism which argues for a broad spectrum of stoic thought, see Robert Voitle, "Stoicism and Samuel Johnson," extra series, no. 4 (1967), 107–27.

this chapter it appeared that Boerhaave, the scientist with a European reputation, and Boerhaave, the modest Christian Stoic, were almost coincidentally the same man. But his learning and his virtue share the same relationship to time. One might draw from the "Life of Boerhaave" a catalogue of temporal virtues. Boerhaave displays "steady adherence," "patience," "constancy." His intellectual pursuits are distinguished by "long and unwearied observation"; his behavior in sickness by "fortitude and steady composure of mind" (*Works*, VI, 285, 284).

The qualities that make a great poet are also characterized in Johnson's work by a sense of the importance of time. In the definition of genius quoted earlier the operative words, repeated a total of six times, are "still" and "always." Johnson throws his emphasis on the persevering qualities. No wonder he said, agreeing with Locke, that "the widest excursions of the mind are made by short flights frequently repeated" (*Rambler* No. 137, *Yale*, IV, 361). The man of genius must continually snatch graces. The Romantics could admire far, far better things and single intense moments, but for Johnson the things that one can do day in and day out are more important. And he tends to think of his subjects' accomplishments in terms of customary excellence.

Finally, we can see why the writer becomes a central hero for Johnson: "Statesmen and generals may grow great by unexpected accidents, and a fortunate concurrence of circumstances, neither procured nor forseen by themselves: but reputation in the learned world must be the effect of industry and capacity" ("Boerhaave," *Works*, VI, 289). And if the ideal of heroism described in Johnson's "Prologue to *Irene*" ("the virtuous mind / Daring, tho' calm; and vigorous, tho' resign'd")—a stance clearly related to that recommended at the conclusion of *The Vanity of Human Wishes*—seems to be most nearly approached in such modest polymaths as Boerhaave and Watts, his very definition of genius is heroic and applies most fully by his own standards to Pope, Dryden, and Milton.

It is perhaps best to end with Milton, for if Johnson has little but scorn for his republicanism, the conclusion of the *Life of Milton* surely describes the poet as hero:

He was naturally a thinker for himself, confident of his own abilities and disdainful of help or hindrance; he did not refuse admission to the thoughts or images of his predecessors, but he did not seek them. From his contemporaries he neither courted nor received support; there is in his writings nothing by which the pride of other authors might be gratified or favour gained, no exchange of praise nor solicitation of support. His great works were performed under discountenance and in blindness, but difficulties vanished at his touch; he was born for whatever is arduous; and his work is not the greatest of heroick poems only because it is not the first. [I, 194]

This is the *aretē* of the poet. All the heroic qualities Johnson denies Milton in his active life are absorbed into this portrait of the contemplative man. (The traditional dichotomy, however, may not be apt. The poet is in a sense active: his poem is characteristically for Johnson a "performance.") Here we see the destined task of the hero, the aspiration and endurance, the isolation and independence, the overcoming of limitations both physical and social, and all issue in an almost unequaled human achievement. If Johnson's final presentation of Milton is not heroic, where, we may ask, is heroism to be found?

CHAPTER 4

Interpretation

In a letter to Giuseppe Baretti detailing a disillusioning visit to Lichfield, Johnson says that "as nothing is little to him that feels it with great sensibility, a mind able to see common incidents in their real state, is disposed by very common incidents to very serious contemplations."[1] I have remarked during the course of this study the importance of "common incidents" to Johnson, and I think he explains here why he is so particularly well suited to the writing of biography. In the details of individual lives (the "kindred images" of *Rambler* No. 60) he finds a significance that leads to moral perceptions valuable to all men. Johnson is a great moral interpreter, and the brilliance of his judgments, the moral aphorisms which critics such as Walter Raleigh and Mark Longaker have disinterred from his biographies as though they were brushing the mud off diamonds, depends on their function as comments on empirical realities.[2]

Johnson's purpose in writing biography is frankly moral, and he is antipathetic to the doctrine that the biographer's or the historian's proper task is only, in Herbert Butterfield's words, "to show how men came to differ rather than to tell a story which

1. *Letters*, I, 140. James Joyce might have said something like this in explaining his "epiphanies."
2. Raleigh excerpts eight "good sayings"; Longaker, ten aphorisms. "Johnson's Lives of the Poets," in *Six Essays on Johnson* (Oxford: Clarendon Press, 1910), p. 133; *English Biography in the Eighteenth Century* (Philadelphia: University of Pennsylvania Press, 1931), p. 360.

is meant to reveal who is in the right."[3] History has gone through a dehumanization analogous to that which Ortega finds in the arts. The scientific historians, to adopt the language of Johnson on the metaphysical poets, sometimes write "rather as beholders than as partakers of human nature; as beings looking upon good and evil, impassive and at leisure; as Epicurean deities making remarks on the actions of men and the vicissitudes of life, without interest and without emotion." It is no wonder that scientific history is under attack in some quarters today as both inadequate and impossible (value judgments will intrude, for the writers are men). Butterfield's statement is purposely oversimplified and loaded, but though Johnson would insist on the necessity of both tasks, he would come down firmly, if forced, on the side of moral judgment.

And yet we should also notice that Johnson is not merely naive by modern historical standards. Isaiah Berlin would seem to be arguing for much the same reasons as Johnson against scientific determinism. Berlin says: "The invocation to historians to suppress even that minimal degree of moral or psychological evaluation which is necessarily involved in viewing human beings as creatures with purposes and motives (and not merely as causal factors in the procession of events), seems to me to rest upon a confusion of the aims and methods of the humane studies with those of natural science."[4] He goes on to call this determinism "one of the greatest and most destructive fallacies of the last hundred years."

For Johnson, not to condemn a bad act is to condone it. "Historians," he says in *Rambler* No. 79, "are certainly chargeable with the depravation of mankind, when they relate without censure those stratagems of war by which the virtues of an enemy are engaged to his destruction" (*Yale*, IV, 54). And ten years earlier in his "Life of Blake," a thoroughly sympathetic study of the Puritan admiral written to encourage a nation at war, he had

3. *The Whig Interpretation of History* (1931; rpt. New York: W. W. Norton, 1965), p. 130.

4. *Historical Inevitability* (Oxford: Oxford University Press, 1954), p. 53. It is no surprise to find him saying earlier in the book, on the subject of free will, "Dr. Johnson, as in other matters affecting commonsense notions, here too seems to have had the last word" (p. 27n.).

had occasion to take his predecessors to task for not criticizing Blake's foolhardy conduct in engaging a far superior enemy at great cost in men and ships (*Works*, VI, 301-2). In fact, as Johnson was to say later, the necessity to condemn the faults of the generally good man is greater than to condemn those of the bad, for the readers is in more danger imitating him:

It is particularly the duty of those who consign illustrious names to posterity, to take care lest their readers be misled by ambiguous examples. That writer may be justly condemned as an enemy to goodness who suffers fondness or interest to confound right with wrong, or to shelter the faults which even the wisest and the best have committed from that ignominy which guilt ought always to suffer, and with which it should be more deeply stigmatized when dignified by its neighbourhood to uncommon worth, since we shall be in danger of beholding it without abhorrence, unless its turpitude be laid open, and the eye secured from the deception of surrounding splendour. [*Rambler* No. 164, *Yale*, V, 109-10]

In an age that valued perspicuity and was unabashedly didactic there was a distinct taste for moralizing interpretation. A reviewer of John Jortin's *Life of Erasmus* (1758) complained that the author was "too sparing of his comment, for want of which the narrative is, in many places, dry and tedious."[5] After all, unless a historian had new materials, he could only, according to Johnson, "decorate known facts by new beauties of method or of style, or at most . . . illustrate them by his own reflections" (*Idler* No. 94, *Yale*, II, 291).

When the *Lives of the Poets* appeared, the reviewers did not fail to appreciate this aspect of Johnsonian biography. One reviewer referred to Johnson's "happy art of moralization by which he gives to well known incidents the grace of novelty and the force of instruction."[6] One can imagine few tributes which would be more apt to please him.

Johnson's great predecessor as a moral biographer was, of course, Plutarch, and at least one critic noticed that the two had something in common. Although he seems to have been thinking primarily of the lighter side of Johnson's commentary, he

5. Quoted in another context by Longaker, *English Biography*, p. 219.
6. "Review of *Prefaces, Critical and Biographical*," *Gentleman's Magazine*, 51 (1781), 276.

preferred the English moralist to the Greek for the "vein of pleasantry interspersed."[7]

The moral biographer's task is particularly difficult because though presumably judging actions he is actually judging intentions: "The morality of an action depends on the motive from which we act. If I fling half a crown to a beggar with intention to break his head, and he picks it up and buys victuals with it, the physical effect is good; but, with respect to me, the action is very wrong" (*Life*, I, 97–98). Johnson is highly conscious of this distinction and of the problems it creates for the biographer. Since he believes that the psychological basis of moral judgment can only be clear (if ever) when a man is writing of his own actions, he ultimately prefers autobiography to biography. The temptation of the biographer to permit his own personal emotions to color his conjectures—"and by conjecture only can one man judge of another's motives or sentiment"—is all the greater because the biographer may not be aware of the deception perpetrated. The situation of the autobiographer is, according to Johnson, quite different, for he has a surer knowledge of his own motives and "that which is fully known cannot be falsified but with reluctance of understanding, and alarm of conscience" (*Idler* No. 84, *Yale*, II, 263). Johnson is also aware, as his continual emphasis on the danger of self-deception demonstrates, that, as he puts it in the *Life of Dryden*, "we do not always know our own motives" (I, 458), but compared to the autobiographer, the biographer is groping in the dark.[8]

Johnson's practical solution of this problem in his biographies is to present alternative motives for a single action. Even when directed by a general knowledge of the character of his subject, the alternatives may be numerous. Edmund Smith, who might have had the patronage of Halifax, "by pride, or caprice, or indolence, or bashfulness, neglected to attend him, though doubtless warned and pressed by his friends, and at last missed his reward by not going to solicit it" (II, 15–16). Sometimes Johnson will find two motives for an action which have as little in

7. W. B., "Remarks on Dr. Johnson's *Lives of the Poets*," *Gentleman's Magazine*, 51 (1781), 563.
8. See also *Idler* No. 84, *Yale*, II, 262–64; *Rambler* No. 87, *Yale*, IV, 95.

common as wishing to hit a man on the head with a coin or intending to treat him to dinner. And occasionally, he may even juxtapose two possible motives for satiric effect. Having discussed Dryden's inability to write a persuasive religious tract, Johnson explains that he called poetry to his aid, and "actuated . . . by zeal for Rome, or hope of fame," he published *The Hind and the Panther* (I, 380). [9]

This is not to say that Johnson merely sets down alternatives and lets the reader take his pick. He always prefers the most probable motive if he has a basis for choice. One of the almost obsessive motifs of the *Life of Savage* is engendered by Johnson's attempt to explain the motivation of the Countess of Macclesfield. Early in the life he says, "it is not indeed easy to discover what Motives could be found to overbalance that natural Affection of a Parent, or what Interest could be promoted by Neglect or Cruelty" (*Savage*, p. 6). He is left even more bewildered by the fact that she seems otherwise to be kind and charitable. Some thirty pages later he returns to the subject when Savage, having attempted to visit her, is accused by the Countess of intending her murder. "It is natural to enquire upon what Motives his Mother could prosecute him in a manner so outragious and impacable," says Johnson. And his answer is motiveless malignity: "only this can be said to make [such a lie] probable, that it may be observed from her Conduct that the most execrable Crimes are sometimes committed without apparent Temptation" (*Savage*, pp. 38, 39).

Johnson will occasionally force a knowledge of the difficulty of determining motives upon his reader, and then leave him with the facts. Having quoted the reasons which Wood and Sprat assigned for Cowley's retirement, he says, "So differently are things seen and so differently are they shown; but actions are visible, though motives are secret. Cowley certainly retired . . ." (I, 15). And of Addison's "preparatory criticism" for *Cato* he says,

9. Both Harold Bond and Leo Braudy have found this method characteristic of Gibbon. Braudy calls it "a kind of epistemological doublet." See Braudy, *Narrative Form in History and Fiction*: *Hume, Fielding, and Gibbon* (Princeton: Princeton University Press, 1970), p. 216, and Bond, *The Literary Art of Edward Gibbon* (Oxford: Clarendon Press, 1960), pp. 77–78. And see Hoyt Trowbridge, "Scattered Atoms of Probability," *ECS*, 5 (1971), 1–38.

"The fact is certain; the motives we must guess" (II, 99). In essence all depends on probability and circumstances: "We cannot prove any man's intention to be bad. You may shoot a man through the head, and say you intended to miss him; but the judge will order you to be hanged" (*Life*, II, 12). And the biographer, himself a judge, is often forced to decide more difficult cases. During Johnson's time there were many, perhaps under the influence of Descartes, who believed that a "Science of mankind" which would enable them to understand the springs of man's actions, was fast approaching. Johnson was not among them. He believed that they were responding to a false analogy: "It seems to be almost the universal errour of historians to suppose it politically, as it is physically true, that every effect has a proportionate cause. In the inanimate action of matter upon matter, the motion produced can be but equal to the force of the moving power; but the operations of life, whether private or public, admit no such laws. The caprices of voluntary agents laugh at calculation."[10]

Long before he wrote these words he was putting this knowledge to good use in his biographies. In attempting to discover why Roger Ascham, a Protestant, was given a place of honor at Queen Mary's court, Johnson casts aside the weak conjectures of the *Biographia Britannica* and admits the futility of the case: "Nothing is more vain, than, at a distant time, to examine the motives of discrimination and partiality; for the inquirer, having considered interest and policy, is obliged, at last, to admit more frequent and more active motives of human conduct, caprice, accident, and private affections."[11]

Johnson's pessimism concerning our knowledge of specific human motivation leads to a healthy skepticism and a careful tentativeness in his discussion of the meaning of actions. "The heart cannot be completely known," he says in his life of Zachary Pearce, "but the nearest approach which can be made is by op-

10. "Thoughts on the Late Transactions Respecting Falkland's Islands," *Yale*, X, 365–66.
11. "Life of Ascham," *Works*, VI, 515. This is a favorite theme. See, for example, *Lives*, I, 2; *Rambler* No. 184, *Yale*, V, 202; *Idler* No. 55, *Yale*, II, 172. It is also a major theme in *Rasselas*.

portunities of examining the thoughts when they operate in secret, without auditors and beholders." The difficulty of obtaining such testimony is, of course, great, but in the case of Pearce,
Johnson finds a not very good piece of poetry "which can be
supposed to be only a soliloquy, nothing more than his own
thoughts, written down for his own gratification," and which
corroborates his public statements about his retirement.[12] When
he does not possess such evidence, he cedes his jurisdiction to a
higher court. He attempts to explain Dryden's conversion to
Catholicism by saying: "It is natural to hope that a comprehensive is likewise an elevated soul, and that whoever is wise is also
honest. I am willing to believe that Dryden, having employed his
mind, active as it was, upon different studies, and filled it,
capacious as it was, with other materials, came unprovided to the
controversy, and wanted rather skill to discover the right than
virtue to maintain it. But enquiries into the heart are not for
man; we must now leave him to his judge" (I, 378). Johnson
begins with rational expectation, goes on to sympathetic interpretation, and concludes by emphasizing the speculative quality of his remarks and the uncertainty of human knowledge.

2

D. T. Starnes has set forth the major objections to the historian as moralist: "the use of history for moral guidance, so common in the Renaissance, prejudiced humanist history as a serious subject, either of inquiry or of instruction. History became
fragmentary, artificial, a *cento* of examples, of commonplaces,
of biographical idealizations. Critical study tended to be shirked
as spoiling good illustrations; and the art of the historical writer
was limited to clothing accepted versions of facts in novel and
ingenious forms."[13] The example of Johnson proves that moral
purpose need not prejudice the historian. Both truth and
morality provide much of the power of Johnsonian biography.
And if we have to make a choice between the two, truth will win:
"Whether to see life as it is will give us much consolation I know

12. "The Life of the Author," in Zachary Pearce, *A Commentary on the Four
Evangelists*, ed. John Derby (London, 1777), I, xxxvii.
13. "Purpose in the Writing of History," *MP*, 20 (1922–23), 299.

not, but the consolation which is drawn from truth, if any there be, is solid and durable, that which may be derived from errour must be like its original fallacious and fugitive" (*Letters*, I, 111).

The famous *Rambler* No. 60 begins with a description of the way in which the reader of any narrative may, through "an act of the imagination," identify with the protagonist. Johnson ends, however, with the warning, quoting (probably from memory) the great jurist Matthew Hale, that the biographer must not let sympathy overcome judgment: "'Let me remember,' says Hale,'when I find myself inclined to pity a criminal, that there is likewise a pity due to the country.' If we owe regard to the memory of the dead, there is yet more respect to be paid to knowledge, to virtue and to truth" (*Yale*, III, 323). This primary allegiance to absolute values outweighs personal considerations. When Boswell said that Robert Sibbald, whose manuscript autobiography he possessed, reconverted to Protestantism because he disliked fasting, Mrs. Thrale, a child of her age, quickly suggested that he should not publish the work: "To discover such weakness exposes a man when he is gone." But Johnson brushed this opinion aside as essentially irrelevant: "Nay, it is an honest picture of human nature. How often are the primary motives of our actions as small as Sibbald's for his reconversion" (*Life*, II, 228). And even in cases in which the biographer and his subject "lived in intimacy" Johnson is unequivocal. When a hospitable Scot implied that Orrery had done wrong in exposing Swift's flaws, Johnson said nothing was wrong with such an action "after the man is dead and it is done historically" (*Hebrides*, p. 202).

In fact, unless the truth is told, the danger is that biography will not have its moral effect. Edmond Malone broached the subject of Johnson's inclusion in the *Life of Addison* of Addison's execution of Steele's debt:

I then mentioned to him that some people thought that Mr. Addison's character was so pure, that the fact, *though true*, ought to have been suppressed. He saw no reason for this. "If nothing but the bright side of characters should be shown, we should sit down in despondency, and think it utterly impossible to imitate them in anything. The sacred writers (he observed) related the vicious as well as the virtuous actions of men; which had this moral effect, that it kept mankind from *despair*, into which otherwise they would naturally fall were they not supported by the recollection that others had offended like themselves, and by penitence and amendment of life had been restored to the favour of heaven."[14]

There is no special pleading here. This passage reveals Johnson's settled and long-held opinion. Thirty years before, in *Rambler* No. 4, he insists that fictional narratives should present in their heroes "the most perfect idea of virtue"; but he adds by way of qualification that this should be "virtue not angelical, nor above probability, for what we cannot credit we shall never imitate.[15] And even earlier the *Life of Savage* showed how uncompromising his conception of truth was, even where his personal sympathies were most thoroughly engaged. In Johnson's view, therefore, truth and moral efficacy both demand the inclusion of a man's flaws.

His uncompromising attitude was, of course, characteristic of the critical as well as the biographical sections of his *Lives*. When Boswell asked if Johnson, then under contract to the booksellers, would write the life of any dunce, Johnson replied, "Yes, and say he was a dunce." This was not simply the retort unanswerable, but one more break with the practice of his predecessors. Until Johnson's biographies appeared, the author of collective biography was apt to write the life of any dunce and say he was "the prodigy of his time" (Winstanley on John Ogilby), "of the first rank of wit and gallantry" ("Cibber" on Colonel Coddrington) or "allowed to be a good dramatick Poet of that Age" (Giles Jacob on Henry Glapthorn). Winstanley's customary rhetoric, with its use of litotes for nonironic effects, gives something of the flavor of these largely uncritical writers. According to him, Henry Bradshaw writes "a not bad chronicle," Charles Aleyn is "no despicable poet," and Dr. Robert Wild is "not the meanest of the

14. *Life*, IV, 53. Malone was not alone. Reviewing the *Lives of the Poets* in the *Gentleman's Magazine*, W. B. says, "I am sorry that our author has acquainted us with this action [Addison's execution of Steele's debt] of such a pattern of virtue and beneficence" ("Remarks," p. 508).
15. *Yale*, III, 24. And see *Rambler* No. 164.

Poetical Cassock." Revealing too is his use of the cant phrase "has obliged the world with" for "has written." Johnson was always a master of the blunt truth.

As we can gather from the attitudes of Malone's friend, Mrs. Thrale, and MacLeod, Johnson's Scottish host, the ethics of suppression which we commonly associate with the Victorian era were already in evidence.[16] On the basis of my readings in biography and criticism of biography in the later eighteenth century, I would conclude that the real difference between this age and the Victorian with respect to biographical suppression is that the more highly unified, almost monolithic, society of the nineteenth century led to an unwritten code which was far more pervasive. Just after the middle of the century a bit of Podsnappery is apparent in Mrs. Montagu's reaction to Thomas Birch's biography of Queen Elizabeth: "I shall hate these collectors of Anecdotes if they cure one of that Admiration of a great character that arises from a pleasing deception of sight. . . . I cannot forgive Mr. Birch."[17] Mrs. Montagu is, however, at least superior to Dickens' character in her consciousness that she wishes to evade the truth. Similarly, in his "Life of Fielding" (1763), Arthur Murphy's long-winded declaration of intentions lets the reader know that he will not "disturb the Manes of the dead"; nor will he give a detailed account of the misfortunes resulting from Fielding's imprudence, nor "infer the character of his heart from the overflowing of sudden and momentary passions," nor "tear off ungenerously the shroud from his remains, and pursue him with a cruelty of narrative, till the

16. Joseph W. Reed, Jr., has shown in *English Biography in the Early Nineteenth Century: 1801–1838* (New Haven: Yale University Press, 1966) that the attitude we call Victorian can be seen from the very start of the century. In Maurice J. Quinlan's *Victorian Prelude: A History of English Manners, 1700–1830* (New York: Columbia University Press, 1941), the general tone of the Victorian age is shown to extend even farther back. Quinlan's study, however, does not touch specifically on the problem of biography. James L. Clifford discusses the problems Boswell encountered in "How Much Should a Biographer Tell? Some Eighteenth-Century Views," *Essays in Eighteenth-Century Biography*, ed. Philip B. Daghlian (Bloomington: Indiana University Press, 1968), pp. 67–95.

17. Quoted by Katherine G. Hornbeak, "New Light on Mrs. Montagu," in *The Age of Johnson: Essays Presented to Chauncey Brewster Tinker* (New Haven: Yale University Press, 1964), p. 361. Professor Hornbeak sees this as a minority view.

reader's sense is shocked."[18] Portraying the candid biographer as ghoul (and implying that a great deal about Henry Fielding needed to be buried), Murphy would fit neatly into the Victorian frame of mind. Although his biography of Fielding does not follow this credo religiously, it is clear that Murphy expected his reader to respond favorably to the suppression of unflattering material.[19] In fact, all of the Victorian arguments for suppression were adumbrated in the later eighteenth century: the need for ideal heroes, the moral value of unrelieved goodness, the right to privacy, due consideration for the feelings of the subject's relatives and friends.[20] The fact that each critic of the *Lives of the Poets* invariably finds something he wishes Johnson had omitted because of the way it reflects against the character of the subject suggests the prevalence of such arguments at this time.

Johnson's general attitude toward suppression can be seen in miniature by examining his use of one topic, drinking, as a touchstone for the treatment of moral issues in biography. Although both truth and morality are served by presenting the man as he is, a strong tension between the two may lead sometimes to the kind of works that Starnes discusses. The tension in its theoretical form can be observed in Boswell's account of Johnson's "varying from himself" on the question of "whether a man's vices should be mentioned" in biography. At one time Johnson suggests, though on the whole in a hypothetical manner, that the revelation of Parnell's and Addison's drinking might set a bad example for the reader and ease his conscience should he be inclined to drink. At another time, however, and in a more assertive vein, he had insisted that "if a man is to write *A Panegyric*, he may keep vices out of sight; but if he professes to

18. "The Life of Henry Fielding," *Works of Henry Fielding* (London, 1821), 1, 6.

19. It is a tribute to Johnson's biographical principles that Murphy's "Essay on the Life and Genius of Samuel Johnson" (1792) speaks of the necessity of giving "the lights and shades of the character" (*Works*, I, i). This would certainly not disturb the *manes* of Samuel Johnson.

20. It is not correct to assume, as Joseph W. Reed, Jr., does in *English Biography*, that the only real force operating for suppression in the eighteenth century was the "doctrine of dignity." This term was, in the sense in which Robertson, Hume, and Voltaire used it, to be applied to history in order to exclude almost all biographical material except great good or evil deeds.

write *A Life,* he must represent it really as it was"—a virtual anticipation of Ranke's *"wie es eigentlich gewesen."* And when Boswell offered the example of Parnell's drinking, Johnson countered by saying that "it would produce an instructive caution to avoid drinking, when it was seen, that even the learning and genius of Parnell could be debased by it" *(Life,* III, 155). Although this last was his general opinion, it would be a mistake to see the first position simply as Johnson "talking for victory" or, as Leon Edel suspects, being ironic at the expense of an obtuse Boswell.[21] The problem is deep and real, one that any man committed to both truth and morality has to contemplate. And the lives themselves show very clearly how Johnson coped with it.

Most biographers before Johnson suppressed all mention of their subjects' drinking. Johnson is able to satisfy both truth and morality by giving the context. His disquisition on Addison's drinking explains cause and effect in a paragraph that marks this vice as an outgrowth of weakness of character which destroys freedom of will:

From the coffee-house he went again to a tavern, where he often sat late and drank too much wine. In the bottle discontent seeks for comfort, cowardice for courage, and bashfulness for confidence. It is not unlikely that Addison was first seduced to excess by the manumission which he obtained from the servile timidity of his sober hours. He that feels oppression from the presence of those to whom he knows himself superior will desire to set loose his powers of conversation; and who that ever asked succour from Bacchus was able to preserve himself from being enslaved by his auxiliary? [II, 123]

Tickell, Addison's authorized biographer, could tell the reader about Addison's irregular pulse, but not about this. In the *Life of Collins,* Johnson portrays Collins' drinking as one of the concomitants of incipient madness. Collins, "with the usual weakness of men so diseased, eagerly snatched that temporary relief with which the table and the bottle flatter and seduce" (III, 340–41). Only in the *Life of Parnell* does Johnson really attempt to mitigate the charge of inebriety which he scrupulously lodges. Parnell's bibulousness deserves more sympathy because it was

21. *Literary Biography* (Garden City, N.Y.: Doubleday, 1959), pp. 19–20.

probably caused by the death of his son or of his wife. And Archbishop King's preferment of him leads Johnson to believe that "the vice of which he had been accused was not gross, or not notorious" (II, 51). Goldsmith had already mentioned Parnell's drinking and attributed it to the loss of his wife.[22] Johnson is the first biographer who discussed the drinking of Addison or Collins.[23] Though this is clearly not a new *topos* for biography, Johnson's candor, his unflinching payment of what was due to both truth and morality, marks a new realism in the biographical presentation of human beings.

Interestingly, Roger North had argued earlier in the century for the inclusion of such failings on moral grounds: "What signifies it to us, how many battles Alexander fought. It were more to the purpose to say how often he was drunk, and then we might from the ill consequences to him incline to be sober." North's words, in his intended "General Preface" to the "Life of the Lord Keeper North," went unpublished until recently, and by the middle of the nineteenth century the topic itself seems to have become unmentionable. This attitude, needless to say, has changed drastically. Reminding his readers that at the beginning of the twentieth century Edmund Gosse—in many ways a champion of more candid biography—"arrived at the conclusion that the one horrendous fact about his subject which a biographer should under no circumstances reveal is his addiction to drink," Mark Schorer, the biographer of Sinclair Lewis, adds, "If we were today to eliminate this phenomenon, what would the biographers of American writers have to write about?"[24]

22. "Life of Parnell," *Collected Works of Oliver Goldsmith*, ed. Arthur Friedman (Oxford: Clarendon Press, 1966), III, 442.

23. For Addison see James Lyons Battersby, Jr., "Samuel Johnson's *Life of Addison*: Sources, Composition, and Structure" (Ph.D. diss., Cornell, 1965), p. 419. The charge had appeared in print and was an open secret, but none of his numerous biographers thought it mentionable. Langhorne's "Memoirs of the Author" in *The Poetical Works of Mr. William Collins* (1765), the most recent contemporary biography, contains no hint that Collins drank.

24. North, *Biography as an Art*, ed. James L. Clifford (New York: Oxford University Press, 1962), p. 31. For the Victorians, see A. O. J. Cockshut, *Truth to Life: The Art of Biography in the Nineteenth Century* (London: Collins, 1974), pp. 35, 137, and *passim*. Schorer, "The Burdens of Biography," in *The World We Imagine* (New York: Farrar, Straus, and Giroux, 1968), p. 234.

After observing Johnson's skillful voyage between the Scylla of suppression and the Charybdis of giving bad examples, one must add that he admitted reluctantly to the need for one form of suppression and, on a very small scale, practiced another. In a famous passage in the *Life of Addison* he says:

> The necessity of complying with times and of sparing persons is the great impediment of biography.... What is known can seldom be immediately told, and when it might be told it is no longer known. The delicate features of the mind, the nice discriminations of character, and the minute peculiarities of conduct are soon obliterated; and it is surely better that caprice, obstinacy, frolick, and folly, however they might delight in the description, should be silently forgotten than that by wanton merriment and unseasonable detection a pang should be given to a widow, a daughter, a brother, or a friend. [II, 116]

And he resolves to tell the truth about his contemporaries, but not the whole truth. Ironically, this resolve seems to have been carried out most firmly in the *Life of Lyttelton*, a biography which brought the whole Lyttelton coterie swarming about him. He had attempted unsuccessfully to have Lyttelton's brother, Lord Westcote, employ someone to write the life, as Herbert Croft wrote the biographical section and the character for Johnson's *Life of Young*.[25] When this reluctantly written life appeared, the reviewer for the *Gentleman's Magazine*, quoting part of the above passage from the *Life of Addison*, expressed the wish that Johnson had suppressed his criticism of Lyttelton's "anxiety" over the publication of his *History of Henry the Second*.[26] The reviewer, like the Victorian public which was to follow in his footsteps, was far more susceptible to "pangs" than was Johnson, who prided himself, perhaps in reaction to the negative criticism of this life, on having foregone the mention of Lyttelton's table manners; and, according to an anonymous contemporary account, possibly by George Steevens, "he assured a friend ... that he kept back a very ridiculous anecdote of [Lyttelton] relative to a question he put to a great divine of his time."[27] To the Lytteltonians the

---

25. For Johnson's attempt to have Westcote sponsor the biography—a logical if weary extension of his belief that the best biographies are written by those who knew the subject personally—see *Letters*, II, 383, 385.

26. *Gentleman's Magazine*, 51 (1781), 275.

27. *Johnsonian Miscellanies*, ed. G. B. Hill (Oxford, 1897), II, 417. And see *Lyttelton* (*Lives*, III, 454, n. 6).

cruelest cut of all was Johnson's phrase "poor Lyttelton." They might have reflected that he uses the same adjective to describe Prior, Gay, and Dryden.

Johnson will sometimes suppress a detail or an anecdote because it is indecent or malicious, and because no positive good will come from the telling of it. Even in such cases, however, he usually lets his reader know that the material exists. He had once heard "a single line too gross to be repeated" from Edmund Smith's lampoon on Dr. Aldrich (II, 13). And he is unwilling to relate Cibber's "idle story of Pope's behaviour at a tavern" (III, 185; undoubtedly Cibber's account of Pope's putative nonperformance in a brothel). This is decorum, not suppression. No one could ever confuse Johnsonian biography with the *histoire scandaleuse*. In the *Life of Savage* he seems to act the part of Savage's literary executor. He refrains from quoting a lampoon which Savage left unpublished because "no other person ought to prosecute that revenge from which the person who was injured desisted" *(Savage*, pp. 100–101).

Only in questions of religion was Johnson likely to suppress some material without hinting at its existence. His treatment of Mallet is merely vague. After mentioning Mallet's personal appearance and conversational abilities, he says, "The rest of his character may without injury to his memory sink into silence" (III, 410). Most notably this would include his freethinking. Mallet was memorably described by Johnson in conversation as the "beggarly Scotchman" whom Lord Bolingbroke had left to fire the "blunderbuss against religion and morality" which he himself had charged *(Life*, II, 268). There is no mention of irreligion in the *Life of Mallet*. Another example, though less significant, of his suppression of material on religious grounds is the deleted expletive "Good God" in a letter from Prior to Swift (II, 195).[28] The *Lives* were, he indicates in his diary, "written I hope in such a manner, as may tend to the promotion of piety."[29]

For the most part, however, his omissions are more properly matters of selection than suppression. Suppression is an act of

28. But quotations in general are treated rather loosely. Johnson freely condenses and recasts.

29. *Yale*, I, 294. Such statements should not be overemphasized, however; Johnson attempts to consecrate all his energies to God in his private writings.

concealment—usually in conformity with social or religious doctrine; exclusion is an artistic act. Johnson was far less prone to suppress anything than was his age, and his contemporaries attacked many of his lives, particularly those of Dryden, Addison, and Pope, for not suppressing details, anecdotes, and events.

Like much eighteenth-century poetry, Johnsonian biography derives part of its strength from its exclusion of the irrelevant and the unnecessary, from the demands it makes upon its material. It achieves unity and coherence, though not at the expense of truth or moral complexity. In order to appreciate Johnson's biographies fully, one must recognize what they are free from as well as what they include. Here we will find no harangues, outlandish conjectures, or panegyric strains. Johnson rarely uses the biographical possessive, that rhetorical form that leads the biographer to appropriate his subject and refer to him as "our bard," "our author," and "our poet" (Ruffhead's *Pope* in a single page) or "our young nobleman" (Maty's *Chesterfield*).[30] Long before Lytton Strachey complained of "those two fat volumes with which it is our custom to commemorate the dead," Johnson was attacking the mealy-mouthed panegyrics of his day and writing himself with "a becoming brevity." At the same time, however, the scholarly attack on Stracheyan liberties in our century is in some ways a reprise of Johnson's attack on the fanciful in history. Sir John Dalrymple indulged in a pre-Stracheyan form of psychological narrative which Johnson, on the occasion of an invitation to dine with him, extemporaneously parodied. Imagining Dalrymple's anxiety at the nonappearance of his guests, Johnson portrays his worries as ending in suicide. This parody was justified with a few prefatory remarks: "Let me try to describe his situation in his own historical style. I have as good a right to make *him* think and talk as he has to tell us how people thought and talked a hundred years ago, of which he has no evidence. All history, so far as it is not supported by contemporary evidence, is romance" (*Hebrides*, p. 392).

30. He does, however, speak of "our young student" in the "Life of Boerhaave," *Works*, VI, 272. Owen Ruffhead, *The Life of Alexander Pope, Esq.* (London, 1769), p. 14; Matthew Maty, "Memoirs of Lord Chesterfield" in *Miscellaneous Works by the Late . . . Earl of Chesterfield* (London, 1777), I, 12.

Johnson's shrewd historical sense is often put to the service of interpreting the meaning of certain facts (usually literary ones) in his biographies. As he insists in the *Life of Pope*, "Time and place will always enforce regard" (III, 238). He doubts that Otway's *Don Carlos* had a first run of thirty nights because "so long a continuance of one play upon the stage is a very wide deviation from the practice of that time" (I, 244). He also accounts for what seems to be the small sale of *Paradise Lost* by explaining that the number of readers was not large and supporting his statement by reference to the paucity of editions of Shakespeare in the seventeenth century (though in some ways he overlooked the question of Shakespeare's relative popularity before the time of Dryden). "Those who have no power to judge of past times but by their own," he adds, "should always doubt their conclusions" (I, 143). He also notes that the sale was kept down by the political climate ("its admirers did not dare to publish their opinion") and for what we would consider sociological reasons ("the opportunities now given of attracting notice by advertisements were then very few").

Johnson sets Dryden's successive poems on Cromwell and Charles in their historical contexts: "The reproach of inconstancy was, on this occasion, shared with such numbers that it produced neither hatred nor disgrace; if he changed, he changed with the nation" (I, 334). And he defends Congreve's depiction of Foresight in *Love for Love* by giving instances of famous men of the day who believed in astrology and deciding that Foresight therefore exhibits "real manners" (II, 218). Although Johnson is not writing life-and-times biography—he is collectively writing literary history—he sometimes uses a general knowledge of the age to help him over the bare spots: "The particular character of Tonson I do not know, but the general conduct of traders was much less liberal in those times than in our own; their views were narrower and their manners grosser" (I, 407).

In addition to basing many of his judgments on historical knowledge, Johnson willingly employs computation, if not to the extent that a modern cliometrician might desire. He figures that "the value of money and the customs of life" of Waller's time made his yearly £13,500 equivalent to £110,000 in the later eighteenth century. And responding to the preposterous claim that King had read over 22,000 books and manuscripts in eight years at Christ Church, Oxford, he remarks, "The books were certainly not very long, the manuscripts not very difficult, nor the remarks very large; for the calculator will find that he dispatched seven a day, for every day of his eight years, with a remnant that more than satisfies most other students" (II, 26).

Many of Johnson's critics have commented upon his selection of facts from a large body of material. James Battersby, having exhaustively studied all of the possible sources for the *Life of Addison*, concludes that "Johnson apparently did not aim for fullness; indeed, the sources available to him contain many details that he did not choose to include in his account."[31] In a comparison of Johnson's *Life of King* with that of John Nichols, whose biography Johnson abridged, Edward Hart finds that "Nichols was striving for accuracy and completeness of detail; Johnson for elegance of style."[32] And Donald A. Stauffer, who calls Johnson the greatest of all English biographers "at drawing the general truth from the individual fact," accuses many of his followers of failing to see "that Johnson maintained that the small detail should be selected with unusual care because it must be significant."[33] Battersby's general account of what Johnson includes is revealing: "In his brief survey of Addison's life and writings, only those works and events which reveal genius, concerning which dispute has arisen, in which excellence or originality is manifested, which are important as early intimations of later and more complete realizations, which signify important stages in political, social, or literary advancement, and by which individual uniqueness is revealed deserve attention.... Neither each writing, nor each reported action warrants notice."[34] Battersby's list is generally sound, but his limitation to one life has its drawbacks as well as its advantages. The *Life of Addison* is a good

31. "Samuel Johnson's *Life of Addison*," p. 194.
32. "Some New Sources of Johnson's *Lives*," *PMLA*, 65 (1950), 1111.
33. *The Art of Biography in Eighteenth-Century England* (Princeton: Princeton University Press, 1941), p. 401.
34. "Samuel Johnson's *Life of Addison*," pp. 222–23.

representative life in that Johnson had a wealth of information from which to draw, and therefore his choices were much freer than in some of the lives with skimpier source materials. But the *Life of Addison* also has a coherence that some of the other lives lack simply because of the nature of Addison himself, and some of the facts included in the *Life of Addison* would not have been mentioned in the life of a less eminent man or of one who interested Johnson less. For these reasons, as well as others which will become apparent, it is worth examining the process of selection in Johnsonian biography as a whole.

Johnson discusses the use of details in *Rambler* No. 60, where he ridicules Tickell's mentioning the irregularity of Addison's pulse. Johnson is interested in the moral, not the physiological. If the first principle of the eighteenth century was "The proper study of mankind is man," Locke had earlier stated its corollary: "morality is the proper . . . business of mankind."[35] Johnson also objects to the remarks in the Marquis de Racan's biography of François de Malherbe as irrelevant to the subject as a focus of our concern. Malherbe's opinion of the effects of a woman's promiscuousness upon her social status, as well as his decision that the phrase "noble gentleman" is a solecism, do not, for Johnson, elucidate Malherbe's character, nor do they provide us with any useful information. It may be noted in passing, however, that these opinions are precisely the sort of thing, assimilated into a rich personal context and placed in time and space, on which Boswellian biography thrives. A glimpse of the difference between Johnson's attitude toward the minutiae of a literary life and that of later ages can be seen in his comment on his predecessors' enumeration of Milton's houses: "I cannot but remark a kind of respect, perhaps unconsciously, paid to this great man by his biographers: every house in which he resided is historically mentioned, as if it were an injury to neglect naming any place that he honoured by his presence" (I, 127). For him the biographers' scrupulosity is more revealing than the mundane facts themselves, and he probably would have marveled at the nineteenth-century enshrinement of authors' homes (includ-

35. *An Essay Concerning Human Understanding*, ed. Alexander Campbell Fraser (1894; rpt. New York: Dover, 1959), II, 351:

ing his own) and the concomitant popularity of literary pilgrim-ages.[36]

In the *Lives of the Poets*, the specific kind of biography Johnson is writing has a bearing on the process of selection. Despite his disquisitions and digressions, the explicit awareness that he is writing literary biography, that his lives are proportioned to the literary importance of his subjects and that his topics are chosen for the light they will throw on the poet, is to be found in a number of the *Lives of the Poets*. The *Life of Halifax* is very short, although Johnson had a great deal of material to work with. The first paragraph is, in a sense, a defense of that shortness: "The life of the Earl of Halifax was properly that of an artful and active statesman employed in balancing parties, contriving expedients, and combating opposition, and exposed to the vicissitudes of advancement and degradation: but in this collec-tion poetical merit is the claim to attention; and the account which is here to be expected may properly be proportioned not to his influence in the state, but to his rank among the writers of verse" (II, 41). Johnson is a master at preterition, at "getting on the record" information which is putatively ignored as irrelevant (e.g., "Cheynel," *Works*, VI, 413–28), and this highly generalized summary gives us some idea of the nature of Halifax's political activity. After this introduction it is not surprising to find that the critical section of the life is devoted not to Halifax's poetry but to an explanation of why he was so overrated in his own time. The very shortness of Johnson's account at once counter-balances the excessive estimate of Halifax in Queen Anne's time and "places" him in comparison to the other poets in the *Lives*.

Of course, the great failures of proportion in the *Lives of the Poets* are the *Life of Savage* and the *Life of Dryden*. The *Savage*, which Johnson neglected to rewrite for its new context, bulks far too large in the *Lives*, and the printer may have been playing literary critic when he set it in reduced type. (I am not suggest-

36. Harlan W. Hamilton has shrewdly noted Boswell's suppression of the paragraph on Tickell and Racan from a series of four paragraphs quoted in sequence in the *Life of Johnson*. See "Boswell's Suppression of a Paragraph in *Rambler* No. 60," *MLN*, 76 (1961), 218–20. On the cult of the author see Richard D. Altick, *Lives and Letters: A History of Literary Biography in England and America* (New York: Alfred A. Knopf, 1964), ch. iv.

ing, however, that the *Life of Savage* is a failure itself; quite the contrary, as we shall see in Chapter 9.) The odd shape of the *Life of Dryden* may have been caused by the discrepancy between the importance of that biography and the relatively little material Johnson could find. Padding is not a charge one is inclined to raise against Johnson, but here he seems to have thrown in some things simply to give himself a chance to say more about Dryden. Most of his memorable complaints about the difficulty of biographical scholarship come in this life, and even the combined researches of modern scholarship have issued only in a relatively short biography by Charles Ward.

On the whole, however, Johnson's sense of proportion is strong, especially at a time when most biographers lacked standards for proportioning their works. The fact that a number of Johnson's contemporaries thought the *Life of Dryden* his best is good evidence that proportion was not one of their main criteria for biography. Today, when we reel from one "definitive" biography to another, we may doubt if the situation is entirely improved.

Sometimes Johnson uses an explicit statement to remind us that a difference exists between biographical and historical relevance: "my business is not the history of the peace, but the life of Prior" (II, 189). Sometimes he uses this call in order to keep himself from criticizing certain beliefs of the poet. Discussing Akenside's "The Pleasures of Imagination" he says, "With the philosophical or religious tenets of the author I have nothing to do; my business is with his poetry" (III, 417).[37]

This attitude, with which Johnson's critics rarely credit him, seems to be consistent with his conception of the relation of poem to poet and with his practice in the *Lives*. At another time a variation of the same remark ("My business is only with his poems") keeps him from the necessity of discussing Sprat's prose writings (II, 38).

Another form of exclusion that is immediately evident from a

37. Donald J. Greene, after quoting a political attack by Johnson on Akenside, adds: "But such *obiter dicta* are not very frequent, and not so important in the plan of the *Lives* as the number of times they have been quoted might suggest" (*The Politics of Samuel Johnson* [New Haven: Yale University Press, 1960], p. 221).

study of Johnson's sources is his reluctance to name or even mention minor characters. He likes to work with a smaller *dramatis personae* than do most of the prefatory biographers of his day. He seems to adhere to a variety of the belief he imputes to Milton: he considers the naming of a person a preservative from oblivion, and one qualifies for such an honor not through reflected glory but by achievement.

A number of the sources Johnson used are thick with names, the sort of accounts over which modern positivistic scholarship would smack its lips. Johnson found much of their material unpalatable and chose not to garnish his biographies with facts from which no sustenance could be obtained. Names are deleted by the bushel unless they have some close relationship to the subject or some importance of their own. Johnson is far from the life-and-times conception of Sir Walter Scott's *Dryden* or, for that matter, of Boswell's *Johnson*. In his account of Cambridge at the time of Ascham's matriculation only Smith, Cheeke, and Pember are chosen for inclusion from the dozen professors of note mentioned by Grant in his Latin funeral oration. In a biography of Savage written in 1727 Savage is committed to jail by "Nathaniel Blakesley and two other of his majesty's justices of the peace."[38] In Johnson's life they become "three justices," and the time of Savage's removal from the gatehouse to Newgate is omitted. Minor patrons and all but the most important friends fall by the way. Patrick Murdoch's "Life of Thomson" mentions the Reverend Mr. Gusthart, who aided Thomson's mother in family affairs; Sir William Bennet, who invited Thomson to spend a number of summers with him; and several friends, including the painter Aikman, whom Thomson had celebrated in an extant poem.[39] Johnson retains none of these names. In the *Life of Prior* he excludes—here perhaps "suppresses" would be the better word—any mention of Elizabeth Cox or Anne Durham, two ladies whose names appeared in Prior's will, and at least one of whom, as Johnson undoubtedly knew, was Prior's mistress.[40]

38. Richard E. Lyon, "The Life of Richard Savage: An Edition" (Ph.D. diss., University of Chicago, 1958), p. 9.

39. *The Works of James Thomson* (London, 1788), I, ix-xxx, *passim*.

40. The will is given in *A New Collection of Poems on Several Occasions by Mr. Prior and Others* (London, 1725), pp. 10–11.

Since he does not name Hammond's mistress either, though he has something to say of her, it is possible that delicacy, or indignation, accounts for his reticence.

A good example of this process of exclusion can be found in Johnson's accounts of the families of his subjects. The brothers and sisters of the subject are rarely mentioned and even more rarely named by Johnson, despite the sharp awareness he exhibits in his essays and conversation of the effects of siblings on one another. Speaking of Ascham's mother, he says, "She had three sons, of whom Roger was the youngest, and some daughters; but who can hope, that of any progeny more than one shall deserve to be mentioned."[41] His source, Edward Grant's *Vita Aschami*, names all the boys. Even when he finds that the relationship between the subject and a sister helps, as in the lives of Fenton and Thomson, to demonstrate the benevolence of his subject, he does not name the sister. One notable exception is his short discussion of the brother and sister of Milton. Christopher Milton is named because he remained loyal to the king and might have shielded his brother from the wrath of the restored royalists. Anne Milton was the mother of the two nephews who attended Milton's school; and "the only authentic account of his domestick manners" comes from his nephew John Phillips.

This treatment of the subject's brothers and sisters is not as striking as it would be in the Victorian or our own post-Freudian age, but it is at variance with the practice of Johnson's predecessors and contemporaries. The normal procedure of seventeenth- and eighteenth-century biographers is to give short accounts of the brothers and either name the sisters or merely mention that they exist. The male bias which prohibits more than mentioning sisters *en masse* is a fairly consistent trait of the biographies of the time. The passage quoted above from the "Life of Ascham" is typical, as is the information in Johnson's *Life of Addison* that Addison left "no child but a daughter" (II, 218). This attitude is conditioned by the inferior status of women and the fact that they did not continue the family name. Johnson's own sources frequently contain references to brothers

41. "Ascham," *Works*, VI, 504. Those interested in the relationship of Samuel Johnson and his wayward brother Nathaniel may want to ponder the statement.

and sisters which do not find their way into his accounts. All six of Addison's siblings are mentioned in Thomas Birch's article in the *General Dictionary* (1734) and none of them in Johnson's *Life of Addison*. Sprat discusses Cowley's treatment of his brothers, but Johnson omits this information.

Apart from specific incidents, the brothers and sisters of the subject seem to be mentioned only when they are sufficiently numerous. Johnson tells us that Watts was the eldest of nine children, Fenton the youngest of twelve. Only in the *Life of Thomson* does he use the number of children in the family as a detail with consequences for the future poet: "The revenue of a parish in Scotland is seldom large; and it was probably in commiseration of the difficulty with which Mr. Thomson supported his family, having nine children, that Mr. Riccarton, a neighbouring minister, discovering in James uncommon promises of future excellence, undertook to superintend his education, and provide him books" (III, 281–82). This conjecture is not to be found in Murdoch, Johnson's principal source, nor does anyone else, to my knowledge, motivate Ricaltoun in this way.

Easy as it would be to quibble over the reasons for Johnson's decisions to add or omit information and commentary in the lives he writes, this examination of Johnson as interpreter should demonstrate something more important: that he is impressing his own vision on his materials. A comparison with Lytton Strachey may show that Johnson's franchise as interpreter was more limited, and illustrate the creative tension between his own view of things and his adherence to truth, impartially delivered. "Uninterpreted truth is as useless as buried gold," asserts Strachey, perhaps remembering Johnson's use of the same figure in *Idler* No. 84 to make a point at once close to Strachey's and significantly different: "Between falsehood and useless truth there is little difference. As gold which he cannot spend will make no man rich, so knowledge which he cannot apply will make no man wise" (*Yale*, II, 62). Strachey's idea of interpretation, which he places foremost in his theory of biography, cuts off much of what Johnson and most modern historians would consider truth. Putting a fair face on Strachey's

method, his best modern biographer admits that "his theory of
artistic uniformity forbade him from putting at his readers' disposal the evidence necessary for them to come to their own
opinion or to reach a reasonable assessment of his."[42]

The practice which Michael Holroyd defends by reference to
presumed theory is rather different from Strachey's professed
intention to "row out over that great ocean of material and lower
down into it, here and there, a little bucket, which will bring up
to the light of day some characteristic specimen, from those far
depths, to be examined with a careful curiosity."[43] The activity
implied is in some ways that of the scientist and yet akin to the
act of social judgment which would leave the subject fixed and
wriggling on a pin. But it also implies a readiness for the contradictory nature of the findings which Strachey's point of view
(sometimes taken firmly in advance of his research) belies.

Johnson, for all the formidable power with which he holds
and states his position, enables his readers to come to conclusions different from his own. An instructive example is the life
of Francis Cheynel, surely of all his subjects the one with whom
he had the least sympathy. In 1775, the same year the "Life of
Cheynel" was reprinted in the *Gentleman's Magazine*, Samuel
Palmer complains that Johnson's biography is "drawn up in such
a manner as might be expected from a man of his avowed principles in religion and politics. The narrative is indeed a satyr
both upon *Dr. Cheynel* and the times. From the writer's conces-
sions, however, the reader will remain possessed of the idea that
Dr. Cheynel's was a truly great character, tho' from undeniable
facts he will be constrained to own it was not without its
blemishes."[44] That the biography contains satire (and indeed
excellent satire) of a man who might easily have served as the
model for Swift's Jack in *A Tale of a Tub* is beyond dispute. What
Palmer fails to recognize, however, and a reading of the earlier

42. Michael Holroyd, *Lytton Strachey, The Years of Achievement* (New York: Holt,
Rinehart, and Winston, 1968), p. 272.
43. Preface to *Eminent Victorians*, in *Biography as an Art: Selected Criticism,
1560–1960*, ed. James L. Clifford (New York: Oxford University Press, 1962), p.
121.
44. *The Nonconformist's Memorial; Being an Account of the Ministers Rejected or
Silenced* (London, 1775), II, 467–68.

biographies of Cheynel establishes, is that Johnson's praise is not
extorted from him, but develops through an exploration of
Cheynel's character which goes far deeper than the acidulous
Anglican accounts of Wood and Maizeau or even that of
Cheynel's defender, Edmund Calamy, whose *Nonconformist's
Memorial* Palmer revised. Despite Johnson's indubitable an-
tipathy for his subject (strategically chosen to drive home a lesson about education), he is more sympathetic than any other
high church biographer, willingly accepts Cheynel's own account
of many things, and unquestioningly includes almost all the
praise of his foremost defender. In Cheynel he portrays a churchman who missed his *métier*: he should have been a soldier.
Palmer pays an unconscious debt to Johnson as biographer, for
the major part of the praise of Cheynel in his own book derives
from Johnson.

  Johnson's biographies are at once highly personal and broadly
humane. In the next chapter I hope to show that what he takes
from his predecessors and the form of his biographies also de-
velop from his own conception of biography.

CHAPTER 5

Precedents and Form

Naming the predecessors of Johnsonian biography is an easy task, but pointing to specific influences is much more difficult. Speaking of the *Life of Savage* in what is perhaps the most circuitous passage in a very forthright book, Joseph Wood Krutch says that "if Johnson had had occasion to mention the models for the sort of biographical writing which he admired he might well have cited Plutarch and Tacitus, with possibly even an allusion to Suetonius or Diogenes Laertius."[1] If Johnson's reading or his allusions in his own biographies could be used in evidence, Suetonius would seem to have been a favorite. In the *Lives of the Poets* he quotes the *Caligula* and brilliantly adapts Suetonius' praise of Augustus (*Pope*, III, 166; *Dryden*, I, 469). The year he began writing the *Lives* (1777) we find him reading the biographies of Galba, Otho, and Vitellius (*Yale*, I, 275).

Johnson's interest in Suetonius suggests that he may have used Suetonius as a biographical model. Paul Fussell notes that Johnson could find in Suetonius "an exhibition of triumphant auctorial control: . . . a cool detachment which avoids cynicism only by the speaker's awareness that being human, he is deeply implicated in the follies he is depicting."[2] But this tone, important as it is, may be of less importance to Johnson than the form

1. *Samuel Johnson* (1944; rpt. New York: Harcourt, Brace, and World, 1963), p. 81.
2. *Samuel Johnson and the Life of Writing* (New York: Harcourt, Brace, Jovanovich, 1971), p. 265.

of Suetonius' biographies. Friedrich Leo argued at the turn of the century that there were essentially two kinds of ancient biography, the Suetonian and the Plutarchean. "The Suetonian type," in the words of Arnaldo Momigliano, "is the combination of a tale in chronological order with the systematic characterization of an individual and his achievements. As such it is naturally well suited to lives of writers."[3] This is not a bad description of Johnson's formula in the *Lives of the Poets*. Leo sees the Suetonian biography as a development from the Alexandrian grammarians by way of Aristotle and looks upon Suetonius as chiefly a grammarian who wrote of both writers and emperors. Like Suetonius, Johnson gains some of his effects from the serial consideration of a group of men representing a single professional type, and one of Johnson's most impressive and characteristic passages, the conclusion of the *Life of Dryden*, places Dryden's poetic achievement by using metaphorically the phrase that Suetonius had applied to Augustus.

In his letters Johnson quotes Tacitus' *Agricola* (though he was no admirer of his style) and perhaps Plutarch's "Life of Caesar" (*Letters*, III, 30; II, 378). Though he was interested in the accomplishment of Plutarch—he planned to translate his lives and to write "Lives of Illustrious Persons, as well of the active as the learned in imitation of Plutarch" (*Life*, IV, 382n.)—he did not quote, as did Sir Philip Warwick in his *Memoirs of... King Charles I*, or Dryden in his "Life of Plutarch," or as Boswell would in his *Life of Johnson*, the passage from the "Life of Alexander" in which Plutarch says: "It must be borne in mind that my design is not to write histories, but lives. And the most glorious exploits do not always furnish us with the clearest discoveries of virtue or vice in men; sometimes a matter of less moment, an expression or a jest, informs us better of their characters and inclinations, than the most famous sieges, the greatest armaments, or the bloodiest battles whatsoever."[4] Although Johnson's heroes are, for the most part, vastly different from Plutarch's soldiers and

3. *The Development of Greek Biography* (Cambridge, Mass.: Harvard University Press, 1971), p. 18.

4. *The Lives of the Noble Grecians and Romans*, trans. John Dryden and Arthur Hugh Clough (New York: Modern Library, n.d.), p. 801.

statesmen, these are sentiments with which he agrees, and the expression of them by this "Prince of biographers" (Boswell's phrase) unquestionably made his own emphasis on morality, particularly in the private and domestic realm, more readily acceptable.[5] Plutarch was the biographer *par excellence* for the eighteenth century.

There is no questioning Johnson's familiarity with the biographies of classical antiquity. On the other hand, I find the presence of any but a very generalized classical influence difficult to establish. We might speak of his affinities with the Plutarchean emphasis on the private man and the small detail, and the love of anecdotes of Suetonius, Diogenes Laertius, and Cornelius Nepos. We might perhaps even suggest that the dignified, monochromatic Christian Stoicism of the early "Life of Boerhaave" owes something to that monument of Roman Stoicism, the *Agricola*, and that Johnson's use in the *Life of Savage* of a general truth as a point of departure for the biography that follows owes something to the Plutarchean model.[6]

The classical writer with the most discernible influence on Johnson's biographies, however, is not a biographer at all, but Sallust. (Johnson's translation of part of the *Catilinian Wars* is in the Hyde Collection.) In *Rambler* No. 60 he praises Sallust as "the great master of nature," and uses as an example of the kind of biographical detail he admires Sallust's observation that Catiline's "walk was now quick, and again slow" (*Works*, II, 288). He thought that Sallust was one of the writers we can trust because he knew the men he wrote about (*Life*, II, 79). In a few of his early biographies Johnson uses details in a Sallustian fashion. The "Life of Blake" (1740) dramatically presents the Puritan captain upon the receipt of an insulting refusal by the

5. James William Johnson has suggested that the systematization of Plutarch by Vossius may have paved the way for Johnson and Boswell. See *The Formation of English Neo-Classical Thought* (Princeton: Princeton University Press, 1967), p. 151.

6. This last practice had become common property. It is used effectively by Vasari, and English homiletics probably gave it an added impetus. Dr. Samuel Parr told Boswell that he "had found out forty points of similarity between [Johnson] and Plutarch" (*The Journal of James Boswell 1765–1768*, ed. Geoffrey Scott and Frederick A. Pottle, in *The Private Papers of James Boswell* [n.p.: Privately printed, 1930], VII, 94. Dr. Parr may have overstated his case.

Spanish to let him draw water for his men: "Fired with this inhuman and insolent treatment, he curled his whiskers, as was his custom when he was angry" and quickly took the city of Tunis (*Works*, VI, 305). But Sallust's main influence appears in the portraiture within the "character."

2

David Nichol Smith finds that the spirit of biography is inimical to the art of the historical character. Since the biographer need not depend upon the character alone to give the sense of a man, he is apt to ignore the lapidary touches which the character needs. "The truth is," Smith continues, "that a life and a character have different objects and methods and do not readily combine. It is only a small admixture of biography that a character will endure."[7] This estimate seems sound, but a large amount of biographical knowledge often lies behind successful historical characters.

In Johnson's *Lives of the Poets*, the biographical section and the character complement one another. When he disdainfully dismisses Sprat's *Cowley* as "the character, not the life of Cowley; for he writes with so little detail that scarcely anything is distinctly known," Johnson is not rejecting the genre altogether but pointing out its inadequacies. He wrote one character for separate publication, although he evidently thought that the character gave a very tenuous impression of the man if it stood alone.[8]

One might enumerate a series of opposed but complementary elements in the life and the character. Though they will not hold good in every case, they should give the tendencies of the two forms. The life presents process; the character, essence. The life is chronological; the character topical. The life presents circumstances, actions in sequence, and is therefore detailed. The character, with the exception of the portrait, is highly general,

7. *Characters from the Histories and Memoirs of the Seventeenth Century* (1918; rpt. Oxford: Clarendon Press, 1963), pp. ix, li.
8. His character of Collins appeared in Francis Fawkes's and William Woty's *The Poetical Calendar* (London, 1763), XII, 110-12. The death notice of the Reverend Zachariah Mudge, which Boswell refers to as a character, appeared in the *London Chronicle*, April 29 to May 2, 1769, p. 410, col. 3 (reprinted in *Life*, IV, 77). He also wrote several other death notices.

and the particulars are used to illustrate general truths. The life deals with a man's fortune, in several senses of the word, with his achievements and failures. The character deals with a man's abilities and gifts, with the qualities that determine his actions. The life focuses on a man's struggle in the world; the character is more psychologically oriented. The character, then, cannot be considered merely as the summing up of the life. Sacrificing temporality, the character writer is free to reconstruct the controlling forces behind his subject's actions.

Emphasizing the flexibility of the Johnsonian character, Lawrence Lipking says it gives "unique opportunities for covert literary criticism" and sees it as a technical means by which "a biographer can mediate between the poet and his poetry with all the subtlety and resourcefulness at his command."[9] Indeed, he sees Johnson's development of the character to prominence as the most distinctive formal element of the *Lives*. Johnson is able to call his central section the "character," "intellectual character," or "literary character" and proceed accordingly.

Johnson may be considered a student of the historical character. Langton told Boswell that Johnson "apprehended that the delineation of characters in the end of the first book of [Xenophon's] 'Retreat of the Ten Thousand'" was the first instance of the kind that was known. Johnson also thought that Dryden's critical character of Shakespeare was the finest example of "encomiastick criticism" he knew. Despite the fact that he distrusted characters given by those who did not personally know the subjects, his own characters of Dryden and Pope (and not just that of Savage) are memorable.

To quote a major character in full would take too long, but one can gain an idea of Johnson's powers in miniature from the thumbnail characters of featured players within the biographies. Take Warburton:

About this time Warburton began to make his appearance in the first ranks of learning. He was a man of vigourous faculties, a mind fervid

9. *The Ordering of the Arts in Eighteenth-Century England* (Princeton: Princeton University Press, 1970), p. 420. For an interesting account of the "literary character" see Jean H. Hagstrum, *Samuel Johnson's Literary Criticism* (1952; rpt. Chicago: University of Chicago Press, 1967), pp. 38–41.

and vehement, supplied by incessant and unlimited enquiry, with won-derful extent and variety of knowledge, which yet had not oppressed his imagination nor clouded his perspicacity. To every work he brought a memory full fraught, together with a fancy fertile of original combina-tions, and at once exerted the powers of the scholar, the reasoner, and the wit. But his knowledge was too multifarious to be always exact, and his pursuits were too eager to be always cautious. His abilities gave him an haughty confidence which he disdained to conceal or mollify, and his impatience of opposition disposed him to treat his adversaries with such contemptuous superiority as made his readers commonly his enemies, and excited against the advocate the wishes of some who favoured the cause. He seems to have adopted the Roman Emperor's determination, "oderint dum metuant"; he used no allurement of gentle language, but wished to compel rather than persuade. [III, 165–66]

One-quarter of the *Lives of the Poets* contain no personal characters. This figure is somewhat deceptive because most of the biographies without characters are short, the longest among them being *Denham, Congreve*, and *Blackmore*, which run to forty-odd paragraphs apiece. Johnson is unwilling to include or adapt characters which were not written from personal knowl-edge of the subject. Although he paraphrases Goldsmith's "Life of Parnell," for example, he does not use the character. Con-versely, he frequently quotes contemporary characters on the grounds that characters are of value when they come from one who knew the subject.

Johnson's usual though not invariable practice in presenting a character of his subject written by a contemporary is to alert his reader to the partiality of the writer. He quotes James Wel-wood's character of Rowe, remarking that it seems to be pro-duced by "the fondness of a friend" (II, 73–74). Having applied the same phrase to Steele's account of Addison as a companion, he says "let us hear what is told us by a rival," and gives cor-roborating testimony from Pope (II, 119). His strongest attack on a character written by a contemporary appears in the *Life of Smith*. The lengthy character of Smith by Oldisworth—really a biographical sketch in which the description of character predominates—had been subjected to witty disparagement ear-lier in the century. Johnson exonerates Oldisworth from any possible accusation of disingenuousness but exposes the decep-

tiveness of his panegyric: "Such is the declamation of Oldisworth, written while his admiration was yet fresh, and his kindness warm; and therefore such as, without any criminal purpose
of deceiving, shows a strong desire to make the most of all
favourable truth. I cannot much commend the performance.
The truth is often indistinct, and the sentences are loaded with
words of more pomp than use. There is little however that can
be contradicted, even when a plainer tale comes to be told" (II,
11).[10] Johnson's "plainer tale" is really a counterbiography that
substitutes an unsavory human being of some ability for the
exemplary plaster cast of Oldisworth's creation.

In some cases, however, Johnson does not make a bias clear.
Dr. Joseph Towers' early biography of Johnson contains a valid
criticism of his failure in his *Life of Waller* to mention Clarendon's obvious contempt for the man.[11] Johnson also fails to mention that Prior's character of Dorset originally appeared in a
dedication of Prior's *Poems on Several Occasions* to Dorset's son.
The fact that Prior was "familiarly known" to Dorset makes the
character worthy of inclusion, but to describe it as an "encomiastick character" in the *Life of Prior* and not in the *Life of Dorset* is
surely a mistake (II, 186; I, 303).

His own characters sometimes begin with a "portrait" of the
subject. In the great age of English portraiture, the biographer,
like the artist, was apt to present his subject formally posed
and at rest. Johnson's *Lives* contain relatively few portraits.
I suspect that his notoriously poor eyesight had little to do with
this lack. The difficulty of finding evidence he considered
satisfactory probably held him back. In his biographies he
avoids the evidence of paintings and engravings and relies
solely on printed materials for his pen portraits. Engraved
portraits appear as frontispieces to the fifty-six volume edition of
the *English Poets* ("very impudently called mine," said Johnson)
for which his *Prefaces* were commissioned. He complained several
times in conversation that the painters of his day excessively
idealized their portraits; he sought likenesses.

10. And see p. 49 above.
11. *An Essay on the Life, Character, and Writings of Dr. Samuel Johnson* (London,
1786), p. 56.

The portraits we do have will not be much admired by readers who are looking for novelistic descriptions replete with minute details. Johnson thought that the use of details was appropriate in biography, but, like most of the historians and biographers of his day, he conceives them in terms of deviations from a normative human figure. Typically, we are presented with a sketchy full length. The subject is "above," "below," or of "the middle size." His girth is considered. Most of the poets are "corpulent" —Thomson is described in his own words as "more fat than bard beseems"—and few, such as Savage with his "thin habit of body," fit the stereotype of the poet. One should also notice that the objective and subjective descriptions of the subject blend. Johnson mentions that the "diminutive" Mallet was "regularly formed" and that Shenstone had "something clumsy in his form," but we are usually given the "appearance" of the subject, the effect of seeing him upon an observer. Thomson was of a "gross, unanimated and uninviting appearance." The increasing subjectivity here is particularly appropriate because it provides a transition to Thomson's social behavior. His "uninviting appearance" is both justified, for he was "silent in mingled company," and deceptive, for he was "cheerful among select friends" and loved by them (III, 294). The generality of Johnson's descriptive adjectives is typical. Savage was "of a grave and manly deportment" (II, 429). Collins' "appearance was decent and manly." Clothing, an item of great importance in that social age, is usually mentioned in similarly general terms: Shenstone was "very negligent of his cloaths"; Mallet permitted his small frame "to want no recommendation that dress could give it" (III, 354, 409). The biographical section of the *Life of Milton* contains a more detailed version of his subject's dress, but only in the character of Pope is any fullness of detail to be found.[12]

12. See Ch. 2, p. 40, for some remarks on the portrait of Pope. For accounts of literary portraiture in history and the novel see B[lanchard] W[esley] Bates, *Literary Portraiture in the Historical Narratives of the French Renaissance* (New York: G. E. Stechert, 1945); Sean Shesgreen, *Literary Portraits in the Novels of Henry Fielding* (DeKalb, Ill.: Northern Illinois University Press, 1972); and Peter Brooks, *The Novel of Worldliness* (Princeton: Princeton University Press, 1969), especially pp. 57 ff.

What a biographer ran into if he gave more particulars than
Johnson does can be best seen in Peter Pindar's satire of Boswell:

> Who will not, too, thy pen's *minutiae* bless,
> That gives posterity the Rambler's dress?
> Methinks I view his full, plain suit of brown,
> The large grey bushy wig that graced his crown,
> Black worsted stockings, little silver buckles,
> And shirt that had no ruffles for his knuckles.[13]

This passage, filled with footnote references to Boswell's *Tour to
the Hebrides*, is intended to point to self-evidently foolish details.
We who have been brought up on the particularity of the novel
need a Peter Pindar to recapture the historical objections.

In describing the faces of his subjects Johnson sticks to typify-
ing phrases except when there is some specific reason for being
more particular. He has no Aubreyan interest in the brute fact.
He will not describe eyes as blue, grey, or hazel, but he will
mention that Pope's eyes were "animated and vivid" in order to
explain the attractiveness of this otherwise misshapen man. He
also mentions that Milton's eyes, before his blindness, must have
been "quick," for he was a skillful fencer. Milton's hair is likewise
described because it helps to explain why he was called "the lady
of his college" and because he has given the same hair style to
Adam. Shenstone's grey hair is mentioned because "he was remarkable for wearing it in a particular manner, for he held that
the fashion was no rule of dress, and that every man was to suit
his appearance to his natural form" (III, 354). What that manner was Johnson does not tell us (and very likely did not know,
since his source, Robert Dodsley, does not tell us either). The
details Johnson gives us, then, are those that reflect the nature
and abilities of the subject. They are more likely to be a part of
the ethical stance of the subject than simply matters of fact (like
those in Sallust). He wants to do what he claimed Hogarth did:
to see the "manners in the face."

In the character the "familiar day," a description of the typical

13. [John Wolcot], "A Poetical and Congratulatory Epistle to James Boswell,
Esq. on his Journal of a Tour to the Hebrides with the celebrated Doctor
Johnson," in *The Works of Peter Pindar, Esq.* (London, 1794), I, 313–14.

daily activities of the subject, also finds its place. Given Johnson's emphasis on quotidian realities, this is a congenial task. He usually alerts his reader to the time from which such a description is drawn. The course of Addison's day "before his marriage" (he married three years before he died) appears in the character. In the *Life of Milton* Johnson gives quick accounts of daily activities at different times before presenting a sketch of his familiar day more fully:

In his youth he studied late at night; but afterwards changed his hours, and rested in bed from nine to four in the summer, and five in the winter. The course of his day was best known after he was blind. When he first rose he heard a chapter in the Hebrew Bible, and then studied till twelve; then took some exercise for an hour; then dined; then played on the organ, and sung, or heard another sing; then studied to six; then entertained his visiters till eight; then supped, and after a pipe of tobacco and a glass of water, went to bed. [I, 152]

The account is far more blunt and peremptory than Johnson usually gives. The anaphoric use of "then" (varied only at the end by the pipe and water) and the interchangeability of "sung, or heard another sing" prepare us for the paragraphs that follow:

So is his life described; but this even tenour appears attainable only in Colleges. He that lives in the world will sometimes have the succession of his practice broken and confused. Visiters, of whom Milton is represented to have had great numbers, will come and stay unseasonably; business, of which every man has some, must be done when others will do it. [I, 152]

These are the observations of the skeptical biographer. He not only thought such systematic behavior unlikely but also, in its more extreme forms, as several passages in his writings make clear, not human. As Nekayah says to Rasselas of marriage, "wretched would be the pair, above all names of wretchedness, who should be doomed to adjust by reason every morning all the minute detail of a domestick day" (*Rasselas*, ch. 29, p. 132). In the following paragraph from the *Life of Milton* Johnson constructs an account that is more in keeping with human variety, and ends with a strikingly informal picture of the great poet:

When he did not care to rise early he had something read to him by his bedside; perhaps at this time his daughters were employed. He composed much in the morning and dictated in the day, sitting obliquely in an elbow-chair with his leg thrown over the arm. [I, 152]

Interestingly enough, according to Benjamin Boyce, on the few occasions when the fictional character in its heyday was handled chronologically, it suggested "an individual person on a particular day."[14] Historical writers made full use of the technique as well. In the *Decline and Fall of the Roman Empire*, for example, Gibbon includes typical days in the lives of a number of his emperors.[15]

3

The "life" section of Johnson's biographies, though much longer than the character which follows it and precedes the critical section, requires less explanation. In the narrative of the subject's life Johnson gives, whenever he can, the place and date of birth, the father's name and occupation. He often gives the mother's name and, if the occasion warrants, as in the case of noblemen or very old families, an account in small compass of the ancestry. Brothers and sisters, as I have indicated earlier, are infrequently mentioned and less frequently named. He usually attempts to name the subject's grammar school and master, his college and tutor, but he seems to be more concerned with the earlier schooling, possibly because he believed in good Lockean fashion that the first impressions and the initial training are most important. His own experience as an Oxford dropout may have reinforced such an opinion.

This section of the life includes finances and friendships, marriage and offspring, the events of the subject's life taken for the most part in chronological order. In *Idler* No. 102 he had suggested that "the gradations of a hero's life are from battle to battle, and of an author's from book to book" (*Yale*, II, 312). And

14. *The Theophrastan Character in England to 1642* (Cambridge, Mass.: Harvard University Press, 1947), p. 182.

15. H. L. Bond (*The Literary Art of Edward Gibbon* [Oxford: Clarendon Press, 1960], p. 91) notes that he does this for Julian, Saper, Attila, Theodoric, and others.

his own practice would seem to bear out this contention. The landmarks in his accounts are the publications, and we frequently observe the changes in status of the subject as his reputation grows and his wealth increases.

This is not to say that the narrative form of biography was a matter of indifference. In that genre-conscious age the writer, as two biographers of Swift will attest, was aware that a certain sort of rhetorical development was called for. Orrery introduces some remarks on Stella by saying that "according to the rules of biography, I ought perhaps to have delayed the account till we arrived at that period of his life when he married her." And Deane Swift says, "I suppose, according to the rules of biography I should in the former chapter have mentioned the name of Sir WILLIAM TEMPLE, before I had contrived to make Dr. Swift a master of arts in the university of Oxford."[16] Some theorists, like Vossius, had attempted to codify biography, but the "rules" to which these rivals refer were hardly ironclad. They were neither so rigid nor so precise as the "rules" of the stage, which were called into question well before Johnson's "Preface to *Shakespeare*." It is significant that both Orrery and Swift refer to the "rules of biography" while breaking them.

Under "biography" in his *Dictionary* Johnson quotes Watts's *Logick*: "In writing the lives of men, which is called *biography*, some authors place every thing in the precise order of time when it occurred." Perhaps we can say no more about the ordering of a life in biography than Johnson says in a letter to Edward Cave: "a history . . . ranges facts according to their dependence on each other, and postpones or anticipates according to the convenience of narration" (*Letters*, I, 20). In the *Life of Savage*, to take one skillful example, Johnson purposely withholds the anecdote of Savage's entering his mother's house and being accused of an attempt upon her life in order to insert it at the point when she used the incident to have the Queen deny him a pardon. (His apology for the delay indicates the sway of chronology.)

Johnson may break chronology to discuss a particular friend-

16. John, Earl of Orrery, *Remarks on the Life and Writings of Dr. Jonathan Swift*, 3d ed. (London, 1752), p. 14; Deane Swift, *An Essay upon the Life, Writings, and Character of Jonathan Swift* (London, 1755), p. 32.

ship like that of Addison and Steele, or he may, as in the *Life of Rowe*, follow a full chronological account of the works with a short account of lesser events out of chronological order. The narrative of Addison's life, on the other hand, mingles poetry and politics because his literary skill led to political preferment and both activities were of great importance in his life.

Johnson usually focuses on the personal consequences of the author's activities in this section, but he may also include a digression on the genesis of a work (*Paradise Lost* or Pope's translation of the *Iliad*), predecessors in the field (the account of books on manners before the *Tatler* and the *Spectator*), and the effect of the work on contemporaries. It should be noted that digressions are a rhetorically expected part of history and biography. All the theorists agree that one should use them, and disagree only on when and how. As William Hayley put it in his versified *Essay on History*:

> Of all the parts, that History's volume fill,
> The just Digression claims the nicest skill.[17]

Johnson himself praises his favorite historian, Richard Knolles, for "digressions without ostentation" (*Rambler* No. 122, *Yale*, IV, 290). And under "digression" in his *Dictionary* Johnson quotes Dryden's translation of Dufresnoy: "To content and fill the eye of the understanding, the best authors sprinkle their works with pleasing digressions, with which they recreate the minds of their readers." (This, incidentally, helps to explain the age's higher tolerance for what we consider padding.) The *Life of Cowley* was the biography he liked best of all his *Lives* because of "the dissertation which it contains on the *Metaphysical Poets*" (as Boswell put it), possibly the most famous digression in the history of criticism.

Johnson may have used, as some critics claim, a formula in structuring the *Lives*, but he certainly did not have a checklist of topics. One thing that will strike the reader of his biographies is that despite the continuity of Johnson's interests, he is not systematic. He does not, as far as I can tell, make use of any of the topical schemes that were available to him in the works of Aristo-

17. *An Essay on History* (London, 1781), Epistle III, ll. 297-98, p. 73.

tle, Cicero, Quintilian, and various Renaissance rhetoricians. His belief that the literary biography should include an account of the subject's "studies, his manner of life, the means by which he obtained to excellence, his opinion of his own works, and such particulars" at once suggests that he had given thought to the topics of literary biography and that his thought was not systematic (*Hebrides*, p. 204). Frequently he allows his main source to determine the order in which he takes up various topics. We might select two for special attention: the first, childhood, because Johnson's treatment is different from that of the modern biographer; the second, death, because his treatment is different from that of his contemporaries.

Childhood plays a small role in Johnson's biographies, though not by choice. In his early "Life of Sydenham" he expresses his disappointment at not finding any knowledge of Sydenham's childhood:

Under whose care he was educated, or in what manner he passed his childhood, whether he made any early discoveries of a genius peculiarly adapted to the study of nature, or gave any presages of his future eminence in medicine, no information is to be obtained. We must, therefore, repress that curiosity, which would naturally incline us to watch the first attempts of so vigorous a mind, to pursue it in its childish inquiries, and see it struggling with rustick prejudices, breaking, on trifling occasions, the shackles of credulity, and giving proofs, in its casual excursions, that it was formed to shake off the yoke of prescription, and dispel the phantoms of hypothesis. [*Works*, VI, 406; cf. 310]

This passage displays what Johnson wishes to find in the childhood of a great man: the evidence of his future greatness. In the next paragraph he expresses the opinion that in those relatively few lives which have been presented in full the "same proportion of intellectual vigour" is displayed at all stages of life. Johnson is looking not for development but for acts that will shadow forth the essential being of the subject. His interest in childhood is displayed elsewhere in his biographies. The "Life of Barretier" concerns a child prodigy who died at the age of twenty. Johnson is generally alert for early signs of genius, as we see in the lives of Pope and Cowley. In his "Review of an Essay on the Writings and Genius of Pope" he suggests that had Warton "happened to think on Baillet's chapter of Enfans célèbres, he might have made . . . a very entertaining dissertation on early excellence" (*Works*, VI, 41).

Deathbed scenes were almost obligatory in the biographies of the age, and Johnson's early "Life of Boerhaave" contains the heartfelt presentation of a pious and humble end. His description of Pope on his deathbed is the more moving for its simplicity of narration. He gives us Pope's hallucinations, the tears of Bolingbroke, Pope's agreement to take the sacraments, his last words in praise of friendship and virtue, the placid death itself—all in a quiet tone of voice with no heightening or commentary (III, 190-92). In the *Life of Lyttelton* he recommends and quotes "a very affecting and instructive account" of Lyttelton's death given by his doctor. There is, however, reason to think that his feelings toward deathbed comportment were, at the very least, equivocal.

Speaking of the style of the hapless Sir John Dalrymple, Johnson complains "nothing can be poorer than his mode of writing: it is the mere bouncing of a school-boy. Great He! but greater She! and such stuff." He has in mind a deathbed scene from *Memoirs of Great Britain and Ireland* (1771-73): "With a deep and noble silence, with a long and fixed look, in which respect and affection, unmingled with passion, were expressed, Lord and Lady Russell parted for ever; he great in this last act of life, but she greater" (*Life*, II, 210 and n. 3).

The death of Savage in prison is the most fully realized of Johnson's deathbed scenes because it gives us a human pathos which immediately eclipses all the stagy dying speeches and silences that filled the biographies of the time: "The last time that the Keeper saw him was on *July* the 31st, 1743; when *Savage* seeing him at his Bed-side said, with an uncommon Earnestness, *I have something to say to you, Sir*, but after a Pause, moved his Hand in a melancholy Manner, and finding himself unable to recollect what he was going to communicate, said *'Tis gone*. The Keeper soon after left him, and the next Morning he died" (*Savage*, p. 135). The ineffectuality of Savage's attempt to communicate with his jailer is an authentic reminder of the frailty of man. The action is complete and needs no comment. Johnson, whose obsessive fear of death led him to believe that men who showed no fear when they were about to die generally dissembled,[18] seems to treat deathbed scenes without the fervor that one so often encounters. In the best known and most melodramatic of all the deathbed scenes of the century, Addison attempted, like his own Cato, to face death with a *sententia* on his lips so that he might point a moral for his profligate young stepson, the Earl of Warwick. Tickell's elegy alluded to it, and Young gave the line its fame: "See in what peace of mind a Christian can die." Johnson, a Christian who thought most of his life that he would not die in peace of mind, refers to "this moving interview" as the last "experiment" in Addison's program of changing the earl. His comments following his account of the meeting are brief and telling: "What effect this awful scene had on the earl I know not; he likewise died himself in a short time" (II, 117).

The account of the death of Otway brings up another aspect of Johnson's response to death in biography:

He died April 14, 1685, in a manner which I am unwilling to mention. Having been compelled by his necessities to contract debts, and hunted, as is supposed, by the terriers of the law, he retired to a publick house on Tower-hill, where he is said to have died of want; or, as it is related by one of his biographers, by swallowing, after a long fast, a piece of bread which charity had supplied. He went out, as is reported, almost naked, in the rage of hunger, and, finding a gentleman in a neighbouring coffee-house, asked him for a shilling. The gentleman gave him a guinea, and Otway going away bought a roll, and was choaked with the first mouthful. [I, 247]

"All this, I hope, is not true," adds Johnson, and he recounts a story of Pope's that Otway died of a fever following the hot pursuit of a thief who had robbed a friend. Johnson's narrative of the end of Otway is worth comparing to his better known terror at the death of Cordelia. He does not want to tell the story of Otway's death, he hopes on the basis of other testimony that it is not true, and he relates it with references to his authorities which let us know that he does not want the responsibility for

18. *Life*, II, 106–7. For the deathbed in nineteenth-century biography, see A. O. J. Cockshut, *Truth to Life: The Art of Biography in the Nineteenth Century* (London: Collins, 1974), ch.3.

telling it. Yet he does not pass over it. It appears with the best authority available. On the other hand, he is willing to see Tate's conclusion to *King Lear* rather than Shakespeare's because the terrible death of Cordelia is fiction (Shakespeare's "historical" sources do not sanction such treatment), and we need not, in Johnson's view, be put unnecessarily to such terrors. If this attitude seems to disable him at times as a critic of tragedy, we must at the same time recognize that as biographer he does not shirk the tragedies and absurdities of life.

4

It would, I think, be supererogatory to go one by one through earlier biographical collections attempting to determine what each had to offer Johnson formally. This has effectively been done by a series of students whose studies comment sometimes on the history of literary biography and sometimes on the excellence of Johnson.[19] By the time Johnson wrote the *Lives* most of those elements which did not originate with him had long been taken for granted. Indeed, after examining the various claims to influence of Phillips, Winstanley, Langbaine, Jacob, Mrs. Elizabeth Cooper, and "Cibber's" *Lives*, Lawrence Lipking finds that the differences between Johnson and his predecessors are most striking and attributes them to Johnson's formal as well as intellectual superiority.[20] Perhaps, however, by examining the nature of the work with the greatest claim to influence, I can indicate most fully my objections to taking these collections as formally related to Johnson's in any but the most general way.

In seeking literary models for the structure of Johnson's *Lives*

19. See Sir Walter Raleigh, "Early Lives of the Poets," in *Six Essays on Johnson* (Oxford: Clarendon Press, 1910), pp. 98–127; George Lorant Lam, "Johnson's *Lives of the Poets*: Their Origin, Text and History, with Remarks on Sources and Comment on His *Life of Cowley*," (Ph.D. diss., Cornell, 1938); René Wellek, *The Rise of English Literary History* (1941; rpt. New York: McGraw-Hill, 1966), pp. 142–43; William R. Keast, "Johnson and 'Cibber's' *Lives of the Poets*, 1753," in *Restoration and Eighteenth-Century Literature: Essays in Honor of Alan Dugald McKillop*, ed. Carroll Camden (Chicago: University of Chicago Press, 1963), pp. 89–101; Lawrence Lipking, *The Ordering of the Arts in Eighteenth-Century England*, pp. 415–28.

20. Lipking's full examination of all of these figures appears in an earlier version of his book, his 1962 Cornell doctoral dissertation. See especially p. 642.

of the Poets, George Watson, like George L. Lam and Lipking,[21] turns to the intriguing remarks of Sir John Hawkins:

When Johnson had determined on this work, he was to seek for the best mode of executing it. On a hint from a literary lady of his acquaintance and mine, he adopted, for his outline, that form in which the Countess D'Aunois has drawn up the memoirs of the French poets, in her "Recueils [*sic*] des plus belles pieces des Poètes François"; and the foundation of his work was, the lives of the dramatic poets by Langbaine, and the lives of the poets at large by Winstanley, and . . . their lives by Giles Jacob.[22]

Watson points out that the *Recueil* was actually written by Fontenelle and discerns Johnson's tripartite form, "biography, character, criticism," in Fontenelle's little prefaces.[23] But Fontenelle's claim to strong influence seems untenable. Each sketch starts with the birth of the man, but from there it may move immediately to the king's bounty to the full-grown poet or to some other poet's praise of him. There is no "character," as I have described that form (most of these prefaces are in their entirety no longer than most characters). The "critical" section is usually composed of testimony to the poet's excellence. Watson mentions that Fontenelle's criticism "is often confined to a few valedictory phrases, and painfully general phrases at that."[24] But he does not mention what the passage he quotes from Fontenelle betrays: this is not for the most part criticism, but the citation of authorities. In fact, testimony was the standard form of "criticism" in many of the biographical collections of the time. An indication of the triteness of the practice can be observed in Dryden's rejection of it at the conclusion of his "Life of Plutarch": "And now, with the usual vanity of *Dutch* prefacers, I could load our Author with the praises and Commemoration of Writers . . . but to cumber pages with this kind of stuff were to raise a distrust in common readers that *Plutarch* wants them."[25]

21. "Johnson's *Lives*," pp. 346 ff.; *Ordering*, p. 415.

22. Hawkins, *The Life of Samuel Johnson, LL.D.*, 2d ed. (London, 1787), pp. 533–34.

23. *The Literary Critics: A Study of English Descriptive Criticism* (1962; rpt. Harmondsworth: Penguin Books, 1964), pp. 94–95.

24. *Literary Critics*, p. 96.

25. *The Works of John Dryden*, ed. Sir Walter Scott and George Saintsbury (Edinburgh: William Patterson, 1892), XVII, 76.

To say that Fontenelle's form is similar to Johnson's is to ignore the most significant way in which Johnson differs from all
of his predecessors: the distinct separation of the biographical
and critical sections. A better way to speak of the structure, and
one that Watson considers in passing, is by reference to
Johnson's early biographical practice. Watson observes that
some of Johnson's early lives contain the gist of the later structure: "The anonymous 'Life of . . . Boerhaave' for example, . . .
already reveals the characteristic structure of a Fontenelle
notice."[26] Or, he might have added, of lives by many
seventeenth-century writers, for this form was not particularly
novel.

When Johnson began to write his biographies for the *Gentleman's Magazine*, there were no periodical biographies to provide
precedents, and almost nothing beyond a few loosely linked
anecdotes in the magazine itself. The form Johnson devised was
simply an account of the life of his subject followed by a shorter
section giving the character. His first biography, the "Life of
Sarpi," was quarried from the long prefatory life by Le
Courayer. It was obviously intended to serve as a puff for
Johnson's translation of *The History of the Council of Trent* and
may well have been destined to serve as his own prefatory life,
had that abortive project come to birth. The short catalogue of
the writer's works in the "Life of Boerhaave"—the only essential
difference between his first and second biographies—was also a
staple of the biographies of the time and appeared in such works
as Anthony a Wood's *Athenae Oxonienses*. Any number of prefatory lives in English had a similar structure, and, but for their
length and the cannibalistic Baylean footnotes, which threatened
to devour the text, so did the biographical dictionaries.

The structure of the *Lives* was arrived at by the simple expe-
dient of adding a critical section to this traditional short biography of life and character. The difference between the "Life of
Roscommon" as it originally appeared in the *Gentleman's
Magazine* (1748) and as it appeared in the *Lives of the Poets* was
brought about by Johnson's incorporating the footnotes within

26. *Literary Critics*, pp. 94-95.

the text and adding some criticism of Roscommon's poems. Johnson thought of the biographical and critical sections of the *Lives* as separate undertakings. In a famous letter to Boswell he refers to them as "little Lives, and little Prefaces, to a little edition of the English Poets" (*Letters*, II, 170), and while working on the *Life of Cowley* he refers in a letter to Mrs. Thrale to "little lives and little criticisms" (*Letters*, II, 231). Even the actual title of his work, *Prefaces, Biographical and Critical, to the Works of the English Poets*, may be misleading if we put the emphasis on *Prefaces* rather than on the split between life and writings. In a letter to John Nichols he proposed two possible titles: "An Account of the Lives and Works of some of the most eminent English Poets" and "The English Poets biographically and critically considered" (*Letters*, II, 426).

Hawkins' comments on the *Lives* gloss Johnson's statement, in the "Author's Advertisement," that he had "first planned to write an 'advertisement' for each poet like those in what he calls the 'French Miscellanies.'"[27] But it is not clear from Watson's account that such an undertaking would have included, according to Johnson, only "a few dates and a general character" (I, xxvi). Johnson does not suggest any formal similarities between Fontenelle's work and what he has actually done ("I have been led beyond my intention"). Hawkins' comments, then, refer to Johnson's original intention and not to his finished work. Hawkins' fallibility is readily apparent from his naming of Langbaine, Winstanley, and Jacob as the principal sources of the *Lives*; for apart from Johnson's choice of primary source for each individual life, his major debt is to the *Biographia Britannica*.[28]

Johnson intentionally lays out the sections of a biography separately because the life and the work are essentially different things, though conduct and poem are products of the same human agency. Hence Watson's criticism of "the total absence of bridge-passages" in the *Lives* misses the point. "He is writing to a

27. *Literary Critics*, p. 93.
28. Bergen Evans' full study of the sources determines this conclusively. "Dr. Johnson as a Biographer" (Ph.D. diss., Harvard, 1932).

recipe," says Watson, "and he does not stir his ingredients."[29]
But Watson does not realize that to mix these ingredients is to
mix them up. In order to make proper discriminations, Johnson
must be wary of easy transitions from life to art. The fact that
Johnson, a skillful writer of transitions, frequently abjures them
in his lives should warn the critic that he has a positive reason for
doing as he does. In the next chapter I shall discuss this most
neglected and original aspect of Johnson's literary biographies,
the discrimination between life and art.

29. *Literary Critics*, p. 95.

CHAPTER 6

Art and Life: Discriminations

Rambler No. 14 opens, like so many of Johnson's essays, with an empirically grounded generalization: "Among the many inconsistencies which folly produces, or infirmity suffers in the human mind, there has often been observed a manifest and striking contrariety between the life of an author and his writings" (*Yale*, III, 74). These observations, however, are part of a strong minority report. The major literary tradition concerning the relationship between a poet and his poems held that a good work can only be the product of a good man. This theory of the *bonus orator*, which received its impetus in the Renaissance from Minturno, was based on Plato's defense of the philosopher and Cicero's and Quintilian's of the rhetorician.[1] Strabo had explicitly applied it to the poet in late classical antiquity, and in the sixteenth and seventeenth centuries it had such adherents as Ronsard, Ben Jonson, and Milton. In the eighteenth century, reinforced by the recently popularized doctrines of Longinus, this idea was a commonplace. Shaftesbury, after quoting Strabo, uses an elaborate neoplatonic musical analogy: "The moral artist who . . . is thus knowing in the inward form and structure of his

1. My account of the *bonus orator*, a term which I shall use generically to characterize this theory, is indebted to J. E. Spingarn, *Literary Criticism in the Renaissance* (1899; rpt. New York: Harcourt, Brace, and World, 1963), p. 34; W. J. Bate, *From Classic to Romantic* (1946; rpt. New York: Harper and Brothers, 1961), p. 4 and *passim*; Herschel Baker, *The Image of Man* (1947; rpt. New York: Harper and Row, 1961), p. 271; M. H. Abrams, *The Mirror and the Lamp: Romantic Theory and the Critical Tradition* (1953; rpt. New York: W. W. Norton, 1958), p. 229.

fellow creature, will hardly, I presume, be found unknowing in himself or at a loss in those numbers which make the harmony of a mind. For knavery is mere dissonance and disproportion. And though villains may have strong tones and natural capacities of action, it is impossible that true judgment and ingenuity should reside where harmony and honesty have no being."[2] The rhetoric indicates allegiances different from Ben Jonson's or Milton's, but the import is the same: the good poet must be a good man.

Nor does Samuel Johnson subscribe to the alternate tradition: *Lasciva est nobis pagina, vita proba*. Cowley used this defense,[3] but Dryden probably spoke for the majority in rejecting it: "*Vita proba est* is no excuse, for it will be scarcely admitted that either a poet or a painter can be chaste, who give us the contrary examples in their writings and their pictures."[4] This proposition is the converse of our original: the immoral poet is a bad man. But this is not quite Johnson's way either. In order to find the poet guilty of immorality, we must examine his life as well as his page. And he is even willing to believe, when no evidence of vice exists, that, as in the *Life of Duke*, the licentious poet "rather talked than lived viciously in an age when he that would be thought a wit was afraid to say his prayers" (II, 24). The *Life of Dryden* clarifies his stand. After suggesting that the "dissolute licentiousness" of Dryden's works was merely "artificial and constrained," he points out that acquittal on the count of actual immorality leaves Dryden open to an equally serious charge: "Of the mind that can trade in corruption, and can deliberately pollute itself with ideal wickedness for the sake of spreading the contagion in society, I wish not to conceal or excuse the depravity" (I, 398). Such an action is in itself immoral, regardless of one's personal conduct.

The tradition of the *bonus orator* is attacked implicitly in a number of Johnson's biographies and explicitly in some of his essays. He thinks that good poems are not necessarily written by good men, for as he says in the *Life of Addison*, "to write and to

2. *Advice to an Author*, I, iii, in *Eighteenth-Century Critical Essays*, ed. Scott Elledge (Ithaca: Cornell University Press, 1961), I, 183.
3. See Abrams, *Mirror and Lamp*, pp. 229, 372 n. 8.
4. "A Parallel of Poetry and Painting," in *Of Dramatic Poesy and Other Critical Essays*, ed. George Watson (London: J. M. Dent and Sons 1962), II, 187.

live are very different" (II, 125). His distinction would seem to
rest on a Christian framework and particularly on his personal
sense of man's fallen nature. The genesis of Johnson's treatment
of the relationship between poet and poem, as well as its logic, is
perhaps best revealed in his answer to a lady who had complained that a certain writer "does not practice what he teaches":

"I cannot help that, madam. That does not make his book the worse.
People are influenced more by what a man says, if his practice is suitable
to it, because they are blockheads. The more intellectual people are, the
readier will they attend to what a man tells them. If it is just, they will
follow it, be his practice what it will. No man practices so well as he
writes. I have, all my life long, been lying till noon. Yet I tell all young
men, and tell them with great sincerity, that nobody who does not rise
early will ever do any good. Only consider! You read a book; you are
convinced by it; you do not know the author. Suppose you afterwards
know him, and find that he does not practice what he teaches; are you
to give up your former conviction? At this rate you would be kept in a
state of *equilibrio* when reading every book, till you knew how the author
practised." [*Hebrides*, p. 169]

This is perhaps the definitive rejection of one form of the doctrine of sincerity. Johnson's belief may be summed up by a short
passage from the works of John Whitgift, the Tudor archbishop,
which he quotes in the *Dictionary* under "prejudice": "Neither
must his example, done without the book, prejudice that which
is well-appointed within the book." Although quick to call a man
a liar in conversation, Johnson was slow to call a writer a hypocrite. His humorous reference to himself as a slothful proponent
of early rising has its darker analogues in the pages of the *Prayers
and Meditations*.

The sense of his own culpability seems to have haunted
Johnson throughout that part of his life with which we are familiar. In a letter to Mrs. Thrale he suggested that his failings put
him in a better position to know the value of the precepts he
espoused but could not follow. Shortly before his death he told
Sir John Hawkins that "he had written as a philosopher, but had
not lived like one."[5] And at the conclusion of their discussion,
says Hawkins, "He uttered this passionate exclamation,—'Shall
I, who have been a teacher of others, myself be a castaway?' "

5. Sir John Hawkins, *The Life of Samuel Johnson, LL.D.*, 2d ed. (London, 1787),
p. 564.

This outburst is slightly adapted from St. Paul (I Corinthians 9:27)—"But I keep under my body and bring it into subjection: lest that by any means, when I have preached to others, I myself should be a castaway!"—lines which also roused fear and trembling in William Cowper. The passage did not enter Johnson's mind only *in extremis*. In 1781, two months after the completion of the *Lives of the Poets*, Johnson discussed some of the same points with Boswell, concluding with St. Paul's doubts. Indeed, nearly thirty years before his death Johnson had quoted the same passage under "castaway" in his *Dictionary*. The role of individual guilt and the split between public and private consciousness remained continuously alive for him. Other Pauline texts, such as II Corinthians 10:10 and Romans 7:19, also seem to emphasize this dualism. In a footnote to the deathbed colloquy Hawkins, though unaware of the allusion to Paul, points to the similarity between some of Johnson's arguments and the writings of William Law. Both Paul and the Pauline morality of Law's perfectionist doctrines certainly exacerbated Johnson's awareness that "to write and to live are very different."

Such a distinction can be found earlier as the familiar Renaissance idea of the difference between the "erected wit" and the "infected will," but the tentative way in which Sir Philip Sidney introduces this distinction in *The Defense of Poesy* tells us that literary criticism had an easier time dealing with the *bonus orator*:

Neither let it be deemed too saucy a comparison to balance the highest point of man's wit with the efficacy of Nature; but rather give right honor to the heavenly Maker of that maker, who, having made man to his own likeness, set him beyond and over all the works of that second nature; which in nothing he sheweth so much as in poetry, when with the force of a divine breath he bringeth things forth surpassing her doings, with no small arguments to the incredulous of that first accursed fall of Adam, since our erected wit maketh us know what perfection is, and yet our infected will keepeth us from reaching unto it. But these arguments will by few be understood, and by fewer granted.[6]

Here we have the poet as maker, the poem as heterocosm, the divine afflatus and the effect of the fall on human nature in the purview of a paragraph. Sidney expects his reader to under-

6. In *The Renaissance in England*, ed. Hyder E. Rollins and Herschel Baker (Boston: D. C. Heath, 1954), p. 608.

stand this conception of the poet only with great difficulty if at all.

As with most of Johnson's thought, his ideas about the *bonus orator* are far from systematic. Yet his dual awareness leads to important consequences for literary biography. Johnson believed that the theory of the *bonus orator* had much to recommend it abstractly, but that it simply would not bear up under the weight of empirical observation. The beginning of the *Life of Savage* makes this point most emphatically: "It seems rational to hope that intellectual Greatness should produce better Effects; that Minds qualified for great Attainments should first endeavour their own Benefit; and that they who are most able to teach others the Way to Happiness should with most Certainty follow it themselves. But this Expectation, however plausible, has been frequently disappointed" (*Savage*, p. 4). The discrepancy between Savage's poetic morality and his dissolute life becomes one of the main themes of the biography. It enables Johnson to arrive at a judgment of him which is at once sympathetic and critical: "The reigning Error of his Life was, that he mistook the Love for the Practice of Virtue, and was indeed not so much a good Man as the Friend of Goodness" (*Savage*, p. 74). The distinction Johnson makes in theory and in practice between life and writings is important and has occasionally been misinterpreted by critics who judge him by their own theories of unity. In his biographical study of Johnson, Joseph Wood Krutch uses a key passage from the *Life of Savage* to expose what appears to him as fuzzy thinking:

Like many other writers of the eighteenth century, Johnson was much more ready than we to give credit for good intentions even when they got nowhere near performance. To consider professed "respect for virtue," even in the absence of any practice of it, surprisingly important was one of his conspicuous foibles. . . .Hence he can say of Savage: "His actions which were generally precipitate, were often blameable; but his writings, being productions of study, uniformly tended to the exaltation of the mind, and the propagation of morality and piety." In all seriousness he can even regret that Savage never carried into effect an intention to compose a poem called the *Progress of a Freethinker*.[7]

7. *Samuel Johnson* (1955; rpt. New York: Harcourt, Brace, and World, 1963), pp. 83-84. Johnson does speak of Savage's "literary hypocrisy," but he restricts the term to refer to a difference in what Savage thought of specific people, such

Although we may not regret the loss of the poem, our judgment of the quality of Savage's work is not at issue here. Dismissing such passages as "unintentional satire," Krutch fails to see that Johnson is making a distinction between life and art which is meant not to "excuse" Savage but to explain the validity of his poems. Johnson is judging not the goodness of his intentions but the usefulness to others of his productions, and in this sense Savage is a benefactor of mankind.[8] In fact, Johnson is keenly aware that "a man who acts in the face of light is worse than a man who does not know so much" (*Hebrides*, p. 169) and that it is natural for men to be angry at "those, who neglect the duties which they appear to know with so strong conviction the necessity of performing" (*Rambler* No. 77, *Yale*, IV, 41). He thinks, however, that the writer who fails to live up to his writings may "sometimes incur censures too severe, and by those, who form ideas of his life from their knowledge of his books be considered as worse than others, only because he was expected to be better." "No man," he tells us, "has the power of acting equal to that of thinking" (*Yale*, IV, 41). Hence writing, though in some ways an action like any other, is a privileged act, one in which a man can temporarily insulate himself against the thousand natural shocks that flesh is heir to, and rise above his quotidian morality.

Thus when a friend asked him to introduce her to a well-known writer, he replied, "Dearest Madam, . . . you had better let it alone; the best part of every author is in general to be found in his book."[9] And several remarks he made when he first met Boswell are in the same vein: "People . . . may be taken in once, who imagine that an author is greater in private life than other men. Uncommon parts require uncommon opportunities for their exertion" (*Life*, I, 393). Imlac's well-known admonition to

---

as Dennis, Walpole, and Lord Tyrconnel, and what he wrote about them. It is not extended to the difference between his mean actions and his noble ideals.

8. Edward A. Bloom makes the complementary error of believing that Johnson "inflexibly insisted that a man's life must be as exemplary as his writings." He is therefore hard pressed to explain Johnson's defense of Savage's "propagation of morality and piety." See *Samuel Johnson in Grub Street* (Providence: Brown University Press, 1957), pp. 80, 113.

9. "Anecdotes by Wm. Seward, F.R.S.," in *Johnsonian Miscellanies*, ed. G. B. Hill (Oxford: Clarendon Press, 1897), II, 310. Hawkins recounts the same incident but makes Johnson's statement categorical.

Rasselas is a variation on this theme: "Be not too hasty... to trust, or to admire, the teachers of morality: they discourse like angels, but they live like men" (*Rasselas*, ch. 18, p. 85). It is quite possible, therefore, that the author, in private life, may neither please nor instruct. And so we may in opposition to the *bonus orator* adopt Johnson's own emblematic figure, the "vicious moralist," who, as we are told in *Rambler* No. 77, "may be considered as a taper, by which we are lighted through the labyrinth of complicated passions: he extends his radiance farther than his heat, and guides all that are within view, but burns only those who make too near approaches" (*Yale*, IV, 41).

Far from being prejudiced against a man's poems by his life, Johnson was only too ready, for the taste of his contemporaries, to distinguish them from his life. Such passages as the following from Owen Ruffhead's *Life of Pope* were as common in literary biography as nude scenes in modern films.

> In truth, his morals are the best comment on his writings: and they will be read with infinitely more pleasure and profit, when it is known that he felt and practised himself what he recommended to others. If we have reason to suspect from a writer's conduct in life, that he disregards the most essential principles which he inculcates with his pen, the mind revolts from his doctrine, and it hurts our pride to be the dupes of hypocrisy. To be truly useful and entertaining, a good writer should likewise be a good man. Such was Mr. Pope.[10]

Johnson's conception of the vicious moralist permits him to come to some much harsher conclusions about Pope as a man and at the same time to find his poetry great. Although he is happy when, as with Boerhaave and Addison, the morality of the man lives up to that of the writer, he is not driven to reconcile them. The biographers trapped by the doctrine of moral correspondence often were forced to distort either the man or his work to bring them into conjunction; Johnson's ability to make separate evaluations is at great variance with their practice. Those who made hasty assumptions about the unity of life and work were quickly dispatched. "He allowed high praise to Thomson as a poet," says Boswell, "but when one of the company said he was also a good man, our moralist contested this

10. *The Life of Alexander Pope, Esq.* (London, 1769), pp. 483–84.

with great warmth, accusing him of gross sensuality and licentiousness of manners" (*Life*, II, 63). And in the *Lives of the Poets* he finds Prior's beliefs praiseworthy, but his life "irregular, negligent, and sensual" (II, 200). In anonymous reviews of the *Lives of the Poets* in the *Monthly Review*, Edmund Cartwright noticed Johnson's readiness to separate poet and poems: "In characterizing Thomson's merit as a poet, his Biographer nearly coincides with the general opinion. As a man, however, the representation of his character is not so favorable." And again: "Through the whole of his narrative Dr. Johnson seems to have no great partiality for Milton as a man: as a poet, however, he is willing to allow him every merit he is entitled to."[11] If one wishes to see the importance of this tendency for Johnsonian biography, perhaps the best example, as the last quotation may suggest, is the *Life of Milton*.

Critics from Johnson's time to our own have found the *Life of Milton* troublesome when they have failed to recognize the distinction he makes between life and art. Such confusion ranges from prejudices based on a priori conceptions of the nature of Johnson's thought ("Johnson disliked Milton's politics so violently," asserts one modern critic, "that he could scarcely be expected to treat his poetry with critical calm")[12] to subtler misunderstandings of his method. In his *Essay on the Life, Character, and Writings of Dr. Samuel Johnson* (1786), Dr. Joseph Towers claims, "There is something curious in tracing the conduct of Johnson with respect to Milton, and in observing the struggle which there was in his mind concerning him, resulting from his reverence for him as a poet, and his rooted dislike against him as a political writer."[13] And recently George Watson in *The Literary Critics* uneasily discussed Johnson's putative "indiffer[ence] to the paradox (for Johnson) that Milton, with his republican sentiments, wrote the greatest of English Epics."[14] The paradox,

11. *Monthly Review*, 1779, 1782; now collected in *Johnson: The Critical Heritage*, ed. James T. Boulton (New York: Barnes and Noble, 1971), pp. 264–65, 261.

12. W. Powell Jones, "Johnson and Gray," *MP*, 56 (May 1959), 96.

13. *Essay on the Life, Character, and Writings of Dr. Samuel Johnson* (London, 1786), p. 57.

14. *The Literary Critics: A Study of English Descriptive Criticism* (1962; rpt. Harmondsworth: Penguin Books, 1964), p. 96.

however, is to be found in Johnson's conception of the nature of man and not in his treatment of Milton in particular.

In fact, a close look at the *Life of Milton* shows that Johnson consistently resisted those approaches which would appeal to one who permitted his political opinions to affect his literary judgments. The Romantics' interpretation of Satan as the hero of *Paradise Lost* and of Milton as a member of the devil's party had been anticipated well before Johnson's biography appeared. Blake, Byron, and Shelley, attracted by the Promethean figure of Satan, came to some of the same conclusions as did a number of late seventeenth- and early eighteenth-century monarchists repelled by the politics of Milton.[15] Dryden, Chesterfield, and Voltaire had called Satan the hero for technical rather than political reasons; Johnson chastised Dryden for "petulantly and indecently den[ying] the heroism of Adam because he was overcome" (I, 176).

The temptation to identify Satan with Milton must have been even stronger. We tend to forget that models for such identifications, though not plentiful, were close at hand. Dryden, comparing Homer to Achilles and Virgil to Aeneas, says, "The very heroes shew their authors."[16] Of less critical importance, though more to the point, were several poems commending Milton the poet and attacking Milton the politician by making explicit comparisons between him and Satan or his minions. A good example is a couplet from "On the Reprinting of Milton's Prose Works with his Poems" by Thomas Yalden, one of the happy few whose poetry was added on Johnson's recommendation to the edition prefaced by the *Lives*:

> Like the fall'n angels in their state
> Thou shar'dst their nature, insolence and fate.[17]

15. In "Milton among the Augustans: The Infernal Council" (*SP*, 48 [1951], 15–25), John Robert Moore mentions that "in the minds of many Tories Milton was equated with his Prince of Darkness," though he does not illustrate this contention (p. 22). My experience in reading poetic tributes to Milton written by Tories would seem to corroborate his statement.

16. "Preface to the Fables," in *Critical Essays*, ed. Watson, II, 276. Abrams, who quotes this passage, believes that no writer went further in this mode of thought for one hundred years (*Mirror and Lamp*, p. 232).

17. Quoted by John Walter Good, who gathers all the poetical tributes to Milton before 1800, but rarely comments on them. See *Studies in the Miltonic Tradition* (Urbana: University of Illinois, 1915), p. 59.

Johnson does not comment on this passage, but we can imagine what he must have thought of such analogies. In the *Life of Milton* he paraphrases the little-known strictures of John Clarke on Satan, agrees with Clarke's psychological reasoning, but exonerates Milton from his charges:

Milton has been censured by Clarke for the impiety which sometimes breaks forth from Satan's mouth. For there are thoughts, as he justly remarks, which no observation of character can justify, because no good man would willingly permit them to pass, however transiently, through his own mind. To make Satan speak as a rebel, without any such expressions as might taint the reader's imagination, was indeed one of the great difficulties in Milton's undertaking, and I cannot but think that he has extricated himself with great happiness. [I, 173]

Johnson is not merely paying lip service to Clarke's assumptions, for he had applied the same standard in criticizing Shakespeare fifteen years earlier, and in the *Lives* he finds that Dryden's "writings exhibit many passages, which, with all the allowances that can be made for characters and occasions, are such as piety would not have admitted" (I, 104). We must also remember in reading this passage that for Johnson Milton's defense of regicide was wrong but not impious: Johnson was no believer in the divine right of kings.

2

Along with the tradition of the *bonus orator* Johnson is wary of another conception of the relationship between the poet and his poem which might logically appear to be connected to it. This doctrine asserts that the character of the man is to be found in his works. It is a broader conception than that of the *bonus orator* for it deals not with morality as such but with all the various personal traits a man possesses. In the *Poetics* Aristotle subscribes to it in a matter-of-fact way: "Poetry . . . soon broke up into two kinds according to the differences of character in the individual poets; for the graver among them would represent noble actions, and those of noble personages; and the meaner sort the actions of the ignoble."[18] Such an assumption was inherent in the Greek conception of character, a conception that becomes

18. *The Rhetoric and the Poetics of Aristotle*, trans. Ingram Bywater, ed. Friedrich Solmsen (New York: Random House, 1954), p. 227, 1448a–1449b.

apparent when we remember that our word "character" is a dead metaphor (the *charaktēr*) is an instrument for engraving). Thus an agent would naturally be thought to leave his "stamp" on a product of his making.

Aristotle's broader conception of the relationship between man and work, despite its relevance for poetic theory and literary biography from the eighteenth century to the present, plays a small part in his own system and does not seem to have influenced aesthetic speculation. Statements similar to Aristotle's, when articulated by Englishmen, seem to be traceable to a concern for national and individual differences, and do not—despite his authoritative standing—make use of his position.

When Johnson gives a short account of the beginnings of literature in the "Preface to *Shakespeare*," the difference between his treatment of the relationship between the poet and his choice of poem and Aristotle's treatment of the same problem is suggestive. Though they both agree that there was an immediate division into tragic and comic poets, Johnson says that poets "selected some the crimes of men, and some their absurdities," not because of any individual preferences, but "according to the laws which custom had prescribed" (*Yale*, VII, 66). Thus the choice of a genre is not determined by inner necessities, but by conventions. The importance of this difference for literary biography is that Johnson is not likely to leap to any hasty conclusion about a writer's character on the basis of his choice of genre.

In the *Life of Thomson* Johnson makes a distinction between life and art at the expense of Dr. Patrick Murdoch:

The biographer of Thomson has remarked that an author's life is best read in his works: his observation was not well-timed. Savage, who lived much with Thomson, once told me how he heard a lady remarking that she could gather from his works three parts of his character, that he was "a great lover, a great swimmer, and rigorously abstinent," but, said Savage, he knows not any love but that of the sex: he was perhaps never in·cold water in his life, and he indulges himself in all the luxury that comes within his reach. [III, 297–98]

This retort has been quoted frequently. M. H. Abrams uses it as convincing evidence that Krutch was wrong when he said that Johnson had a tendency to look in poetry for the character of the poet.[19] And the New Critics, recognizing an ally of sorts, enlisted it in their cause. Like the doctrine of the *bonus orator*, this tendency, which Abrams has dubbed "literary physiognomy," has implications worth exploring.

First, Murdoch was consciously stating a commonplace: "It is commonly said, that the life of a good writer is best read in his Works."[20] Second, Johnson refutes him not by attacking the theoretical premises of his statement, but by recounting Savage's refutation of an anonymous lady's conclusions about Thomson's character from reading his works. Dryly understating his objections, Johnson says that Murdoch's observation "was not well-timed." The question of the comparative deductive abilities of Murdoch and the lady does not arise; the dangers of Murdoch's stance are made abundantly clear.

If Johnson's Christian sense of man's fallen state is the wedge, this skepticism, with its firm empirical basis, is the hammer by means of which Johnson separates life and art. It is frequently observable in his squelching of conversationalists who attempt to take poets' words as indicative of their beliefs.[21] The shock to which Johnson exposes his auditors is like that which Mann's Felix Krull experiences when he goes backstage after the delightful performance of Müller-Rosé and sees the ugly satyr with his makeup half off. I bring up this modern instance because Johnson's own favorite word for the act of writing is "performance," a term that points both to an act like any other and to a specially heightened and rhetorical state which may have nothing to do with one's offstage behavior.

In the *Ciceronianus*, a book with which he was in general agreement, he found that "once or twice Erasmus somewhat unskillfully entangles Cicero's civil or moral, with his rhetorical character" (*Letters*, III, 185). Though he does not specify the location, I believe that his criticism can only refer to two passages in the colloquy. In the more revealing of the two, Bulephorus,

19. *Mirror and Lamp*, pp. 233–34.
20. "An Account of the Life and Writings of Mr. James Thomson," in *The Works of James Thomson* (London, 1788), I, ix.
21. See his treatment of the Bishop of St. Asaph on Young and William Seward on Horace (*Life*, III, 251; IV, 215).

Erasmus' mouthpiece, has warmed to his task of berating Cicero
and finally adds, "I do not know in which he was the more
intemperate—in boasting of himself or in censuring others."
Nosoponus, the fanatical Ciceronian, tries to change the subject:

> Nosoponus. Let us leave off talking of mores, of men and revert
> to the discussion of strength and beauty of speech.
> Bulephorus. I should gladly do so if the rhetoricians did not
> declare that one cannot be a good orator who is not also a
> good man. [*nisi retores ipsi contenderent bonem oratorem esse non
> posse qui non sit idem vir bonus*].[22]

With an ironic touch Erasmus turns the theory of the *bonus orator*
against its progenitor. What Johnson would find objectionable,
besides the theory itself, is the identification of Cicero's boasting
and censoriousness with personal characteristics. Used in a
speech, they are dubious examples of "intemperance."

In yet another area, the relation of the work of art to the
author's experience, Johnson often makes discriminations, but
here, as we shall see in the next chapter, he is as apt to think in
terms of the conjunctions. Again, his skeptical empiricism is evident. Proud of his produce, Monboddo maintained "that Virgil
seemed to be as enthusiastic a farmer as he, and was certainly a
practical one. JOHNSON. 'It does not always follow, my lord,
that a man who has written a good poem on an art has practised
it. Philip Miller told me that in Philips's *Cyder, a Poem* all the
precepts were just, and indeed better than in books written for
the purpose of instructing, yet Philips had never made cider'"
(*Hebrides*, p. 54). Johnson does not respond to the question of
Virgil's enthusiasm. But once again he uses a known fact about a
particular poet to discourage someone from improperly deduc-
ing facts about another poet.

In the *Life of Pope* Johnson generalizes in a kindred spirit.
"Poets," he says, "do not always express their own thoughts" (III,
228). And he contrasts Pope's ignorance of music and his inability to appreciate it with his glorification of it in the "Ode on
St. Cecilia's Day." The statement is not pejorative; the poem
itself is inferior of its kind only to Dryden's.

22. Trans. Izora Scott (New York: Columbia Teachers' College, 1908), p. 45. I
have amended the translation somewhat to make it more literal.

Johnson's skeptical attitude toward the biographical validity of literary statements plays an important part in his biographies and accounts for the caution with which he draws inferences from a literary text. Frequently he insists that the criterion for taking certain statements in poetry as biographically significant is the presence of external evidence. In the *Life of Waller* he invokes the *argumentum e silentio* to discredit (with an appropriate metaphor) Fenton's assumption that Waller was on an expedition to the Bermudas: "From the verses written at Penshurst it has been collected that he diverted his disappointment by a voyage, and his biographers, from his poem on the Whales, think it not improbable that he visited the Bermudas; but it seems much more likely that he should amuse himself with forming an imaginary scene than that so important an incident, as a visit to America, should have been left floating in conjectural probability" (I, 254).

But his skepticism is more radical yet; once again in opposition to the dominant opinion of the age, he rejected the contention that letters, particularly those addressed to close friends, reveal a man's true thoughts and feelings. After excoriating this view in the *Life of Pope*, he goes on to compare Pope's professions in his letters to Swift with other evidence: "a friendly letter is a calm and deliberate performance in the cool of leisure, in the stillness of solitude, and surely no man sits down to depreciate by design his own character" (III, 207). This cautious approach marks a distinct break with the traditions, scanty as they were, of English literary biography. From the last years of the sixteenth century, when Speght wrote his *Life of Chaucer* (or before, it we take translations into account), biographers had shown themselves ready to accept poems purportedly autobiographical or merely in the first person, whether they discussed attitudes or events, as statements of fact about the life of the poet.

This, indeed, was the standard practice of biographers in classical antiquity and the middle ages.[23] Pope, who with good reason doubted that Herodotus had written an early life of Homer, noticed that all his other biographers had "guessed out circum-

23. See Domenico Comparetti, *Vergil in the Middle Ages*, trans. E. F. M. Benecke (London: George Allen and Unwin, 1895), p. 135.

stances for a life of him from his own writings."[24] In the seventeenth century such titles as "The Life, Works, and Approof of Ovid, Gathered out of his own Works and the Relations of divers faithful Authours" were not uncommon.[25] As Arnaldo Momigliano says in *The Development of Greek Biography*, while discussing Chameleon, an early Peripatetic, who frequently inferred the "personal circumstances" of poet from poem, "this represented a contribution to the technique of biographical research which cannot be underrated either on the positive or on the negative side."[26]

It would be foolish to think that Johnson alone observed all such distinctions. Discriminations between life and art appear frequently enough throughout the age as discrete insights or satiric thrusts.[27] In some biographies—lives of Steele would be

24. In Joseph Spence, *Observations, Anecdotes, and Characters of Books and Men*, ed. James M. Osborn (Oxford: Clarendon Press, 1966), I, 84.

25. In Ovid's *Festivalls or Romane Calandar, Translated into English Verse Equinumerally* (Cambridge, 1640), A1 ʳ -B2 ᵛ . A variant of the theory that the character of a man was to be found in his works stressed style as the significant factor. Perhaps best known in England through Gibbon's aphorism, "Style is the image of character," this doctrine did not seem to have any particular appeal for Johnson. He certainly believed in the individuality of the artist's style ("infinite *in potestate*, limited *in actu*"), but his comments on style do not suggest that this individuality is deeply related to the poet's character. His most interesting comments on the formation of style occur in a note to *Two Gentlemen of Verona*. There he declares that the "peculiarities" of a writer come "from the desire, natural to every performer, of facilitating his subsequent works by recurrence to his former ideas; this recurrence produces that repetition which is called habit." And he goes on to say that a writer's works may vary a great deal from one another. This should be seen as another of Johnson's tributes to the freedom of the will.

26. *The Development of Greek Biography* (Cambridge, Mass.: Harvard University Press, 1971), p. 70.

27. A good example is Matt Bramble's account of his visit to a successful author: "As I had read one or two of his performances, which gave me pleasure, I was glad of this opportunity to know his person; but his discourse and deportment destroyed all the impressions which his writings had made in his favour." Matt goes on to detail his dogmatic attacks on all other writers. See Tobias Smollett, *The Expedition of Humphry Clinker,* ed. Lewis M. Knapp (London: Oxford University Press, 1966), p. 105. Cf. Johnson in *Rambler* No. 14: "Milton, in a letter to a learned stranger, by whom he had been visited, with great reason congratulates himself upon the consciousness of being found equal to his own character, and having preserved in a private and familiar interview that reputation which his works had procured him" (*Yale*, III, 74). For an intelligent defense of the seemingly immoral poet on the grounds of genre, see Lewis Crusius' "Life of Catullus" in *Lives of the Roman Poets* (London, 1726), I, 41.

obvious examples—the variance of life and art are inescapable, but no other biographer that I have discovered in this period (though the theme fascinated Boswell) makes the "vicious moralist" a central part of his work. As my examples will demonstrate, the other writers at the end of the seventeenth century and during the eighteenth who noticed disparities between the character of the author and that of his work are usually conscious of going against the accepted opinions of the time.

In a late edition of *Les Caractères*, La Bruyere added some atypical observations, which he presents as *"incompréhensible."* These are short "characters" of writers whose lives are at great variance with the abilities they display in their works. One concerns a storyteller: "Un homme paraît grossier, lourd, stupide, il ne sait pas parler, ni raconter ce qu'il vient de voir; s'il se met à écrire, c'est le modèle des bons contes, il fait parler les animaux, les arbres, les pierres, tout ce qui ne parle point: ce n'est que légèreté, qu'élégance, que beau naturel, et que délicatesse dans ses ouvrages."[28] This man, who is himself unable to speak well, makes animals and even the inanimate speak elegantly in his fables. Though the characters are usually idealized types, it is not surprising that this passage is based on La Bruyère's observation of a real man, La Fontaine. In essence such a passage and those that immediately follow it signal the death knell of the Theophrastan character, for they lead to a recognition of complexities it will not support. In one of these passages, referring to Corneille, the description of how the simple, timid, and somewhat scatterbrained man becomes the equal in thought and emotion of kings and heroes ("Laissez-le s'élever par la composition") faintly echoes the old tradition of the afflatus, the divine inspiration which takes possession of a writer and makes him different from his everyday self; but it far more strongly reflects La Bruyère's astonishment (or at least mock-astonishment) when his expectation that a man's literary performance will closely correspond to the characteristics and abilities which he displays in social intercourse is forced to yield to contrary facts. In a subsequent selection we can see the process of fragmentation in

28. *Oeuvres Complètes,* ed. Julien Benda (Paris: Gallimard, 1951), p. 361.

action: "Je commence à me persuader moi-même que j'ai fait le portrait de deux personnages tout différents," and he even thinks that he can find a third.[29]

These observations of La Bruyère at the end of the seventeenth century are similar to those of Johnson many years later. "It is wonderful," said Johnson, with James Beattie's poor conversation in mind, "what a difference there sometimes is between a man's powers of writing and talking" (*Life*, IV, 323). This comment is as close as he ever comes to astonishment at such an occurrence. His empiricism had taught him that what we may reasonably expect does not always happen. In his biographies his rationalism and his empiricism call one another to account:

Of Dryden's sluggishness in conversation it is vain to search or to guess the cause. He certainly wanted neither sentiments nor language; his intellectual treasures were great, though they were locked from his own use. "His thoughts," when he wrote, "flowed in upon him so fast, that his only care was which to chuse, and which to reject." Such rapidity of composition naturally promises a flow of talk, yet we must be content to believe what an enemy says of him, when he likewise says it of himself. [I, 397]

Five years after Johnson commented on the "striking contrariety between the life of an author and his writings" in *Rambler* No. 14, it furnished matter for an essay in Colman and Thornton's *Connoisseur*:

As people are led frequently to judge of a man from his ordinary conversation, so it is common for them to form an idea of the author's disposition from the peculiar turn and colour of his writings: they expect a gloom to be spread over the face of a mathematician; a controversial writer must be given to wrangling and dispute; and they imagine that a satirist must be made up of spleen, envy, and ill-nature. But this criterion is by no means certain and determinate. I know an author of a tragedy, who is the merriest man living; and one who wrote a very witty comedy, though he will sit an hour in company without speaking a word. Lord Buckhurst is celebrated for being "the best good man with the worst natured muse"; and Addison was remarkably shy and reserved in conversation.[30]

29. *Oeuvres*, p. 362.
30. *Connoisseur* No. 114, April 1, 1756; in *The British Essayists*, ed. Lionel Thomas Berguer (London, 1823), XXXII, 106–7.

This essay is instructive both in its assumptions about the common way people thought of the relationship between the artist and his work and in the way it differs from Johnson's handling of the same subject. The correspondence theory is, as one might expect, dominant. People think quite naturally of the satirist, for example, as splenetic. This proclivity, yoked in the nineteenth century to a greater interest in development and flux, led to the pseudo-biographies of Shakespeare, which presented a figure who was gloomy when he wrote the tragedies—his "dark period"—and gay when he wrote the comedies.[31] The Connoisseur opposes this idea simply by referring to the actual dispositions of several writers whom he knows and reinforcing his point with some well-known examples. For Colman and Thornton, however, the empirical fact is an end in itself, an amusing paradox. For Johnson the empirical fact is a starting point, and the discrepancy between the reasonable expectation of a correspondence and the disappointing reality shows that the fact is a manifestation of the nature of man and leads to ethical conclusions.

3

The last aspect of Johnson's discriminations between life and art which I want to consider is his tendency to separate life from work in order to judge the work itself. Although he wished to know the author's personal circumstances in order to estimate the human excellence of his achievement—the man who writes an epic poem while engaged in paltry tasks to earn his bread is more to be admired than the nobleman who writes at his leisure—he recognized the danger, to which so many of his fellow biographers succumbed, of permitting irrelevant biographical information to color his judgment of the poem.

Part of the reason why Johnson can confidently speak of Shakespeare's greatness (at least insofar as any greatness dependent upon comparative judgments can be spoken of) is that the adventitious and extrinsic biographical considerations that

31. For an amusing and useful account of this tendency, see S. Schoenbaum, *Shakespeare's Lives* (New York: Clarendon Press, 1970).

colored Shakespeare's contemporaries' view of him no longer
beclouded a judgment of his works by the time Johnson wrote.
"The effects of favour and competition are at an end; the tradition of his friendships and his enmities has perished; his works
support no opinion with arguments, nor supply any faction with
invectives; they can neither indulge vanity nor gratify malignity,
but are read without any other reason than the desire of pleasure, and are therefore praised only as pleasure is obtained"
("Preface to *Shakespeare*," *Yale*, VII, 61).

The *Life of Milton* may be looked upon, at least from this
vantage point, as an essay in discrimination. When Johnson
snorted at the "honeysuckle" lives of Milton, he probably had in
mind the vague approbation that hovers over all of Milton's acts
and writings in the biographies of Phillips, Toland, and
Richardson. Again and again he distinguishes those things
worthy of admiration from those he finds detestable. As we have
already seen, the foremost distinction is between Milton the poet
and Milton the politician; but Johnson explicitly calls our attention to the error in judgment of those who ignore it: "Such is the
reverence paid to great abilities, however misused: they who
contemplated in Milton the scholar and the wit were content to
forget the reviler of his king" (I, 140). Johnson is also aware of
the tendency to overrate the canon of a writer who has written a
great work. He thinks that "those who admire the beauties of
this great poet sometimes force their own judgment into false
approbation of his little pieces" (I, 163). The mention of "this
great poet" is not a device for disarming the admirers of Milton,
whom Johnson is about to portray as deluded. He is not chastis-
ing particular men, but exposing a foible of the human mind:
"Such is the power of reputation justly acquired that its blaze
drives away the eye from nice examination. Surely no man could
have fancied that he read *Lycidas* with pleasure had he not
known its author" (I, 165). Johnson also thinks that *Samson
Agonistes* profited from its association with Milton's name (and
that *Paradise Regained* was undervalued because it had been written by the author of *Paradise Lost*). This emphasis on the dangers
of letting our reverence for an author overpower our judgment
is certainly not confined to the *Life of Milton*, but it is hardly an

accident that the lesson is brought home most pointedly in the biography of the greatest poet of those whose lives he wrote.

Johnson's strong interest in showing how the judgment is affected by personal considerations takes many forms. Sometimes, as in the case of Ambrose Philips's pastorals, he appears merely to be explaining the workings of the mind: "They are not loaded with much thought, yet if they had been written by Addison they would have had admirers: little things are not valued but when they are done by those who can do greater" (III, 324). As he points out in one of his essays, "the same actions performed by different hands produce different effects, and instead of rating the man by his performances, we rate too frequently the performance by the man" (*Rambler* No. 166, *Yale*, V, 118).

The theme of discrimination appears most frequently with reference to overblown reputations, especially those of noblemen. After describing the esteem in which Dorset's age held him, Johnson says, "If such a man attempted poetry, we cannot wonder that his works were praised" (I, 307). In the *Life of Granville* he provides a *locus classicus* on the entanglements of biographical knowledge with judgment:

Writers commonly derive their reputation from their works; but there are works which owe their reputation to the character of the writer. The publick sometimes has its favourites, whom it rewards for one species of excellence with the honours due to another. From him whom we reverence for his beneficence we do not willingly withhold the praise of genius: a man of exalted merit becomes at once an accomplished writer, as a beauty finds no great difficulty in passing for a wit. [II, 293-94]

And he goes on to cite those characteristics of "illustrious . . . birth," "elegant . . . manners," and consistent principles which led to the overestimation of Granville's work. This facet of poetic reputation is not limited to the effects of good qualities alone; mere celebrity seems to ensure Rochester of some undeserved praise (I, 222).

Nor were noblemen and great poets the only recipients of such praise. Of Hammond's posthumously published elegies Johnson says, "while the writer's name was remembered with fondness they were read with a resolution to admire them" (II, 314). And Addison's poetry was overrated by his contemporaries because of his moral excellence and his political influence (II, 126). We might also notice that Johnson is quick to correct a complementary flaw in judgment, the tendency to let our disdain for a man's writings determine our attitude toward other aspects of his life. His biography of Blackmore, one of the few poets whom he asked the booksellers to include, is an attempt to separate the good from the bad qualities of a man who had been the victim of a smear campaign in Queen Anne's day. Using a Swiftian metaphor, he describes the effects of Blackmore's bad poems on his medical practice: "Contempt is a kind of gangrene, which if it seizes one part of a character corrupts all the rest by degrees. Blackmore, being despised as a poet, was in time neglected as a physician" (II, 250). Johnson is also interested in discerning what he sees as Blackmore's one good poem and in showing that there was morally a great deal to admire in this constant butt of the wits. Appropriately, he chooses to invert a line from Pope, who had done more than any other poet to make Blackmore ridiculous, in order to indicate Blackmore's proper praise. In recounting the anecdote of the old doctor's befriending John Dennis, who had energetically attacked his poetry, Johnson says: "It is remarked by Pope that what 'raises the poet often sinks the man.' Of Blackmore it may be said that as the poet sinks, the man rises" (II, 239). Johnson's own critics, who can scarcely have read this short biography with attention, responded with indiscriminate glee to his inclusion of the *Life of Blackmore* among the *Lives of the Poets*. They failed to see that the standard assessment of Blackmore was lopsided and Johnson—a great redresser of balances—set it right. Johnson distinguishes the wretched poet—and his general remarks on Blackmore's poetry leave no doubt that he thought it on the whole very bad—from the good man. We may have excellent reasons for disagreeing with him on the value of *The Creation*, but only our own stock responses can prevent us from recognizing that the *Life of Blackmore* shows Johnson's humanity and his capacity for discerning the differences between life and art at their best.

In this practice Johnson had philosophical if not biographical predecessors. In *Rambler* No. 93, he says that "Baillet has introduced his collection of the decisions of the learned, by an enumeration of the prejudices which mislead the critick, and raise the passion in rebellion against the judgment. His catalogue, though large, is imperfect; and who can hope to complete it?" (*Yale*, IV, 130). He refers to the vast, unfinished *Jugemens des Savans* (1685–86) of Adrien Baillet, which he also mentions on two other occasions. Under such headings as "Préjugés de la Dignité et de la Qualité des Auteurs," "Préjugés de la Réputation et de l'Autorité des Auteurs," and "Préjugés de l'Humeur des Auteurs," Baillet sorts out many of the critical confusions of life and work which Johnson discusses in his literary biographies.

An English work, greatly admired by Johnson, also makes such distinctions. In his *Logick*, Isaac Watts uses Lockean ideas to explain the divagations of judgment:

A *Mixture of different Qualities in the Same Thing* is another temptation to judge amiss. . . .When we read a book that has many excellent Truths in it and Divine Sentiments, we are tempted to approve not only that whole Book, but even all the writings of that Author. When a *Poet*, an *Orator* or a *Painter* has performed admirably in several illustrious Pieces, we sometimes also admire his very Errors, we mistake his Blunders for Beauties, and are so ignorantly fond as to copy after them.

It is this Prejudice that has rendered so many Scholars perfect Bigots, and inclined them to defend Homer or Horace, Livy or Cicero, in all their Mistakes, and Vindicate all the follies of their favourite Author. . . .

On the other hand, if an author has profess'd heretical Sentiments in Religion, we throw our scorn upon every thing he writes, we dispise even his *critical* or *mathematical* Learning, and will hardly allow him common sense. If a *Poem* has some Blemishes in it, there is a sect of false criticks who decry it universally, and will allow no Beauties there.

This sort of Prejudice is relieved by learning to distinguish Things well, and not to *judge in the Lump*. . . .He should neither *praise nor dispraise by Wholesale*, but separate the Good from the Evil, and judge of them apart.[32]

Watts's examples are general, but their application is chiefly literary.

Baillet and Watts stand well in the shadows of Descartes and Locke, but their work serves to remind us of the importance for criticism and literary biography of the philosophical currents of the time. The eighteenth century was a great age of analysis, and

32. *Logick, or The Right Use of Reason in the Enquiry after Truth*, 3d ed. (London, 1739), pp. 191–93. Johnson illustrates "biography" in his *Dictionary* with a quotation from this work (see p. 108 above).

Johnson insists upon clear and distinct ideas in the realm of literary judgment. Whenever we are tempted to overemphasize Imlac's dictum on tulips, we should remember that Johnson, according to his good friend Sir Joshua Reynolds, "was fond of discrimination."[33]

Johnson's discriminations between life and art, though not systematic, are among the most important elements in his biographies, and are certainly the most overlooked. The historian of biography, staring with a fixed gaze at the connections between art and life, rarely notices this aspect of Johnson's work.[34] And it is just this skeptical approach to the question of the relation of art and life that literary biography most lacks. As we shall see in the next chapter, the ability to make such discriminations does not commit Johnson to a total divorce. The connections between art and life, though not of the sort that some critics have thought, also play a significant role in Johnsonian biography.

33. *Life*, II, 306. Pope bears down on self-serving prejudices and other "causes hindering a true judgment" in *An Essay on Criticism*. The picture of the noble poet closely parallels Johnson's remarks in the *Life of Granville:*

> What woful stuff this Madrigal wou'd be,
> In some starv'd Hackny Sonneteer, or me?
> But let a Lord once own the happy Lines,
> How the Wit brightens! How the Style refines!
> Before his sacred Name flies ev'ry Fault,
> And each exalted Stanza teems with Thought!   [ll. 418–23]

(*The Poems of Alexander Pope*, ed. John Butt [New Haven: Yale University Press, 1966], pp. 156–57.)

34. There are, of course, honorable exceptions. Jean Hagstrum points out that Johnson is not "often found to express—perhaps because he did not always find it to be actually true, however much he may have wanted it to be—that favorite idea of Renaissance criticism, the 'impossibility,' in Ben Jonson's language, 'of any mans being the good *Poet*, without first being a good *Man*' " (*Samuel Johnson's Literary Criticism* [1952; rpt. Chicago: University of Chicago Press, 1967], p. 39). More recently, Lawrence Lipking has noticed that "Johnson faced one insuperable problem in demonstrating the connection between a poet's life and work: he did not trust such connections" (*The Ordering of the Arts in Eighteenth-Century England* [Princeton: Princeton University Press, 1970], p. 420). And Paul Fussell, shifting from his insistence in an earlier book that "ethics and expression are closely allied" in the great Augustans, finds some significant differences in his recent study of Johnson (*The Rhetorical World of Augustan Humanism* [Oxford: Clarendon Press, 1965], p. 7; *Samuel Johnson and the Life of Writing* [New York: Harcourt, Brace, Jovanovich, 1971], *passim*).

CHAPTER 7

Art and Life: Connections

Like other biographers, Johnson draws inferences about his subjects from their writings; but the scope of these inferences is restricted by the skepticism of his approach and the tentativeness of his conclusions.

The care with which he draws such inferences is apparent from the extent to which he qualifies his remarks and the indications of the possibilities he has considered. He is well aware, for example, of the need to take context into account: "Malevolence to the clergy is seldom at a great distance from irreverence of religion, and Dryden affords no exception to this observation. His writings exhibit many passages, which, *with all the allowance that can be made for characters and occasions*, are such as piety would not have admitted, and such as may vitiate light and unprincipled minds" (I, 404; my italics). Such writing is morally reprehensible, but it does not lead Johnson to say that Dryden was a disbeliever. Nor does it lead him to say that Dryden was impious in private life. Instead, he merely concludes that Dryden gave the age what it demanded. Johnson is unwilling to extend the range of his inferences to Dryden's life when he has no external evidence to support him.

The caution with which he works, even when he is fairly certain of his conclusions, can be observed in some changes he made in a paragraph from the *Life of Dryden*. In the first edition of the *Lives* he discusses the likelihood of Dryden's believing in astrology: "Of one opinion he is very reasonably suspected, which will do him no honour in the present age. . . .There is little doubt that he put confidence in the prognostications of judicial astrology. . . .That he had the configurations of the horoscope in his mind, and considered them as influencing the affairs of men, he does not forbear to hint."[1] And he quotes some lines from *Annus Mirabilis* that refer to planetary influence and use astrological terms. But this is not his only evidence. He also mentions that Dryden has similar passages in his other works, probably thinking, as G. B. Hill suggests in a note, of *Absalom and Achitophel* and the "Ode to Mrs. Anne Killigrew" (*Lives*, I, 410, n. 3). Johnson adds that Dryden "in the preface to his Fables had endeavored obliquely to justify his superstition, by attributing the same to some of the Ancients."[2] Although Johnson evidently meant the "Dedication to the Aeneis"—the passage he refers to is not in the *Fables*—this last piece of evidence is the strongest part of his case.

Yet it does not, to his way of thinking, clinch things. In revising his work for the last time he evidently noticed that a letter from Dryden to his sons, probably appended to his biography by John Nichols, who added other material without Johnson's sanction, contained precisely the information he needed. What caught his eye was a prophecy: "Towards the latter end of this month, September, Charles will begin to recover his perfect health, according to his nativity, which, casting it myself, I am sure is true, and all things hitherto have happened accordingly to the very time that I predicted them"[3] Hence, "Of one opinion he is very reasonably suspected" becomes in 1783 "One of his opinions"; "There is little doubt that he put confidence" in astrological prophecies becomes "He put great confidence." And as the last sentence of the paragraph Johnson adds in 1783, "The letter, added to this narrative, leaves no doubt of his notions or practice."[4] Unless Johnson can find sufficient cor-

1. *Prefaces, Biographical and Critical, to the Works of the English Poets*, 10 vols. (London, 1779–81), III, 165–66.

2. *Prefaces*, III, 167.

3. *Prefaces*, III, 347–48. This appears unchanged in *The Lives of the Most Eminent English Poets* (London, 1783), II, 213–14. See *Lives*, I, 481.

4. 1783, II, 101 (*Lives*, I, 409); 1783, II, 102 (*Lives*, I, 410). I have corrected the misprint "latter."

roborating evidence, he generally acknowledges the conjectural nature of his belief.

The limits Johnson usually places on his biographical inferences from literary works are evident in the *Life of Addison*. In the section devoted to Addison's character, he uses the works only for evidence of Addison's learning: "of the Latin poets his *Dialogues on Medals* show that he had perused the works with great diligence and skill" (II, 121). And, following the first seventeen paragraphs of this section, he explicitly states that Addison's "works will supply some information" about his character. The inferences he then proceeds to draw begin with Addison's experience rather than his temper. From his essays Johnson deduces that despite his shyness Addison "had conversed with many distinct classes of men, had surveyed their ways with very diligent observation, and marked with great acuteness the effects of different modes of life" (II, 124). Johnson is always prepared, as the "Preface to *Shakespeare*" also shows, to consider the skillful drawing of characters as the outcome of experience rather than imagination (e.g., *Butler*, I, 213). The rest of the information is really the drawing of Addison's literary character, for Johnson does not extend the remarks to include his empirical behavior. And when he says that Addison's moral conduct was probably similar to that found in his works, he does not ground his assertion on the works but on external evidence. This passage is also the occasion for one of his caveats on reading a man's morality from his writings: "If any judgment be made from his books of his moral character nothing will be found but purity and excellence. Knowledge of mankind indeed, less extensive than that of Addison, will show that to write and to live are very different. Many who praise virtue, do no more than praise it. Yet it is reasonable to believe that Addison's professions and practice were at no great variance" (II, 125). This belief is "reasonable" because, despite the political animosity that hovered about him, none of Addison's enemies ever charged him with immorality. Johnson uses here one of his favorite methods of adducing evidence, the *argumentum e silentio*.

Even at times when modern biographers would leap to draw what would seem an obvious inference, Johnson is cautious. In the *Life of Savage* he says:

> It is probable that these Lines in the *Wanderer* were occasioned by his
> Reflections on his own Conduct.
>> "Though Mis'ry leads to Fortitude and Truth,
>> Unequal to the Load this languid Youth,
>> (O! let none Censure if untried by Grief,
>> Or amidst Woes untempted by Relief,)
>> He stoop'd, reluctant, to mean Acts of Shame,
>> Which then, ev'n then, he scorn'd, and blush'd to name."
>
> [*Savage*, p. 97]

Johnson's grave "it is probable" may make him seem a bit slow. Of course Savage, ever the self-seeking publicist, is talking about his own case. Yet this same caution keeps Johnson from the excesses of biographical assumptions made in his day and ours.

On a few occasions Johnson draws biographical inferences from fiction and poetry with little or no hesitation, but they are mainly devoted to solving certain problems of practice and belief. In the *Life of Swift* he conjectures, probably with the *Directions to Servants* in mind, that "a man . . . with that vigilance of minute attention which his works discover, must have been a master that few could bear" (III, 56). And he even claims that the several anecdotes of Swift's "benefaction" to his servants can hardly be considered representative of his habitual manner. But here he has some empirical evidence, in the form of anecdotes of Swift's conversation, to support his interpretation. In this biography he also decides from his reading of the *Journal to Stella* that "it is easy to perceive from every page, that though ambition pressed Swift into a life of bustle, the wish for a life of ease was always returning" (III, 23). And in attempting to determine the claims of Stella to Swift's "excentrick tenderness," Johnson draws an arch qualification from the *Letter to a Lady on her Marriage:* "if his general thoughts on women were such as he exhibits, a very little sense in a lady would enrapture and a very little virtue would astonish him" (III, 42).

In the *Life of Milton*, however, he uses *Paradise Lost* as the sole evidence for Milton's attitude toward prayer. Opposing those biographers (notably Toland) who, noticing that Milton neither attended church nor appointed a time for private prayers in his home, assume that he did not think prayers were significant, Johnson says, "Prayer certainly was not thought superfluous by him, who represents our first parents as praying acceptably in the state of innocence, and efficaciously after their fall" (I, 156). This is about as far as Johnson goes in drawing explicit conclusions from literature to offset the seeming evidence of a man's empirical existence.

2

Although many critics thought that the supreme quality of the poet was his ability to create his characters *ex nihilo*,[5] Johnson insisted on the importance of experience in forming the poet's conceptions. In this empirical view he follows Locke. By throwing out innate ideas, Locke had put a premium on experience. Johnson consistently attacked those who would have made genius independent of reality. When he protested that "genius" was overrated ("They give to it all, when it can be but a part"), Fanny Burney, using the hackneyed Addisonian example, retorted, "'Certainly, sir; yet there is such a thing as invention: Shakespeare could never have seen a Caliban.'" But Johnson replies that even the Calibans are derived from empirical reality:

"No; but he had seen a man, and knew therefore, how to vary him to a monster.... Suppose you show me a man who is a very expert carpenter; another will say he was born to be a carpenter—but what if he had never seen any wood? Let two men, one with genius, the other with none, look at an overturned waggon:—he who has no genius, will think of the waggon only as he sees it ...; he who has genius, will paint it to himself before it was overturned,—standing still, and moving on, and heavy loaded, and empty; but both must see the waggon, to think of it at all."[6]

Genius, then, always bases itself on the real, and the better poet is inevitably the man who has observed more than another. In

5. M. H. Abrams, *The Mirror and the Lamp: Romantic Theory and the Critical Tradition* (1953; rpt. New York: W. W. Norton, 1958), ch. X, iii, "The Poem as Heterocosm."

6. F. B. D'Arblay, *Diary and Letters*, ed. Charlotte Barrett (London: Macmillan, 1904), II, 271–72. One can trace her example beyond Addison, who popularized it, to Dryden. See "The Grounds of Criticism in Tragedy," in *Of Dramatic Poesy and Other Critical Essays*, ed. George Watson (London: J. M. Dent and Sons, 1962), I, 252–53.

opposition to the writers of his age who portrayed Shakespeare as the child of nature, Johnson portrayed him as the close observer of men and manners, and he even objects to Rowe's contention that Shakespeare's earliest works were best, on the grounds that "Shakespeare, however favored by nature, could impart only what he had learned; and as he must increase his ideas, like other mortals, by gradual acquisition, he, like them, grew wiser as he grew older, could display life better as he knew it more, and instruct with more efficacy, as he was himself more amply instructed" (*Yale*, VII, 88–89). Throughout the *Lives* he is careful to specify the poets' opportunities for increasing their knowledge about the nature of man; Thomson on the Grand Tour and Savage among the Lords are good examples.

Because he believes in the importance of experience to the writer, he will sometimes use literary works as oblique indicators of changes in temper or opinions. Although he is most concerned in his biographies to show those things which are true throughout the life of an individual, to show essence rather than process, he is alive to the possibilities of change (for that matter, the whole program of Johnsonian biography rests on the freedom of the will and the presumed changes which biographical examples may help a reader to achieve). His disbelief in a static conception of character can be seen in his rejection of the "ruling passion" as a valid psychological explanation of human behavior: "Human characters are by no means constant; men change by change of place, of fortune, of acquaintance; he who is at one time a lover of pleasure is at another a lover of money" (III, 174; see also I, 282). The concept of the "ruling passion," which was most memorably expounded by Pope and later employed by Gibbon, was in Johnson's view not only wrong but dangerous. Through its determinism it encouraged the abnegation of moral responsibility.

Johnson shows rather that man is a free agent and responds to his experience through change. Speaking of Addison's state of mind after the resumption of the *Spectator*, he says, "the time that had passed during the suspension of the *Spectator*, though it had not lessened his power of humour, seems to have increased his disposition to seriousness: the proportion of his religious to his comick papers is greater than in the former series" (II, 108). The end of Savage's poem "Of Publick Spirit" "discovers a change which experience had made in Mr. Savage's opinions" (*Savage*, p. 94). In an earlier poem Savage had "declared his resolution either to tower like the cedar or be trampled like the shrub," but here he praises "the middle state of life." And noticing that Edmund Smith's *Phaedra*, a highly unsuccessful tragedy, was followed by the uncompleted *Lady Jane Grey*, Johnson suggests that "his experience of the inefficacy and incredibility of a mythological tale" probably led him to choose a story based on historical fact (II, 17).

Another result of Johnson's belief in the importance of experience to the artist is his solicitude concerning "originals." The wish to discover the "originals" of literary characters is a staple of literary biography. This interest probably arises from the indisputable fact that many characters and events have their basis in the experience of the artist. (The nature and importance of these "real" characters and events embodied in art are problematic.) It was probably reinforced by analogy to the "sister art" of painting. Most of Vasari's *Lives of the Painters*, for example, contain passages identifying the models for the portraits we find in the mythological and religious paintings of his contemporaries.

Johnson's interest in models served various ends. That he was fond of discovering real men and women behind fictional characters cannot be denied. In conversation, he maintained that a "Mr. Nelson" was Richardson's model for Sir Charles Grandison, and in a long letter to the Earl of Orrery he uses external and internal evidence to support Orrery's "slight and uncertain Conjecture" in his *Remarks on Swift* that "Creteus" in the *Aeneid* is Virgil's depiction of Horace.[7] Even more revealing is his confession in a note to *The Merchant of Venice*: "I am always inclined to believe that Shakespeare has more allusions to par-

7. William Seward in *Johnsonian Miscellanies*, ed. G. B. Hill (Oxford: Clarendon Press, 1897), II, 305; *Letters*, III, 265–68. For an accurate copy of Johnson's letter see Paul J. Korshin, "Johnson and the Earl of Orrery," in *Eighteenth-Century Studies in Honor of Donald F. Hyde*, ed. W. H. Bond (New York: Grolier Club, 1970), pp. 34–36.

ticular facts and persons than his readers commonly suppose"
(*Yale*, VII, 218). And he tentatively identifies the Count Palatine
as "Albertus a Lasco, a Polish Palatine who visited England in
our Authour's time," suggests that Bottom was "perhaps the
head of a rival house," and conjectures that the prisoners described in *Measure for Measure* had originals who would have
been recognized by Shakespeare's audience (*Yale*, VII, 218, 150,
204–5). His attempt in the *Lives of the Poets* to ferret out models
tells us that he thinks such identifications are to be valued with
the evanescent personal details which it is the task of Johnsonian
biography to preserve. When he admits to the "fruitless inquiry"
of his search for the "name and adventures" of Pope's "Unfortunate Lady" or when he identifies Waller's Amoret and
suggests that "perhaps by traditions preserved in families more
may be discovered," his interest proclaims the human significance of finding the real behind the fictional (III, 100; I, 253).

In the biographical portions of his *Lives*, Johnson discusses
poems as strategies to enchant a lover or acquire a patron. He
comments on the lack of success of Waller's poems to Sacharissa
and the callowness of Granville's to Mira. Even in the biographical section, however, he does not assume a simple correspondence between model and literary character. He remarks
upon the difficulty of separating the real from the fictitious in
Addison's periodical essays and Pope's poetic epistles. And in his
jaundiced account of Prior's Chloe, who perhaps "stole his plate
and ran away," he recognizes the role of imagination in the
creation of literary characters, but comments obliquely on the
relation of life to art. Although Johnson does not insist upon the
use of personal experience in writing, he has little sympathy with
writers who excessively idealize their subjects or focus exclusively on the marvelous and imaginary. His detestation of most
mythological and pastoral poetry is well known; his biographies
sometimes, as in the case of Shenstone, provide an ironic critique
of the world of an author's poetry by implicitly contrasting it
with the world in which he lives.

The fact that people were responding to poems, particularly
lyrics, by linking the author to his works made the proper discernment of models a necessary task. Johnson is quick to point

out that Shenstone's supposedly autobiographical "Elegy on Jessey," which concerns a "criminal amour," is really based on the episode of Sally Godfrey in *Pamela* (III, 354).

Satire presents a special case. In this genre a knowledge of the specific persons being attacked is especially necessary. Nowhere, however, is Johnson's preference of the general over the particular more to the point than in his dissatisfaction with the satirist's use of real details. Personal satire ultimately weakens the power of a work because "it is of the nature of personal invectives to be soon unintelligible" ("Notes to *Shakespeare*," *Yale*, VII, 274–75). Yet, though the poet "sacrifices the esteem of succeeding times to the laughter of a day," the biographer who wishes to learn all he can about his subject is frequently condemned to search for personal references in obscure satires. Johnson's discussion of the attack on Dryden in *The Rehearsal* focuses on the specific traits and events to which the play alludes. He mentions that Bayes appears in one scene with a patch upon his nose and deduces that this refers to Davenant, whose "nose had suffered . . . diminution by mishaps among the women" (I, 369). Then, noting the contemporary claim that the play attacked Sir Robert Howard, he concludes that "the design was probably to ridicule the reigning poet, whoever he might be." Although he admits that many of the personal elements of the play are difficult or impossible to discern, he conjecturally elucidates the references to Dryden, and, in the case of Bayes's bloodlettings prior to poetic composition, he offers the hearsay evidence of Charles Lamotte that Dryden's "real practice was similar." In this short consideration of *The Rehearsal* Johnson attempts to discover the intention of the play and recover the characteristics of Dryden.

3

One kind of literature, however, appears to enjoy a special status. Whereas a poem's claim to be a personal document is problematic, the familiar letter is composed of the very stuff of the poet's life. Johnson's use of the letter in his biographies calls for special consideration.

The letter form could be used for everything in the eighteenth

century from poetry and the novel to biography itself. Sometimes the supposed form is stretched quite far, as in the two
letters to a friend which comprise Cleland's *Fanny Hill* or the
chapters of Orrery's *Remarks on the Life and Writings of Dr.
Jonathan Swift in a series of Letters to his Son, the Honorable Hamilton
Boyle* (1752). (These last are apt to begin, "I have already told
you, my dear Ham, that the first four volumes of Swift's works
were published together. . . ."

Although overemphasizing any single aspect of Johnson's pro-
tean literary interests is easy, sufficient testimony exists that letters were of concern to him. Among the many literary projects
he contemplated were "a collection of Letters, translated from
the modern writers," "a book of Letters, upon all kinds of subjects," and "a collection of Letters from English authours, . . .
with reasons for selection, and criticism upon styles; remarks on
each letter if needful." Keeping in mind his remarks in *Rambler*
No. 152 on the importance of letters because they are useful and
frequent, we may guess that the second of these abortive projects
was intended for the humble purpose of providing precedents
for those with little education, much as Richardson's *Familiar
Letters* did. In conversation he was as ready to condemn Sher-
lock's French and English letters as he was to insist that Derrick's
letters would have been valued had they been written by a writer
with a better reputation. And Mrs. Thrale claimed—wrongly—
that Lady Mary Wortley Montagu's *Letters* was the only book,
except for those he was required to read, that he ever read
through. The *Dictionary*'s illustrative quotations attest his stylistic
interest. Under "Letter" he quotes Walsh on epistolary style in
general and Swift on the style of Mrs. P. R. The closest thing we
have to a historical survey of letter writing from Johnson is a
short digression on the English letter writers before Pope in the
Life of Pope. In some ways the dismissal of the writers in this
genre parallels his remarks on the "penury of English biography." He was able to yoke a high interest in letters with a low
opinion of those that existed. He mentions Howell, Loveday,
Herbert, Katherine Phillips, and Walsh, only to conclude that
"Pope's epistolary excellence had an open field; he had no English rival, living or dead" (III, 159). This does not mean that he

was impressed with the achievement of the French. Although he does not mention Mme. de Sévigné, the greatest of French letter writers, he refers in *Rambler* No. 152 to the "despicable remains of Voiture and Scarron." The recognition of the letter's significance and the rating of individual letter writers, however, do not determine Johnson's use of letters in biography.

Letters had appeared in English biography from the time of Eddius' early eighth-century Latin life of Saint Wilfrid. In the seventeenth century Walton sometimes dexterously rearranged the letters of his subjects, omitting here and adding parts of other letters there, to create the effect he was after. In the eighteenth century Middleton used many of Cicero's letters, both real and spurious, in his biography of the Roman orator, and Mason, in his *Life of Gray*, actually interspersed a commentary into what was in essence his edition of Gray's letters. Johnson was evidently unimpressed with this practice.

His employment of letters in biography has been seriously criticized by James M. Osborn, who notices that some of Dryden's letters were accessible to Johnson in Derrick's biography, but he did not make use of them: "Probably the best explanation of [his] neglect of them is that the technique of decorating a biography with personal documents had not yet become accepted. . . . Johnson simply did not know how to use letters effectively. Though he had read Mason's *Life of Gray*, it seemed mighty dull to him. He failed to realize the deliberate inclusion of letters was bringing about a great level in the art of biography."[8] Whether one agrees with Osborn's contention about the level of biography or not, there are better explanations to be found for Johnson's practice. First, we tend to overrate Mason's *Gray* because Boswell says, in a well-known passage in the *Life of Johnson*, that he is "enlarging" upon Gray's method. Yet Boswell's method is radically different; Mason has given him the bare hint that personal documents are of primary importance. Boswell's narrative is brilliantly varied by the insertion of Johnson's letters, but Mason is the laconic editor of a series of letters.

8. *John Dryden: Some Biographical Facts and Problems* (New York: Columbia University Press, 1940), p. 28.

A stronger reason for Johnson's exclusion of letters he had at hand is to be found in his judgment of the nature of the letter. A manuscript in the British Museum (Add. MS. 4994), labeled by William Cole, to whom it was given by George Steevens, "Original Notes in Dr Sam: Johnson's Handwriting, on Mr Pope" (and by Johnson simply "Pope"), gives us some insight into the process by which he arrived at his critical remarks on Pope's letters. The passage of interest is not very long—it covers the recto of a 3.8 ″ × 9.3 ″ page—but it is perhaps the longest continuous critical utterance in a memorandum which is chiefly concerned with laying out the chronology of Pope's life by way of outlining the biography. It is as close as we can come to hearing Johnson ruminate before making his critical judgment:

> Amiable disposition—but he gives his own character
> Elaborate. think what to say—say what one thinks.
> Letters in Sickness to Steele on Solitude.
> Ostentatious benevolence
> Professions of Sincerity. Neglect of Fame
> Indifference about every thing. Sometimes gay and airy,
> Sometimes sober and grave. [P. 170 ʳ]

These are Johnson's reactions to the attitude expressed in the letters, if they can be believed; but Johnson, absolving Pope of hypocrisy in the *Life of Pope,* cannot take them straight.

Though letters have significance as common tokens of human commerce, Johnson, going counter to the general opinion of his time, did not believe that "the true character of men may be found in their letters," and his short disquisition on the real nature of the letter ("there is... no transaction which offers stronger temptation to fallacy and sophistication than epistolary intercourse") is a response to the judgment of Pope's "social qualities" which he would be forced to make if he took the letters as illuminations of the heart (III, 207). This, however, does not mean that misleading letters are necessarily insincere. According to Johnson, they are generally the product of self-deception rather than hypocrisy.

A man's letters are to be regarded skeptically. To determine whether Pope's later correspondence accurately registered his feelings, "his book and his life must be set in comparison" (III,

208). And Johnson finds that the Pope of the letters is contemptuous of his own poetry and utterly unruffled by criticism, attitudes that cannot be reconciled with the facts of his life as they
were known to Johnson.

Some of Pope's letters are, according to Johnson, evidently
insincere, both because they are self-contradictory and because
they display traits that strike Johnson as uncharacteristic. He
thinks that Pope protests too much: "His scorn of the Great is
repeated too often to be real: no man thinks much of that which
he despises" (III, 211).[9] Such an attitude toward letters suggests
that Johnson will have a use for them, though not as direct
revelations of the nature of their writer. Letters must be subjected to critical scrutiny and their content must be interpreted.
As opposed to the biographers of his day, therefore, Johnson is
apt to take as true indications of a man's real feelings those
aspects of his letters which show him in a bad light. He is more
likely to trust letters for their oblique references and for the
information they impart in passing than for their ostensibly
heartfelt confessions.

In this spirit Johnson employs a number of Pope's letters. He
quotes mere snippets and full letters and depends on unquoted
letters for assorted factual matters (III, 155–56, 203). Several
letters are quoted in full for their information. A letter from
Pope to Swift, for example, describes the plan of a large unwritten poem, and as an appendix Johnson includes a letter to Ralph
Bridges which gives Pope's opinion of Homer and explains why
he used Chapman and Hobbes in making his own translations
(III, 183, 252). Several others, however, are presented for the
light they throw on Pope's character. Pope's restrained letter to
Halifax is quoted at length because it is the only evidence of the
jockeying that went on between the proud patron and the proud
poet, and Johnson displays a particular interest in the tone of the
letter ("faint acceptance"). He also quotes Pope's letter to War-

9. Johnson may also be influenced by his memory of Pope's behavior toward
noblemen on behalf of Savage. As Savage put it, according to Johnson, "when
you mention Men of high Rank *in your own Character*, they are *those little Creatures
whom we are pleased* to call the Great; but when you address them *in mine*, no
Servility is sufficiently humble" (*Savage*, p. 113).

burton to show "how much he was pleased with his gratuitous defender" (III, 127, 168).

Despite his warning, then, that a man's familiar letters are not likely to be the simple registration of his real feelings, Johnson makes use of letters for facts, opinions, and, to a limited degree, traits of character. His sketchy delineation of Gray's character on the basis of his letters follows a quotation of William Temple's character of Gray (with Mason's additions): "What has occurred to me, from the slight inspection of his letters in which my undertaking has engaged me, is that his mind had a large grasp; that his curiosity was unlimited, and his judgment cultivated; that he was a man likely to love much where he loved at all, but that he was fastidious and hard to please. His contempt, however, is often employed where I hope it will be approved, upon skepticism and infidelity" (III, 431–32). In the narrative section of the life, he had used the letters for information about specific events and had quoted a phrase which Gray used to describe himself when he was about to solicit a professorship from the Prime Minister ("cockered and spirited up") (III, 427). Here it should be noted that Johnson's primary interest is the extent of Gray's mental powers, and that Gray's qualities as a friend—the more apparent substance of familiar letters—and his defense of religion are significant, but not of as much importance.

Sometimes he merely passes judgment on the letters of his subject without quoting them. The letters Cowley wrote as secretary to Lord Jermin are dismissed with praise for their apparently businesslike qualities. Johnson does not agree, however, with Sprat, Cowley's first biographer, that letters, being addressed to particular persons, were of no general value. His tendency rather is to pick out those letters which focused on a man's private life in such a way as to be generally useful. The only letter of Cowley's which he quotes in full is intended by Johnson as a moral lesson to those who "pant for solitude." The letter details Cowley's unhappiness in the retreat which he had long desired. One recognizes once again the vanity of human wishes and pastoral notions. The only other letter he quotes in this biography is used to show that Cowley, like some other

eminent men of his time, was superstitious enough to consult the
Virgilian lots (I, 8, 16).

The *Life of Savage* (1744) contains more letters than most of
his other lives, and they have been selected to a greater extent
for the light they throw on the subject. One of the letters written
by the incarcerated Savage is quoted to show "the Cheerfulness
with which he bore his Confinement" *(Savage,* p. 125). This
judgment displays as well as anything the sympathy with which
Johnson, despite his critical attitude, treats Savage. We might be
more likely to insist—and we would have many Johnsonian sanc-
tions to do so—that this cheerfulness was merely the impression
Savage wished to give. The other letters contain accounts of
Savage's arrest for debt, of the nature of a typical day in prison,
and of his success in obtaining patronage from the Queen—this
last is included because it "was one of the few Attempts in which
Mr. Savage succeeded *(Savage,* p. 76).[10] The fact that Johnson
usually gives his reason for including a letter suggests that he
thinks the practice needs some justification.

Since he is wary of the deceptive nature of letters, he cus-
tomarily qualifies his deductions from them. Even writers who
have left enough letters from which to discern patterns of
thought are treated with care: "Of Swift's general habits of
thinking, if his letters can be supposed to afford any evidence,
he was not a man to be either loved or envied" (III, 61).

In at least one area, however, his strictures on letters do not
seem to apply: the domestic letter. Of all the letters he quotes in
full or at length, three might be considered in this category:
Thomson to his sister; Granville to his father; Lyttelton's father
to Lyttelton (Dryden to his sons is a special case). These letters
are presumably of more interest than most because they are
from one member of a family to another, but Johnson seems to
have included them chiefly because of their moral value. Thomson's letter shows his beneficence to his sisters, Granville's his
regard for both King and church, that of Lyttelton's father the
joy with which he welcomed his son's conversion from atheism.

10. Johnson quotes another letter because it "is too remarkable to be omitted"
(p. 122).

The letters at once distinguish the subjects and are useful to the reader, but Johnson does not quote them primarily, as more modern biographers quote letters, to give the reader a sense of the subject's personality. The inclusion of the letter from Lyttelton's father, for example, and no letters by Lyttelton himself suggests that the general theme (domestic joy at a prodigal's return) is of more importance than Lyttelton's individuality.

Johnson also uses letters as a source of disinterested contemporary testimony: when two people correspond about one of Johnson's subjects he considers their private opinions, if no reason exists to suspect bias, preferable to public testimony. He uses letters this way quoting an exchange between Pope and Swift on Hughes; Pope's letter to Broome on Fenton; and Pope's letter to Blount on Rowe (in the lives of Hughes, Fenton, and Rowe, respectively). There are at least a few unintentionally ironic touches. In the *Life of Shenstone* Johnson makes no use of Shenstone's letters, but he quotes a letter by Gray which gives Gray's impression of Shenstone as formed from a reading of Shenstone's *Letters* (III, 354). And in the *Life of Somerville* he quotes a letter by Shenstone on the death of Somerville (III, 317–18.[11]

Johnson, then, is perfectly aware of the existence of his subjects' letters, though he quotes them frugally. Even when not quoted he may make extensive use of them. His very short biography of Dyer is based on Dyer's letters, and his early "Life of Barretier" is drawn completely from the letters of his subject's father.[12] And if we conclude, as does Osborn, that he lagged behind his contemporaries in the use of letters in biography, we must first see that he had brilliantly stated the case against their uncritical use when his contemporaries hardly recognized the existence of the problem. Despite the fact that letters, unlike most poems, are autobiographical documents, they need careful interpretation. Johnson may have undervalued the speaking

11. James L. Leicester, who thinks that Johnson may not have read Shenstone's *Letters*, does not notice this sole use of them. See "Johnson's Life of Shenstone," *Johnsonian Studies*, ed. Magdi Wahba (Cairo: Privately printed, 1962), p. 215.

12. He was able to add more information from another source at a later date.

voice behind the letter, but the modern biographer has much more to learn from him about the nature of these documents than from the eighteenth century's Middletons and Masons.

4

One of the major links between biography and criticism during the last two hundred years has been the doctrine of sincerity. Under certain conditions and with certain limitations Johnson will invoke this doctrine. The tendency to credit the poet's sincerity was a relatively modern development. As M. H. Abrams warns us, statements that appear to be calls for sincerity often really ask for rhetorical artfulness.[13] But by the time we reach John Dryden we can find sincerity praised as one aspect, though not the *sine qua non*, of poetic excellence. In his "Discourse concerning the Original and Progress of Satire" Dryden finds in Persius "a spirit of sincerity in all he says; you may easily discern that he is in earnest and is persuaded of that truth which he inculcates."[14] There are no such blanket statements in Johnson's works. Jean Hagstrum is right in saying that he "usually applied the theory negatively rather than positively."[15] The question of sincerity arises for Johnson, as his treatment of the "vicious moralist" suggests, only when the poet seems to be speaking of some personal belief or feeling. Hence the lyric is the focus of this question and, to some extent, so are the panegyric and satire.

On a few occasions Johnson finds that an author's expression is self-evidently sincere. Such instances are limited mainly but not exclusively to short passages in controversial writing. Quoting Milton's answer to those who had scurrilously attacked him for being rusticated from Cambridge, Johnson says, "This is

13. *Mirror and Lamp*, p. 72. Henry Peyre's *Literature and Sincerity* (New Haven: Yale University Press, 1963) is weakened by a tendency to assume that "sincerity" means the same thing when employed by different critics at different times. In *The Honest Muse: A Study in Augustan Verse* (Oxford: Clarendon Press, 1967) Rachel Trickett assesses the poetry of honesty but sometimes unfortunately uses "sincerity" as a loose synonym.

14. *Critical Essays*, ed. Watson, II, 123. And see "Preface to *Sylvae*," II, 25.

15. *Samuel Johnson's Literary Criticism* (1952; rpt. Chicago: University of Chicago Press, 1967), p. 46.

surely the language of a man who thinks that he has been injured" (I, 103).[16] And he also finds that Waller in exile "amused
himself with poetry, in which he sometimes speaks of the rebels
and their usurpation in the natural language of an honest man"
(I, 268).

Rosemond Tuve's description of the Renaissance critic's
treatment of "sincerity" remains true, for the most part, of
Johnson's critical practice: "The critical question of 'sincerity' is
neglected in favor of the poetic problem of efficacy through
credibility. The truth of the affections was a serious matter, but
it stood to be answered less in terms of the question 'did the poet
feel it?' than 'will the reader feel it and why should he?'"[17] This
is a good gloss of Johnson's adverse reaction to *Lycidas*. Although
he cautions the reader early in his criticism of *Lycidas* that the
poem "is not to be considered as the effusion of real passion"
and insists that "where there is leisure for fiction there is little
grief," the relation of the poem to its audience is of paramount
importance for him, and he focuses primarily on its deficiencies
in conveying human emotion. The pastoral trappings of the
poem are ineffectual because they obscure the relationship of
Milton and King and because the "inherent improbability" of the
action presented repels the audience. Johnson welcomes artifice
and imagination, but he thinks that "nothing can less display
knowledge or less exercise invention" than a pastoral. The object
of elegy in Johnson's view is to make the reader identify with the
sorrow of the speaker, and this *Lycidas* fails to do (I, 163-64).

His comments on Hammond and Prior are of the same order.
Chesterfield, in a preface to the *Elegies*, had said that Hammond,
"sincere in his love as in his friendship, . . . wrote to his mistresses
as he spoke to his friends, nothing but the true sentiments of his

16. And see "The Life of the Author" in Zachary Pearce's *A Commentary... on
the Four Evangelists*, ed. John Derby (London, 1777), I, xxiv. The practice of
drawing such inferences from writings seems to have been widespread throughout
the century, but Johnson's use of it is strongly circumscribed. See also Thomas
Sheridan's *Life of Swift*, 2d ed. (Dublin, 1785), pp. 296, 314.

17. *Elizabethan and Metaphysical Imagery: Renaissance Poetics and Twentieth-
Century Critics* (1947; rpt. Chicago: University of Chicago Press, 1963), pp. 182-
83.

heart; he sat down to write what he thought, not to think what he should write."[18] After a highly condensed paraphrase of this opinion, Johnson counterattacks: "the truth is these elegies have neither passion, nature, nor manners. Where there is fiction, there is no passion; he that describes himself as a shepherd, and his Neaera or Delia as a shepherdess, and talks of goats and lambs, feels no passion. He that courts his mistress with Roman imagery deserves to lose her; for she may with good reason suspect his sincerity" (II, 315). Johnson's contention, that Hammond has indeed done exactly what Chesterfield says he has not done, is unassailable. Here we may object, as in his criticism of *Lycidas*, to the assumption that a man must feel passion as he writes and that emotion should not be rendered in a literary manner. Even Wordsworth would have the poet recollect his powerful emotions in tranquillity. But when we read Hammond, we hardly feel that Johnson missed the mark. The kindred attack on Prior suggests that in an age glutted with trite mythological imagery and lifeless pastorals Johnson strongly felt the dangers of poetry's dwindling to the level of mere school exercises. Johnson's complaint that Prior "wrote of love like a man who never felt it" is only secondarily a comment on sincerity. What disturbs him most is an improbable poem.

Johnson's use of sincerity as a critical criterion has other distinct limits. In his study of Johnson as a literary critic, Jean Hagstrum says "so committed was Johnson to this principle [of sincerity] that he consulted the author's biography to determine whether he had actually suffered the pangs he sings about."[19] Hagstrum has in mind Cowley's collection *The Mistress*, which I consider a rather special case. Johnson thinks that these poems are full of "enormous and disgusting hyperboles" and a variety of other faults. In fact, more than half of the bad examples from Cowley in the famous catalogue of metaphysical passages can be found in *The Mistress*. Johnson wishes, then, to account for a series of bad poems by a highly talented poet.

18. In *The Works of the English Poets from Chaucer to Cowper*, ed. Alexander Chalmers (London, 1810), XI, 139.
19. *Samuel Johnson's Literary Criticism*, p. 45.

Since Cowley admits in his preface that he considers love poems obligatory, and a contemporary confesses that Cowley had no love affairs, Johnson evidently thinks that the reason for the poems' badness is not far to seek (I, 6). The failure of the series to present a believable lover is probably caused by Cowley's ignorance of the nature of love. The knowledge of the fictive nature of Cowley's lover "cannot but abate in some measure the reader's esteem for the work and the author." It lessens our esteem for the author because of the triviality of such fictions. In the passage attacking Cowley for indulging in his imaginary affairs Johnson seems to be worried about the dangerous prevalence of the imagination. Our esteem for the work is lessened, according to Johnson, because a poem that seems to speak of real events will naturally be thought less powerful if we happen to know that the events are contrary to facts. This assertion is based on the mind's instinctive quest for truth.

Even the "good" poem, however, can sink in value if we find that it is not the unique expression of a truth that we take it to be. Johnson considered both *Lycidas* and *The Mistress* bad poems, but he thought that a panegyric Pope wrote to Thomson was good,[20] and he had no doubt that Pope really liked Thomson. Nevertheless, he speaks, in virtually the same words he uses in attacking *The Mistress*, of the devaluation of this poem caused by Pope's incorporation of it into the *Epistle to Arbuthnot* (III, 291). We can no longer take the poem as a token of Pope's esteem for Thomson when we find that he is able to transfer it to another. By the same sort of reasoning Johnson finds that in *The Dunciad* Pope, who facilely deposed Theobald in favor of Cibber, "reduced himself to the insignificance of his own magpie, who from his cage calls cuckold at a venture" (III, 187). The ridicule which Pope's satire promotes can no longer be effective when we know he has as easy a time applying it to one as to another.[21] Recounting the reasons why a poet may change his attitude at a later time,

20. See *The Correspondence of Alexander Pope*, ed. George Sherburn (Oxford: Clarendon Press, 1956), III, 226, for the letter to Aaron Hill probably containing the lines to Thomson.
21. The modern critic might retort that this backs up Pope's contention that the dunces were made for his poem, and not the poem for the dunces.

Johnson concludes, "But though these Excuses may be often plausible, and sometimes just, they are very seldom satisfactory to Mankind; and the Writer, who is not constant to his Subject, quickly sinks into Contempt, his Satire loses its Force, and his Panegyric its Value, and he is only considered at one Time as a Flatterer, and as a Calumniator at another" (*Savage*, p. 46).

For Johnson, fiction must be employed in the service of truth. He is not demanding literal truth. He knows, for instance, that "exaggerated praise" is allowable in epitaphs, elegies, and panegyrics (*Life*, II, 407). "In lapidary inscriptions," he tells Boswell, "a man is not upon oath." At the same time he insists that such praise should bear a discernible relationship to the actual qualities of the man extolled. In the *Life of Waller* he says that it is impossible "to read, without some contempt and indignation," poems by a single author which praise in turn Charles I, Cromwell, and Charles II. For such insincerity Johnson reserves some of his most scathing language. Responding to Waller's famous quip when Charles II accused him of writing a better poem about Cromwell than the restored king—"Poets, Sir, succeed better in fiction than in truth" (I, 271)—Johnson says that the poet who "has flattery ready for all whom the vicissitudes of the world may happen to exalt must be scorned as a prostituted mind that may retain the glitter of wit, but has lost the dignity of virtue" (I, 271). As he says in another context, "there are laws ⌐f higher authority than those of criticism." But Johnson is not blind to the merits of Waller's poems; he prefers the *Panegyric* to the *Congratulation* because Waller has skillfully chosen his topics in the latter poem and because Cromwell's life was more suitable for heroic presentation.[22] And in the critical section of the biography he praises a number of passages from Waller's encomiastic poetry; the *Panegyric* is singled out as justly preferred by the public, "for such a series of verses had rarely appeared before in the English language" (I, 289).

Johnson's comments on panegyrics are usually jaundiced. As *Rambler* No. 104 makes clear, the "art of pleasing" generally caters to a man's worst instincts toward self-aggrandizement and

22. He also thinks that the choice of hero is "its great fault" (*Lives*, I, 289).

frequently involves the poet in self-deception when he is not consciously hypocritical. In his consideration of Prior's praise of King William, Johnson pulls himself up short in order to avoid giving a false impression: "This year ... produced one of his longest and most splendid compositions, the *Carmen Seculare*, in which he exhausts all his powers of celebration. I mean not to accuse him of flattery; he probably thought all that he writ, and retained as much veracity as can be properly exacted from a poet professedly encomiastick" (II, 84). And he goes on to say that William "was really in Prior's mind what he represents him in his verses" (II, 85). Johnson's test of this sort of sincerity, the correspondence between a man's profession and his belief, is most frequently an appeal to external evidence. He asserts that Waller's poem written after the death of Cromwell was sincere because he had nothing to gain from it and that Fenton's elegy on the death of the Marquis of Blandford was the result of "respect or kindness; for neither the duke nor the dutchess desired the praise, or liked the cost of patronage" (I, 270; II, 259).

Although Johnson is clearly interested in the actual attitude of the poet toward the things he writes about, he never makes the crude mistake of identifying sincerity, ipso facto, with good poetry. The distinction—a crucial one—is explained most fully in the *Life of Pope*:

As Gay was the favourite of our author, this epitaph was probably written with an uncommon degree of attention; yet it is not more successfully executed than the rest, for it will not always happen that the success of a poet is proportionate to his labour. The same observation may be extended to all works of the imagination, which are often influenced by causes wholly out of the performer's power, by hints of which he perceives not the origin, by sudden elevations of mind which he cannot produce in himself, and which sometimes arise when he expects them least. [III, 268]

Though Johnson commends diligence and perseverance, though he thinks it is rational to expect the poem dictated by real feelings to be better than those which have no personal links, he recognizes that the irrational plays a large part in poetic composition.

To see the criticism of such poems in the proper perspective we must remember also that Johnson, unlike the Romantics, thought of "ode and elegy and sonnet" as minor forms. "All that short compositions can commonly attain," he tells us in the *Life of Milton*, "is neatness and elegance" (I, 163). Although he does not emphasize genres in his criticism, he is more interested in large works like *Paradise Lost, Hudibras,* and Pope's *Iliad,* for these display human powers at their peak.

Johnson invokes the doctrine of sincerity because he thinks that poetry should present "human sentiments in human language." And when the poet fails to give him what he is looking for, he will try to account for the failure by examining the relationship between the poet and his material. The inquiry rarely extends very far into the poet's biographical circumstances. On the other hand, he also invokes this doctrine when the poet has given some indication that his real feelings are different from those expressed in his poetry. He recognizes that certain poetry is conventional, but he will only permit convention to go so far. Behind the lyric he wants real emotion; behind the poetry of praise and ridicule he wishes to find an ethical presence. His response is governed by a preference of life to art, of reality to imagination, when reality is sufficient to engross our attention.

5

In his article "Patterns of Significant Action in the 'Life of Addison' " James L. Battersby goes farther than any previous scholar in showing the correspondence between art and life in a biography by Johnson.[23] In a sense his work extends the valuable line of inquiry established by W. R. Keast. Keast's opinion that for Johnson literature is "a mode of activity essentially like activity of any other sort"[24] needs, as I have shown earlier, some qualification, but it does have fruitful practical applications in the work of Battersby. Battersby notices that the negative judgment of one paragraph describes qualities similar to those described positively in another. And, relying on the analytical

23. *Genre,* 2 (1968), 28–42.
24. "The Foundations of Johnson's Criticism," in *Critics and Criticism: Ancient and Modern,* ed. Ronald Crane (Chicago: University of Chicago Press, 1952), p. 184.

methods of Kenneth Burke, he looks for the "equational pat-terns" in Johnson's *Life of Addison*. What he finds is that the man described in the first and second sections of the life bears a strong resemblance to the poet described in the critical section. The prudent, timid Addison wrote poems in which Johnson finds "a calmness and equability, deliberate and cautious, some-times with little that delights, but seldom with any thing that offends" (II, 127). Battersby details a number of these corre-spondences between Addison's actions and the description of his writings. And his study is the more valuable in that he has else-where meticulously compared all the eighteenth-century lives of Addison and found such patterns in none of the other biog-raphies.[25]

Since Johnson does think of literature as a human activity, albeit a privileged activity, he is likely to find certain corre-spondences between the everyday actions of a man and his poetry. Both are productions of the same human agency. Signif-icantly, however, Johnson writes two characters, Addison's "per-sonal character" and his "poetic character," and he neither inte-grates them nor makes explicit reference to the similarities. His intentions in the two characters, we should note, are essentially very different. The personal character establishes the nature of the man as he lived. The poetic character assesses, as Keast has shown, the general ability of the poet in relation to what Johnson himself calls "the general and collective ability of man."[26] The quality of Addison's poetry and the nature of his actions are similar, but Johnson is equally at home discussing poets whose actions are strikingly unlike their poetry, and his treatment of the "vicious moralist" leads us to expect that the latter case is apt to be more frequent.

Generalizing from the *Life of Addison* (and failing to notice here Johnson's caveat on the difference between writing and living; II, 125), Battersby comes to some dubious conclusions about Johnson's conception of the relationship between the writer and his works. He argues that Johnson thought the essen-

25. "Samuel Johnson's Life of Addison: Sources, Composition, and Structure" (Ph.D. diss., Cornell, 1965).

26. *Yale*, VII, 60; quoted by Keast, "Foundations," p. 185.

tial man will be found in his works, and he quotes with approval J. W. Krutch's assertion that Johnson looks in poetry for the revelation of character. But if any lesson is to be drawn from a reading of Johnson's full canon, it is that a man's writings are treacherous documents for the biographer and must be interpreted with the utmost care. Battersby has uncovered significant patterns in the *Life of Addison* which have implications for Johnson's method as literary biographer, but he seems to misjudge the meaning of their presence.

To see some of the possible relationships between character and writings, we may turn once again to the *Life of Milton*. While we should recognize that Milton's fierce integrity, like Addison's timorous caution, may help to give the life a shape that the biography will imitate, it is worth noting here, too, that the structure found in Johnson's *Milton* is not in the earlier biographies. In the best analysis to date of the *Life of Milton* Lawrence Lipking says that Johnson's biography "successively describes, reprobates, and comes to terms with a particular kind of genius." "The *Life of Milton*," he continues, "implies a truth most lovers of poetry would prefer not to admit: that the very independence, impatience, and ardor for fame which make a man impossible to live with or like may help to make a poet great." Lipking details a number of correspondences between the man and the poet and notes that "Johnson does not equate Milton's political independence with his poetic orginality—the one is villainy, the other heroism—but his descriptions of the two are internally consistent and from the *Life of Milton* as a whole we receive an impression of Milton that is indivisible."[27] This seems to me to be an accurate reading of the implied relation of life to art in the *Life of Milton*, but in the critical section I think that Johnson goes even further and implies that the very qualities which make Milton a great poet limit the effectiveness of his poetry.

If such a proposition sounds too paradoxical, it should be remembered that modern critics, such as George Watson, have frequently expressed a dissatisfaction with the relationship of the various parts of the *Life of Milton*. The praise and blame are,

27. *The Ordering of the Arts in Eighteenth-Century England* (Princeton: Princeton University Press, 1970), pp. 439, 438.

on their reading, irreconcilable. Finding himself unable to unify these seeming contradictions, D. M. Hill ingeniously proposes that Johnson's critique of *Paradise Lost* is a kind of "scholastic disputation, arguing at one point wholeheartedly in favour of it, and at another point, wholeheartedly against it."[28] To such lengths are Johnson's critics driven.

Between our criticism and Johnson's lies a great shift in methods of judging poetry and in demands made upon the poet. Before quoting from the second stanza of Donne's "A Valediction of Weeping," Johnson says, "If the lines are not easily understood, they may be read again" (I, 26). The assumption behind his heavy irony is that if one has to read the poem a second time before merely understanding what it is saying, it is presumably a bad poem. (And he may be daring us to reread, complacently feeling that the poem will remain opaque till Doomsday.) Since Coleridge we have been more and more willing to accept this challenge, and the academic study of literature has been strongly influenced by the assumption that if a poem is not easily understood, it *should* be read again (and again).

This opposition points to the shift in the relationship between the poet and his audience which took place in the eighteenth century and is one of the literary turning points that marks the transition from the Renaissance to the modern world. Johnson assumes that a poem should be perspicuous on a first reading because the poet must accommodate himself to his audience. Coleridge (and modern readers are apt to be Coleridgeans in this respect) believes that we must accommodate ourselves to the poet. The reasons for this opposition can be traced to the growth of some now commonplace ideas about the nature of genius and the breakdown of the classical belief, which forms the backbone of Johnson's biographies, that men are basically alike.

We can get a clear view of the implications of this shift by looking at the famous passage in the *Life of Cowley* which provided the foundation for the modern reassessment of the metaphysical poets:

But Wit, *abstracted from its effects upon the hearer*, may be more rigorously and philosophically considered as a kind of *discordia concors*; a combina-

28. "Johnson as Moderator," *N & Q*, 201 (1956), 518.

tion of dissimilar images, or discovery of occult resemblances in things apparently unlike. Of wit, thus defined, they have more than enough. The most heterogeneous ideas are yoked by violence together; nature and art are ransacked for illustrations, comparisons, and allusions; their learning instructs, and their subtilty surprises; but *the reader* commonly thinks his improvement dearly bought, and, though he sometimes admires, is seldom pleased. [I, 20]

My italics are meant to demonstrate that this analysis is made possible only by Johnson's decision to waive his usual requirements and that the unfavorable comment with which he concludes the passage is attributable to the reappearance of the audience as a datum in the evaluation of a poem. This "modern" passage is typical of Johnson only in that he is frequently willing to look at another possibility before passing judgment.

At this point we are ready to encounter those seeming paradoxes that Hill and Watson find in the critical account of Milton. Careful attention to the imagery Johnson uses in describing Milton will show the consistency of his treatment of his subject, and the context of his remarks will explain the variations of his judgments. The imagery used to describe Milton in the critical section is consistent with that earlier in the life. Milton is still higher and greater than other men, but "we desert our master, and seek for companions." Johnson had said in praise that Milton "never fails to fill the imagination," but in Johnson's thought, as in that of Hutcheson and other eighteenth-century writers, one can overfill the imagination, and this, Johnson implies, is what Milton and his superior capacities do to those frail beings, his readers. Milton's "lofty and steady confidence in himself" is "perhaps not without some contempt of others" (I, 94). Johnson presents him again and again in lonely, though not bad, eminence. What Johnson suggests is that Milton, who makes little allowance for human beings in his life, fails to put into his poetry human emotions sufficient to engage his readers or to take human capacities into account. *Paradise Lost* is sublime, "but the passions are moved only on one occasion" (I, 180). "The want of human interest," he says, "is always felt" (I, 183).

In a sense, then, the *Life of Milton* does contain two critiques, though they are not, as D. M. Hill would have it, scholastic disputations pro and con. The first considers Milton's admirable human achievement abstracted from its effect upon the hearer, the second relates the reader to the poem. It is to Johnson's credit that despite the constant warning he gives us, as in his treatment of blank verse, that Milton "like other heroes . . . is to be admired rather than imitated," the balance, even after all qualifications, tips heavily in Milton's favor. Johnson says that Milton "had formed his style by a perverse and pedantic princi- ple" and goes on to claim that this style leads to the condemna- tion of his prose: "But such is the power of his poetry that his call is obeyed without resistance, *the reader* feels himself in captivity to *a higher and nobler mind*, and criticism sinks in *admiration*" (I, 190; italics mine). Johnson prefaces his comments on *Lycidas* (and we ought to remember in reading them that he thought "all that short compositions can commonly attain is neatness and elegance") by saying, "Milton never learned the art of doing little things with grace; he overlooked the milder excellence of suavity and softness; he was a *lion* that had no skill in *dandling the kid*." The consideration of the poem ends as it began with the sugges- tion that Milton's greatness ("the power of reputation justly ac- quired") has caused his readers to overestimate some of his minor poems. When Johnson reaches *Paradise Lost*, his en- comiastic criticism is at its peak:

Before the greatness displayed in Milton's poem all other greatness shrinks away.
    To display the motives and actions of beings thus superior [to humans], so far as human reason can examine them or human imagina- tion represent them, is the task which this mighty poet has undertaken and performed. [I, 172]
    . . . he does not confine himself within the limits of rigorous compari- son: his great excellence is amplitude, and he expands the adventitious image beyond the dimensions which the occasion required. [I, 179]
    The poet whatever be done is always great. [I, 180]

How, one may ask, can such praise be combined with harsh criticism? The answer is that, as in the passage on metaphysical wit, the reader is brought back into the discussion:

The plan of *Paradise Lost* has this inconvenience, that it comprises neither human actions nor human manners. The man and woman who act and suffer are in a state which *no other man or woman can ever know*. *The reader* finds no transaction in which *he* can by any effort of imagination place himself; he has therefore little natural curiosity or sympathy. [I, 181; italics mine]

In Johnson's most forceful comment in this vein, the one which has most exercised Milton's admirers, he remains true both to the terms of his own criticism and his critique of Milton:

Paradise Lost is one of the books which the reader admires and lays down and forgets to take up again. None ever wished it longer than it is. Its perusal is a duty rather than a pleasure. We read Milton for instruction, retire harassed and overburdened, and look elsewhere for recreation; we desert our master and seek for companions. [I, 183–84][29]

To "admire" as Johnson uses the word here means to be impressed with a human accomplishment, and one important purpose of Johnsonian biography is to present exemplary human achievement.[30] On the other hand, Milton's towering excellence in no way accommodates itself to human capabilities. (We might note in passing that one of Milton's staunchest eighteenth-century defenders, Jonathan Richardson, says in his biography of the poet, "a reader of Milton must be always upon Duty.")[31]

Johnson continually depicts Milton as higher and greater than other men— unquestionably, as I argued earlier, the poet as hero. He believed that the first requisite of literary achievement was self-confidence, and he speaks with unqualified approval of Milton's "lofty and steady confidence in himself" (I, 94).

29. Although most admirers of Milton are apt to bridle at the very mention of Johnson's *Milton*, at least one distinguished Miltonist has quoted the last sentence of this passage and confessed, "I can recognize some of my own experience in that formulation. As much as I admire the poem, I cannot live with it constantly; as a non-heroic reader, I find it eventually wearing. With its complexity, its brilliance, its intensity, we cannot lean back in our chairs in its presence; and for most of us there is a limit to how long we can sit forward" (Joseph H. Summers, "The Embarrassments of *Paradise Lost*" in *Approaches* to "*Paradise Lost*": *The York Tercentenary Lectures*, ed. C. A. Patrides [London: Edward Arnold, 1968], pp. 74–75).

30. The *Dictionary* gives as a synonym "wonder," but the quotation from Tillotson under "admiration" is closest to Johnson's meaning. Paul K. Alkon's extensive consideration of the term in "Johnson's Concept of Admiration," *PQ*, 48 (1969), 59–81, covers some of the same ground as I do, though his emphasis on Johnson's subversion of earlier epic theory in his use of the term is different from mine.

31. "The Life of Milton and a Discourse on *Paradise Lost*" (1734), in *The Early Lives of Milton,* ed. Helen Darbishire (London: Constable, 1932), p. 315.

Johnson's comment on *The Reason of Church Government* is fully sympathetic: "In this book he discovers, not with ostentatious exultation, but with calm confidence, his high opinion of his own powers; and promises to undertake something, he yet knows not what, that may be of use and honour to his country. . . . From a promise like this, at once fervid, pious, and rational, might be expected the *Paradise Lost*" (I, 102–3). Johnson's view of Milton's greatness leads him, however, to see another promise as prelude to a pratfall: "Let not our veneration for Milton forbid us to look with some degree of merriment on great promises and small performances—on the man who hastens home because his countrymen are contending for liberty, and, when he reaches the scene of action, vapours away his patriotism in a private boarding school." Johnson sees the disparity as farcical, and John H. Middendorf has shown that the proofsheets of the biography contained at this point an allusion to the *Ars Poetica*: "Let not our veneration for Milton forbid us to look with some degree of merriment upon a human head with a fish's tail."[32] Johnson is attacking neither Milton's greatness nor schoolteaching, for as he says later in attacking Milton's biographers for attempting to exculpate Milton from the charge of schoolteaching, "Milton was not a man who could become mean by mean employment" (I, 109).

From this perspective, then, we can have little doubt that Johnson perceives a relationship between the character of Milton and his writings. Unlike many of his contemporaries, however, Johnson is unwilling to see any sort of deterministic relationship between the two. For Johnson the relation between the life and art of any individual writer is problematic.

6

The "silent reference of human works to human abilities," let it be noted, has little to do with character. And the "enquiry how far man may extend his designs, or how high he may rate his native force, is of far greater dignity than in what rank we shall

32. "Johnson as Editor: Some Proofs of the 'Prefaces,'" in *Eighteenth-Century Studies in Honor of Donald F. Hyde*, p. 103.

place any particular performance" because the individual who surpasses what has been done before enlarges the powers of mankind (*Yale*, VII, 81). His action is exemplary because it proves that man can do things beyond what he thought he could do. Hence originality is of great importance to Johnson in his consideration of the value of literary works.

Originality, as he tells us in the *Life of Congreve*, is "merit of the highest order" (II, 228). It is a human as opposed to a merely poetic excellence. This is the basis for his distinction when he claimed that "Homer was ... the greatest poet, though Virgil may have produced the finest poem" (III, 193). Homer made possible Virgil's achievement by originating the epic form. Frequently in the *Lives* Johnson lets us know who was the first to use a particular innovation. Though he thought little of Gay's poetry he praises him as the inventor of the ballad opera (II, 282). And Denham's "Cooper's Hill" is considered as the first specimen of "local poetry" (I, 77). In order to dismiss Gray's ode "The Bard," he shows that its highly praised beginning is structurally similar to that of *Johnny Armstrong*, and "technical beauties can give praise only to the inventor" (III, 439). He also is interested in those who, like Thomson or Milton, have an original way of seeing and saying things, but as T. S. Eliot shrewdly observes, his conception of originality "does not require the rejection of convention. . . . The originality which Johnson approves is an originality limited by the other qualities which he demands."[33] Hence Johnson can say that Milton's early poems in English "have this evidence of genius, that they have a cast original and unborrowed. But their peculiarity is not excellence: if they differ from verses of others, they differ for the worse" (I, 162).

Johnson's interest in originality, then, is to be distinguished from that of the Romantics. Whereas they valued originality primarily as the expression of a unique personality, he valued it as an exemplary or useful human achievement. His concern is part of a long classical tradition. One of the favorite topics of the Greeks was "who discovered it?" And their etiological interests

33. "Johnson as Critic and Poet," *On Poetry and Poets* (New York: Farrar, Straus, and Cudahy, 1957), p. 209. Eliot does not give any examples.

led them to honor the "first finder."[34] The originality Johnson
seems to credit most is that which elevates the abilities of an
entire group of society. Dryden's establishment of the new ver-
sification, Pope's tuning of the English tongue, Watts's sweeten-
ing of the dissenters' prose: all were original achievements which
gained in value by being transmitted to those who followed (I,
421; III, 238, 306). They are both exemplary and useful. In the
Life of Addison he condemns those who denigrate Addison's critical achievement while profiting from it: "It is not uncommon for
those who have grown wise by the labour of others to add a little
of their own, and overlook their masters. Addison is now despised by some who perhaps would never have seen his defects,
but by the lights which he afforded them" (II, 146; see also I,
294–95).

These remarks remind us that for Johnson any estimate of
human achievement must be put into a historical context. The
popular notion of Johnson's lack of interest in history has been
sufficiently exposed by recent scholars.[35] Anyone whose criticism is committed to honoring originality must know what was
accomplished at any given point and what was yet to be done.
The idea of human excellence implies a judgment based upon a
knowledge of what had gone before. Therefore he can say of
Denham's translation of Guarini, "The excellence of these lines
is greater, as the truth which they contain was not at that time
generally known" (I, 77). On this basis also he will somewhat
mitigate his criticism of certain aspects of a poet's work. The
harshness of Milton's verse is pardoned because his age had not
received the blessings of harmony that Dryden and Pope were to
bestow (I, 318).

Johnson's usual tendency in considering the part played by
history in human excellence is to discriminate the individual

34. Ernst Robert Curtius, *European Literature and the Latin Middle Ages*, trans.
Willard R. Trask (1953; rpt. New York: Harper and Row, 1963), p. 548; B. A.
Van Groningen, *In the Grip of the Past: Essay on an Aspect of Greek Thought* (Leyden:
E. J. Brill, 1953), p. 33.

35. Particularly by William R. Keast, "Johnson and Intellectual History," in
New Light on Dr. Johnson, ed. Frederick W. Hilles (New Haven: Yale University
Press, 1959), pp. 247–56. G. B. Hill had already begun a reassessment before the
end of the nineteenth century.

achievement from the general achievement of his age. "To judge rightly of an author," says Johnson in the *Life of Dryden*, "we must transport ourselves to his time, and examine what were the wants of his contemporaries, and what were his means of supplying them" (I, 411). His tribute to Dryden's elevation of the state of English prose—"He found it brick; he left it marble"—is, therefore, a paradigm for all his high praise. The line's adaptation of Suetonius signals the continuity of the classical measure of human achievement.

CHAPTER 8

"A Plainer Tale": Style

In his excellent study of Johnson's prose style W. K. Wimsatt laid to rest the Macaulayan cliché that Johnson's style grew easier in old age because "he had written little and had talked much," that influenced by his own conversation he stopped writing "Johnsonese." That the *Lives of the Poets* is constructed of shorter, less complex sentences and simpler diction has never been in dispute, but the cause of this "lightness" has. Wimsatt calls attention to the presence of stylistic similarities between some earlier writings and the *Lives*. His conclusion is that "all his life Johnson exhibited different degrees of his own peculiar style both in his talk and in his writing, and that especially in his writing this is to be referred to differences of subject matter." What he means becomes clearer when he discusses specific literary criticism in the *Rambler*: "The reference to this poem and that, the quotation of passages and reference to them, the use of technical terms . . . all conspired to prevent Johnson's logic from taking hold of the theme and carrying it to the realm of elaborate generality. This sort of subject matter in a great measure accounts for the light-ness of the *Lives*."[1]

The description of Johnson's style in the biographies does not seem to be at issue. Warner G. Taylor tells us with precision what all of Johnson's critics had known in a general way: the sentence length decreases strikingly when we move from the *Rambler* to

1. *The Prose Style of Samuel Johnson*, 2d ed. (New Haven: Yale University Press, 1963), pp. 74, 78, 83.

the *Lives* (43.1 words per sentence vs. 30.1).[2] It has also been generally observed that the diction of the *Lives* is simpler than that of the *Rambler* essays, though here Wimsatt notes without bothering to press his point home that Taylor has shown the average syllable length of words in the *Rambler* and the *Lives* to be very close. Wimsatt decides that "this, however, need not persuade us to any further conclusion. There are long words and long words. It is conceivable that Johnson's words should have continued of the same average length yet have become less philosophic. And this, I believe, is what did happen. Certainly, even when they continue philosophic, they are less often exaggerated or freakish."[3] One can only admire Wimsatt's shrewdly observant eye and his refusal to take refuge in statistics that are attractive for his case. I think, however, that the question of style deserves a closer look.

Wimsatt's choice of earlier works to clinch his case against Macaulay consists mainly, though not entirely, of biographies. He does not consider, evidently because of his belief in the consistency of Johnson's style, that the difference in genre might have led Johnson to the *choice* of a different style. Yet I think that an examination of the theories of historical and biographical style which were prevalent in Johnson's day, of Johnson's criticism of style in biography, and finally of the expressive features of Johnson's biographies themselves leads to the conclusion that Johnson's biographies are different in style from his essays through conscious artistry and that a full appreciation of his achievement as a biographer depends on our apprehending those aspects of his work which cannot be accounted for in terms of the *Rambler*'s style, or be judged as a failure to achieve that style.

Johnson himself makes the distinction between the styles characteristic of essays and of historical or biographical writing in the *Life of Swift* and finds that their divergent purposes dictate their differences: "This easy and safe conveyance of meaning it was Swift's desire to attain, and for having attained he deserves praise, though perhaps not the highest praise. For purposes

2. "The Prose Style of Johnson," *University of Wisconsin Studies in Language and Literature*, 2 (1918), p. 35. Reported by Wimsatt, p. 88.
3. *Prose Style*, pp. 87–88.

merely didactick, when something is to be told that was not known before, it is the best mode, but against that inattention by which known truths are suffered to lie neglected it makes no provision; it instructs, but does not persuade" (III, 52). Wimsatt, quoting this passage, concludes that "at best Swift's style is for Johnson but an adequate vehicle for an inferior burden."[4] The burden is "inferior," however, in the sense that a lesser genre is inferior. In the writing of biography, this style is not merely "adequate" but, to use Johnson's words, "the best mode." Johnson's distinction seems to rest on an adaptation of the well-known division of style into the *genus humile* (low style) used to teach, the *genus medium* (middle style) used to delight, and the *genus grande* (high style) used to move. Though we never find these explicit divisions (or exclusive functions) in his work, he clearly believes in the necessity of using different styles for different genres and for different kinds of writing within a genre.

In the first place it should be made clear that Johnson is not systematic. We can hardly expect him to go through books on the writing of history like a Renaissance rhetorician, carefully matching his style to their desiderata. Second, even if he wanted to, he would be faced by the division of theorists on stylistic matters. The familiar opposition of Asiatic and Attic or Ciceronian and Senecan (here better considered as Tacitean or Sallustian) that informed seventeenth-century arguments over style is to be found in treatises on history as well; but the division as to what constitutes proper historical style is an older dispute and appears earlier in fifteenth-century theorists of history, mainly Italian.[5]

Although Johnson was not systematic himself, he was an avid reader and recommender of encyclopedic volumes. He read Baillet and Bayle, Morhof and Moreri. His passing comment on history in *Rambler* No. 152 shows his awareness of historical

4. *Prose Style*, p. 98. For the same distinction without invidious overtones, see *Rambler* No. 3, *Yale*, III, 14–15.

5. The *Artis Historicae Penus*, edited by Johann Wolfius (Basel, 1579), collects a number of such writings. Beatrice Reynolds surveys this literature in "Shifting Currents in Historical Criticism," *Renaissance Essays from the Journal of the History of Ideas*, ed. Paul Oskar Kristeller and Philip P. Wiener (New York: Harper and Row, 1968), pp. 115–36.

theory and its concern with style. "Among the criticks in history," he says, "it is not contested whether truth ought to be preserved, but by what mode of diction it is best adorned" (*Yale*, V, 45). "Diction" is defined in his *Dictionary* as "style; language; expression." For specific theoreticians one could turn to the *Preceptor*, where Johnson recommends that the fledgling student of history should read, among other books, Hearne's *Ductor Historicus*, Degory Wheare's *Lectures* (i.e., his *Methodus*, translated as *The Method and Order of Reading Histories*), and Rawlinson's (i.e., Richard Rawlinson's translation of Nicholas Lenglet du Fresnoy) *Directions for the Study of History*. The comments on history that appear in these books have been described as a recapitulation of Renaissance arguments.[6] A less charitable view would be that du Fresnoy borrows rather freely from Jean Bodin, and so forth. Johnson was highly aware, then, that practical stylistic choices had theoretical implications. We can see this very clearly in some of his definitions in the *Dictionary*. The first definition of "history" is "a narration of events and facts delivered with dignity." The definition of "memoirs" is "an account of transactions familiarly written" ("familiar" here means "easy, unconstrained"). Unfortunately, there is no stylistic comment to be found under "biography" or "life."

Johnson's comments on history proper in *Rambler* No. 122 help to define the upper limits of style in biography. Noticing that other nations have produced great historians and England has few—he writes before the works of Hume, Robertson, and Gibbon appeared—he says that "some have doubted, whether an Englishman can stop at that mediocrity of stile, or confine his mind to that even tenour of imagination, which narrative requires" (*Yale*, IV, 289). This is, of course, a backhanded compliment to the English at the expense of history, but Johnson does think that history requires a middle style, whatever the negative overtones of "mediocrity" may be. As a practicing critic of history he is willing to go beyond his critical boundaries and praise Clarendon's "rude inartificial majesty" (just as he praises *Paradise Lost* despite his general attitude toward blank verse). Yet

6. Leo Braudy, *Narrative Form in History and Fiction: Hume, Fielding, and Gibbon* (Princeton: Princeton University Press, 1970), p. 294.

he begins by saying that Clarendon's "diction is . . . neither exact in itself, nor suited to the purpose of history."

Though some historians were in favor of a higher style, many, particularly those who were writing compilations or histories in which they played a personal role, undertook a "plain" style. In the *Roman History* Goldsmith claims that his "only aim was to supply a concise, plain and unaffected narrative."[7] In conversation Johnson claimed that "Goldsmith's *History* is better than the *verbiage* of Robertson." Johnson's first biographies, written for the *Gentleman's Magazine*, were generally quarried from fuller accounts with that flair for both condensation and commentary that is characteristic of Johnson's *reportage* and his biographic art.

It is easy to go wrong on the question of plain style, for different writers mean different things by the term. In his *History of His Own Times* (published in 1724), a book Johnson praised for its personal account of the age, though he thought the style "mere chit-chat," Gilbert Burnet says, "I have on design avoided all laboured periods or artificial strains, and have writ in as clear and plain a style as was possible, chusing rather a copious enlargement, than a dark conciseness."[8] Plainness here is a middle way between the formality of the periodic structure and the "dark conciseness" (possibly Tacitean) which would lead to obscurity. Johnson's quotations from Jonson and Watts under "conciseness" in the *Dictionary*, like his comments on Swift and Tacitus, leave us in little doubt that he did not admire this stylistic quality in its extreme form, despite his admiration for Sallust. He approves, however, Richard Knolles's "copiousness" without "superfluity" (*Rambler* No. 122, *Yale*, IV, 290).

His comments on narration in poetry may also help to define his stance as a biographer. He criticizes Shakespeare for using an improper style in the narrative parts of his plays: "In narration he affects a disproportionate pomp of diction and a wearisome train of circumlocution, and tells the incident imperfectly in many words, which might have been more plainly delivered in

7. Oliver Goldsmith, *Collected Works*, ed. Arthur Friedman (Oxford: Clarendon Press, 1966), V, 333. And see his preface to *The History of England* (1771), V, 338.
8. Preface, p. 4.

few" (*Yale*, VII, 73). The basis of this argument is that "narration in dramatic poetry is naturally tedious," and he goes on to recommend rapidity and brevity. Though here he is talking about poetry rather than prose, he thinks that "dignity and splendor" are out of place in certain kinds of narration. The criticism of Clarendon touches on some of the same narrative problems. Johnson finds that Clarendon's "narration is not perhaps sufficiently rapid, being stopped too frequently by peculiarities, which, tho' they might strike the author who was present at the transactions, will not equally detain the attention of posterity" (*Yale*, IV, 289–90). Though Johnson sees enough virtues in Clarendon's history to balance this "ignorance or carelessness of the art of writing," an art of writing clearly exists.

2

My comments so far have been mainly on history, a narrative form related to but different from biography. Indeed, most eighteenth-century writers would undoubtedly have agreed with Hugh Blair's description of biography in his highly influential *Lectures on Rhetoric and Belles Lettres* (1783) as "less formal and stately than History." One hundred years earlier Dryden had discussed the relation of these styles more satisfactorily, arguing that the style of biography "is various, according to the occasion. There are proper places in it, for the plainness and nakedness, of narration, which is ascribed to annals; there is also room reserved for the loftiness and gravity of general history, when the actions related shall require that manner of expression. But there is withal a descent into minute circumstances, and trivial passages of life, which are natural to this way of writing, and which the dignity of the other two will not admit."[9]

Since for the most part we are not arguing here about a description of Johnson's style in these biographies, but about the reasons behind that style, I think that Johnson's scattered comments on biography may be of great assistance in showing his intentions. Although my quotations will be selective, an examination of all of Johnson's criticism of biography reveals a ten-

9. Blair, 2d ed. (London, 1785), III, 54; Dryden, "The Life of Plutarch," *Plutarch's Lives* (London, 1683), I, 124–25.

dency to focus on style. This emphasis is a direct result of his belief that style makes one historical work better than another.

Though Johnson was frequently a harsh critic of biographies, particularly literary biographies, his praise of style in biography was generally couched in a few recurrent terms. Foremost of these is "elegance" and its variations. In the *Life of Rochester* he calls Burnet's *Some Passages of the Life and Death of John Earl of Rochester* a book "which the critick ought to read for its elegance, the philosopher for its arguments, and the saint for its piety" (I, 222); he speaks of Fenton's "short and elegant account of Milton" (II, 261); in a letter to George Horne he says that Sir John Hawkins' "Life of Walton" was "very diligently collected, and very elegantly composed" (*Letters*, I, 405); and although he had objections to Mallet's *Bacon*, he thought it "written with elegance" (III, 404). This term, important throughout all of Johnson's criticism, has been studied by Patricia Ingham.[10] Her conclusion that "elegance," as used by Johnson, refers to qualities of concision and energy as displayed primarily in small pieces and minor genres tallies with my own findings. Johnson's *Dictionary* defines "elegance" as "beauty without grandeur," and it defines "elegant" as "pleasing with minuter beauties."

Several other terms of praise recur in his criticism of biography, most often when he is withholding them from the work under consideration. In his "Preface to *Shakespeare*" he attacks Rowe's "Life of Shakespeare" for its lack of "elegance or spirit" (*Yale*, VII, 94). And after deriding John Hackett's *Scrinia Reserata*, he adds that Ambrose Philips' abridgment of that biography of Archbishop Williams "is free enough from affectation, but has little spirit or vigour" (III, 314). "Spirit," "vigour": as Wimsatt warns us, "generalities and epithetical condemnations" or praise may be difficult to pin down or may mean very different things from what the modern reader thinks they mean.[11] These words, especially the latter, were also applied to Johnson's more ornate style. But their affinities in his criticism of biography sometimes leave little doubt as to what he means. Boswell quotes his vehement attack on Carte's *Life of the Duke of Ormonde*

10. "Dr. Johnson's 'Elegance,'" *RES*, n.s. 19 (1968), 271–78.
11. *Prose Style*, p. 90.

as "'ill-written. The matter is diffused in too many words; there is no animation, no compression, no vigour. Two good volumes in duodecimo might be made out of the two in folio.' "[12]

In his own biographies Johnson characteristically abridges or alters quotations—"epitomizes" them, to use his own term from one of his earliest works, the translation of Lobo's *Voyage to Abyssinia*—often in ways unacceptable by the standards of modern scholarship, on stylistic grounds. He is interested, for many reasons, in economy of expression. This concern explains not only his shorter sentences, but the way in which he conflates various accounts and culls significant characters from the larger *dramatis personae* of the earlier biographers of his subject. Comparison of certain comments by Johnson with his sources shows how much more compressed and vigorous, to use his terms, his own writing is. In the *Life of Savage* he quotes Steele as saying of Savage that *"the inhumanity of his Mother had given him a Right to find every good Man his Father"* (*Savage*, p. 13). The original passage in all its turgidity reads *"it ought to be the Care of All, in whose Power it lay, to lift Mr. SAVAGE above a sense of his MOTHER's Cruelty; because a Misery, so undeserved, had intitled him to a Right of finding Every Good Man his FATHER."*[13] In the *Lives of the Poets* this characteristic tendency to compress may have been reinforced by the booksellers' charge to write, according to one of the principals, Edward Dilly, "a concise account of the life of each author." Even though Johnson was "led beyond [his] intention," the result can properly be described as concise. Indeed, Johnson's partiality for conciseness under certain circumstances is apparent from the beginning of his career. His second biography, the "Life of Boerhaave," explicitly contrasts his method with that of his contemporaries: "a close adherence to certainty has contracted our narrative, and hindered it from swelling to that bulk, at which modern histories generally arrive" (*Works*, VI, 270). It should be noted that Johnson achieves his becoming brevity by other than Stracheyan means.

Some of the terms he uses in denigration of various biog-

12. *Hebrides* (printed version), in *Life*, V, 296.
13. *Savage*, pp. 13–14 n.; quoted by Tracy from *Plain Dealer* No. 73 (1724). Johnson, of course, frequently quoted from his capacious memory.

raphies underline the opposing qualities he desired. He complains that Hackett's *Scrinia Reserata* "is written with such depravity of genius, such a mixture of the fop and the pedant, as has not often appeared" (III, 314). A random sample should be enough to show what Johnson has in mind when he abuses Hackett: "A Gentler Hand could not touch a Sore: yet I think of his Judgment in this Point, as Scaliger did of the fine Poet *Fracastorius, Ab sua ipse magnitudine descendisse credi potest aliquando;* he flew lower at the Game, than the pitch of his wonted Wisdom. For the Question did yet hang upon this Pin, whether there were a Sore to be cured?"[14] Metaphors strung together and laced with an ostentatious quotation: this was probably not one of the books that Johnson read through.

He also lodged the charge of "foppery" against Walter Harte's *History of Gustavus Adolphus* (*Life*, II, 120). Though Ambrose Philips was not guilty of "affectation," Johnson thought that Mallet's biography of Bacon was "written with elegance, perhaps with some affectation" (III, 404). The only definition in his *Dictionary* which would seem to apply is "written with over-much study." Foppish, pedantic, affected: these terms stand in opposition to the compression, spirit, vigor, and elegance he admired. If "spirit" and "vigour" are qualities of mind that can be found in all the various styles Johnson employs, "elegance" and "compression" are particularly suitable for genres like biography.

Johnson seeks some form of middle style. If it seems to be "mediocrity" in both senses in his historiographical essay, *Rambler* No. 122, he praises *An Account of the Dutchess of Marlborough* in oxymorons which point to a style between high and low. From this memoir, he says, "the polite writer may learn an *unaffected dignity of style*, and an *artful simplicity* of narration" (*Works*, VI, 6; italics mine).

Yet to see more fully what Johnson is after we will have to return to the quality he sometimes admired even in the more stately and formal historical writings: plainness. Most eighteenth- or late seventeenth-century biographers are likely, if

14. *Scrinia Reserata: A Memorial Offer'd to the Great Deservings of John Williams, D.D.* (London, 1657), p. 66. G. B. Hill prints another example with a passage from Ambrose Philips' abridgment for comparison in *Lives*, III, 314, n. 3.

they make any stylistic comments at all, to praise a plain style. In the preface to Anthony à Wood's *Athenae Oxonienses* John Harrington writes, "It was thought more useful to publish, as you will now find it, in an honest plain *English* dress, without flourishes or affectation of Stile, as best becomes a History of Truth and matter of Fact."[15] One did not need to be English to insist on plainness in biography. The Chevalier Ramsay justifies his style in the preface to the *Life of Fenelon*: "That the Narration may be short, plain, and not too languishing, I touch but lightly such Things as are of little importance, and avoid tedious Reflections, as well as loose general Panegyricks and superfluous Ornaments."[16] And Walton, whose *Lives* Johnson wanted to edit and whose life he intended to write, claims in his introduction to the *Life of Donne* that when he heard Donne's sermons were to be published without a biography *"Indignation or griefe"* led him to resolve *"the World should see the best plain Picture of the* Author's Life *that my artless Pensil guided by the hand of Truth, could present to it."*[17] Walton is hardly artless, but his prose is for the most part plain. We must be wary in such matters, however, for the claim that one is writing a "plain" account may be as much an ethical as a stylistic choice. It designates the writer as a man who is about to deal honestly with his readers, though not all plain dealers write plain prose. We should also notice that many different kinds of writers call their narratives "plain," and we are not likely to find a biographer who claims to present a "diffuse, affected and altogether foppish narrative."

Robert Adolph notes that "for Jonson, Bacon, Savile, and others, the important division is between the plain style and oratory, not between Seneca or Tacitus and Cicero."[18] The distinction between the orator and the historian or biographer is an important one for Johnson. Sometimes he contrasts the panegyrist

15. Quoted by Robert Adolph, *The Rise of Modern Prose Style* (Cambridge, Mass.: M.I.T. Press, 1968), p. 262.

16. Andrew Michael Ramsay, *The Life of François de Salignac de la Motte Fenelon, Archbishop and Duke of Cambray* (London, 1723), p. A3 ʳ⁻ᵛ.

17. *Lives* (London, 1670), p. 10. William Farrell argues interestingly for the existence of biographical style in "Fielding's Familiar Style," *ELH*, 34 (1967), 65–77.

18. *Modern Prose Style*, p. 161.

(especially the funeral orator) as flatterer with the impartial historian, but often the opposition is more specifically stylistic. In trying to account for the unsatisfactoriness of a contemporary life of Ascham, he suggests that perhaps Edward Grant, "preferring the character of an orator to that of an historian, selected only such particulars as he could best express or most happily embellish" ("Ascham," *Works*, VI, 504). After quoting the whole of William Oldisworth's short biography of Edmund Smith, a piece written, according to another eighteenth-century author, John Burton, to show "what fine things one man of parts can say of another," Johnson says: "Such is the declamation of Oldisworth. . . . I cannot much commend the performance. The praise is often indistinct, and the sentences are loaded with words of more pomp than use. There is little however that can be contradicted, even when a plainer tale comes to be told" (II, 11). Here we have plainness opposed to oratory, particulars to "indistinct" generality, and high-flown diction to utility. This passage may remind us of the first paragraph of the *Lives*, where Johnson indicates that his own standards are high and accuses Sprat of producing "a funeral oration rather than a history."

What specifically does Johnson object to in Oldisworth's account? It is not a grotesque work, but it does overflow with laudatory adjectives and adverbs: Oldisworth leaves no noun unmodified. According to him, Smith was the son of an "eminent" merchant who died and left him in the charge of a "faithful and generous" guardian after whose death he was "handsomely maintained" by an aunt. At school he "signally distinguished himself by his conspicuous performances." His college writings "shew a masterly hand; and though maimed and injured by frequent transcribing, make their way into our most celebrated miscellanies, where they shine with uncommon lustre." In contrast, Johnson's version begins: "Edmund Smith is one of those lucky writers who have without much labour attained high reputation, and who are mentioned with reverence rather for the possession than the exertion of uncommon abilities" (II, 1). The conclusion of the biographical portion of the life is, as I have shown earlier, brought about by the combination of an anecdote concerning Smith's death and the bare facts. Smith "swallowed his own medicine, which, in July 1710, brought him to the grave. He was buried at Hartham" (II, 18).The deadly understatement effected by the colorless relative pronoun is the triumph of one Johnsonian voice in these biographies. Such passages show the inadequacy of Wimsatt's otherwise attractive opinion that dates and facts "conspired to prevent Johnson's logic from taking hold of the theme and carrying it to the realm of elaborate generality."[19]

Perhaps a less monistic conception of Johnson's style would bring into prominence characteristics that Johnson's contemporaries found worthy of comment. In Robert Potter's "A Dream" (1789), an imaginary dialogue between Johnson and Joseph Warton, Warton praises the ancients for "strength without point" and accuses Johnson of being "an affected humourist who aim[s] at dryness, slyness, and archness" and whose prose is "patched with witticisms." Potter's Johnson retorts that among others "Virgil's staple works are not strangers to point. Some salt, some zest is required." In his own voice Potter accuses Johnson of "a most pungent sting of contempt" in a passage from the *Life of Yalden*.[20] "Point" and "sting" are both being used in their technical senses. Though it would be difficult to prove that the *Lives* are more aphoristic than the *Rambler* (even if the aphorisms in the biographies are apt to be shorter), the tendency toward point, toward epigrammatic brevity, is characteristic of Johnson's biographies, not his essays.

Before looking at specific passages, I wish to consider two of Wimsatt's assumptions, both useful in the context of his argument, that keep him from recognizing the nature of Johnson's biographical style. First, he is interested in differentiating Johnson's style from other styles, so he finds most characteristic those passages which are most extreme (though he is careful to note their infrequency). Second, he is interested in style as the "last articulation of meaning," and the theoretical thrust of his

19. One can agree with Roger North, whose early eighteenth-century comments on biography have only recently been partially published, that "there is great art, as well as felicity, in making a good description of plain facts" (General Preface to *Life of the Lord Keeper North*, in *Biography as an Art*, ed. James L. Clifford [New York: Oxford University Press, 1962], p. 30).
20. *The Art of Criticism* (London, 1789), pp. 199–201, 110.

book is that syntactical relationships carry *implicit* meanings. As a result he seems to ignore the explicit meanings which arise from style, i.e., the expressive function of the style. In what follows I shall attempt to show something of the nature of Johnson's stylistic repertoire as a way of defining his use of style in biography.

In his anthology *Parodies*, Dwight Macdonald includes a passage from *Rambler* No. 9 under the rubric "Self-Parodies: Unconscious":

Who, when he saw the first sand or ashes, by a casual intenseness of heat melted into a metalline form, rugged with excrescences, and clouded with impurities, would have imagined, that in this shapeless lump lay concealed so many conveniences of life, as would in time constitute a great part of the happiness of the world? Yet by some such fortuitous liquefaction was mankind taught to procure a body, at once in a high degree solid and transparent, which might admit the light of the sun, and exclude the violence of the wind.[21]

Silently cutting fifty-seven words from the last sentence as it appears in the *Rambler*, Macdonald entitles the passage "Lucubrations on Glass." Johnson is fair game for the satirist here, but he is hardly unconscious of what he is doing. Precisely because glass seems to be such a mundane matter he elevates his diction and lengthens his sentence (his rhetorical question is fifty-six words long, twelve words longer than the *Rambler* average, nearly twice as long as the *Lives* average) to convey, uncharacteristically, the sense of wonder at the process by which glass came into being. All the elements of style here are controlled by his expressive purpose. In Johnson's biographies the materials are occasionally more intractable, yet when he writes at his best in the biographies the characteristic excellence of his writing is only occasionally in the *Rambler* style.

The full-blown *Rambler* style can be found in the *Lives*, but not frequently. In the *Life of Cowley* Johnson works through a paragraph opposing Petrarch as a real lover to Cowley, goes on in the next paragraph to attack Cowley for producing insipid love poems that lack a basis in a real love affair, and finally reaches a

---

21. *Parodies: An Anthology from Chaucer to Beerbohm—and After* (New York: Random, 1960), p. 476. My text is from *Yale*, III, 49.

level of generality and indignation that calls forth the extended parallelism of words, phrases, and clauses that is characteristic of Johnson's essay prose:

It is surely not difficult, in the solitude of a college, or in the bustle of the world, to find useful studies and serious employment. No man needs to be so burthened with life as to squander it in voluntary dreams of fictitious occurrences. The man that sits down to suppose himself charged with treason or peculation, and heats his mind to an elaborate purgation of his character from crimes which he was never within the possibility of committing, differs only by the infrequency of his folly from him who praises beauty which he never saw, complains of jealousy which he never felt, supposes himself sometimes invited and sometimes forsaken, fatigues his fancy, and ransacks his memory, for images which may exhibit the gaiety of hope or the gloominess of despair, and dresses his imaginary Chloris or Phyllis sometimes in flowers fading as her beauty, and sometimes in gems lasting as her virtues. [I, 7–8]

The impersonal construction of the first sentence and the categorical statement of the second are typical of Johnson's essay style. As one might expect, a favorite theme, the dangerous prevalence of imagination, leads to the elaboration of parallels. Johnson means to remind us here of things he thinks we ought to know and uses all his rhetorical skill to drive the lesson home.

In the *Lives* this kind of prose is part of a repertoire of styles which gives expressive variety to the whole. The passage just quoted must be seen in its stylistic context for us to appreciate it fully. The next paragraph begins: "At Paris, as secretary to Lord Jermin, he was engaged in transacting things of real importance with real men and real women, and at that time did not much employ his thoughts upon phantoms of gallantry." This sentence brings us back to the "real" world even before Johnson by the repetitions of his adjective (rhetorically, *ploce*) insists upon such a shift. The mention of Paris and Lord Jermin in straightforward prose is opposed to the fictions of the paragraph before. The ornate paragraphs on Cowley's imaginary mistress are effective in part because of their deviation from the plainer base style of the *Lives*, a style which can easily accommodate factual material without sacrificing the possibilities of expressiveness.

This stylistic variety is as much a matter of diction, in our sense, as of sentence length. Although many exceptions can be found, in the *Lives* a polysyllabic phrase frequently points to some aspect of the subject ripe for deflating—Swift's washing himself with "oriental scrupulosity," Pope's thinking himself, while still a teenager, "entitled to poetical conversation," Garrick's "gratitude of exultation" when flattered by Mallet.[22]

In the "Memoirs of the King of Prussia" Johnson satirizes Frederick the First's penchant for tall soldiers:

> The chief pride of the old king was to be master of the tallest regiment in Europe. He, therefore, brought together, from all parts, men above the common military standard. To exceed the height of six feet, was a certain recommendation to notice, and to approach that of seven, a claim to distinction. Men will readily go where they are sure to be caressed; and he had, therefore, such a collection of giants, as, perhaps, was never seen in the world before. [*Works*, VI, 436]

This paragraph begins in a straightforward manner (if we do not inquire too closely into the propriety of Frederick's taking his "chief pride" in such an achievement). The second sentence proceeds logically from the first; but when we reach the third we begin to see that this Brobdingnagian regiment is the product of a Lilliputian mind. Quantity becomes quality as the standard phrases of merit ("a certain recommendation to notice," "a claim to distinction") are applied to mere height.[23] The paragraph takes on the stateliness of form that Johnson usually reserves for more serious matter. The general statement "men will readily go where they are sure to be caressed") is undercut by the language. Why should soldiers, especially brutes verging on seven feet tall, be "caressed?"[24] The values of the king are clearly out of scale. The mock-impressive conclusion ("such . . . as, perhaps, was never seen in the world before") is again turned ironic by a

22. In "The Ironic Tradition in Augustan Prose from Swift to Johnson," Ian Watt makes some characteristically intelligent remarks on irony in Johnson's writings (*Restoration and Augustan Prose: Papers Delivered by James R. Sutherland and Ian Watt at the Third Clark Library Seminar;* [Los Angeles: William Andrews Clark Memorial Library, 1956], pp. 41–46.

23. Johnson had used this trick earlier in the *Life of Savage* to satirize those who were impressed only with fashionable authors. While Lord Tyrconnel was his patron, "to admire Mr. *Savage* was a Proof of Discernment, and to be acquainted with him was a Title to poetical Reputation" (p. 44).

24. "Caressed" means "treated with kindness," but there is the lingering suggestion of our more common meaning, "fondled."

well-chosen word. Johnson's description of the group as a "collection of giants" identifies the king as a royal virtuoso, not much different from collectors of butterflies or seashells. It also suggests that the brethren of these giants are to be found in a freak show at Smithfield or on the stage in Fielding's *Tom Thumb*.

Johnson is not through with the king; he devotes another paragraph to ridiculing his folly:

> To review this towering regiment was his daily pleasure, and to perpetuate it was so much his care, that when he met a tall woman, he immediately commanded one of his Titanian retinue to marry her, that they might propagate procerity, and produce heirs to the father's habiliments.

The last part of this long sentence (long for the genre) contains some of the relatively few "hard words" in Johnson's biographies. Though Johnson had only scorn for imitative form in poetry and did not think that one could suggest height through the length of a line, he satirizes the king's inflated ideas through pomp of diction. Johnson's diction, sentence length and alliteration ("propagate procerity") have an expressive function.[25]

What Geoffrey Tillotson says of writers of the heroic couplet holds good for prose as well: "they know that a reader soon scrambles on to the level of the poem, and that, when he has reached it, that level becomes his norm."[26] Given the normative diction of the biographies, which is not, like the *Rambler*, especially "philosophical," the use of a few hard words provides a strong emphasis. It is noteworthy that Boswell seized on "procerity" as the only instance of *"Brownism"* in Johnson's pieces for the *Literary Magazine* (*Life*, I, 308). The plainer norm of Johnson's prose in the biographies makes possible a wider range of emphatic effects through deviations from that norm. The account of the friendship of the young Pope with the old Wycherley is typical of Johnson's deadly narrative economy. He recognizes Wycherley's high reputation, though he thinks it un-

25. Typically, the next paragraph turns away from satire ("apparent folly") to give us another tone, in this case much darker. See W. Jackson Bate, "Johnson and Satire Manqué" in *Eighteenth-Century Studies in Honor of Donald F. Hyde*, ed. W. H. Bond (New York: Grolier Club, 1970), pp. 145-60, and Watt, "The Ironic Tradition," pp. 42-43.

26. *Augustan Poetic Diction* (London: Athlone Press, 1964), p. 198.

deserved: "Pope was proud of his notice; Wycherley wrote verses in his praise, which he was charged by Dennis with writing to himself, and they agreed for a while to flatter one another" (III, 91). The pride is understandable—the poetry is so favorable that Pope himself was accused of writing it—but Johnson reduces their intentions, the mutual respect of two great literary figures, to a bit of contractual flattery.

Like the reader of Jane Austen, the reader of Johnson's *Lives* has the intense experience of being made to think in more than one direction at once. There is a pervasive irony in his biographies, for what he actually tells the reader is not always the same as what he appears to say. Reading is thus a highly active experience. The largely straightforward informative prose which conveys through an orderly progression the standard topics of life-writing at the same time contains other suggestions that are not taken up and developed as the rapid narrative unfolds:

Pope had now declared himself a poet; and thinking himself entitled to poetical conversation, began at seventeen to frequent Will's, a coffee-house on the north side of Russel-street in Covent-garden, where the wits of that time used to assemble, and where Dryden had, when he lived, been accustomed to preside. [III, 93]

Although this paragraph clearly takes an ironical stance toward the young Pope, it does not merely denigrate him. On another, independent level, we see that the brilliant young man may have found much that was useful for his development in the debris left by Dryden. We draw both of these conclusions from the sentence, and they do not contradict each other. The subordination of the irony to the larger purpose of the writing is total; the passage itself is unremarkable. Neither a brilliant piece of bravura writing nor structured in the way an anecdote is, it serves as part of a larger whole, a passage in a factual narrative, and has no metaphors, no striking images, no "point"—none of the things that make a quotable remark. Yet in the fusion of apparently contradictory elements into a coherent totality by force of an informing style and a sense of general purpose, it expresses the essential nature of the best eighteenth-century writing. Such passages create the intelligence they assume. This is not an anecdote, but it bristles with possibilities. Pope, whose relation to society is one of the prominent themes of this life, thinks himself "entitled to poetical conversation," a minor presumption. The image of Dryden giving his little senate laws is raised only after we see him as already dead. Johnson's power over his narration enables him to throw away lines which another writer would attempt to turn into a more obviously pointed account, if he recognized their possibilities at all. The fact that he can afford to mute such effects gives us the impression of a speaker who has at once enormous intelligence and great control. Maynard Mack pays tribute to this effect in Johnson's comment on Pope's grotto: "[His] excavation was requisite as an entrance to his garden, and, as some men try to be proud of their defects, he extracted an ornament from an inconvenience, and vanity produced a grotto where necessity enforced a passage" (III, 135). Mack remarks, "Johnson shows here his characteristic lack of sympathy with the *furor rusticus*, but his fine intelligence catches in passing at an ethical analogy that is highly characteristic of him and contains an important truth about Pope."[27]

Perhaps I can best demonstrate the typical excellence of style in Johnson's biographies by examining several successive paragraphs that display the contrasted styles of which I have been speaking. They come from one of the better short biographies, the *Life of Shenstone*:

Whether to plant a walk in undulating curves, and to place a bench at every turn where there is an object to catch the view; to make water run where it will be heard, and to stagnate where it will be seen; to leave intervals where the eye will be pleased, and to thicken the plantation where there is something to be hidden, demands any great powers of mind, I will not enquire; perhaps a sullen and surly speculator may think such performances rather the sport than the business of human reason. But it must be at least confessed, that to embellish the form of nature is an innocent amusement; and some praise must be allowed by the most supercilious observer to him, who does best what such multitudes are contending to do well. [III, 350-51]

Ian Watt notices, in an excellent analysis of this passage, Johnson's unwillingness "to range the full force of his mind against Shenstone and the multitudes who are contending in the

27. *The Garden and the City: Retirement and Politics in the Later Poetry of Pope, 1731-1743* (Toronto: University of Toronto Press, 1969), p. 61.

sports of human reason," but what we have, as so often in Johnson, is an implicit judgment against Shenstone, followed by a turning upon himself and his own position. Watt says of the multiplied parallels and antitheses, "the very complication of the syntax is necessary to enable Johnson to re-enact all the gradations of attitude in the judging mind, and to allow of such incidental ironic felicities as 'stagnate where it will be seen,' where the formidable analytic power is shown easily constrained to a suitably comic antithesis."[28] In some ways what Johnson has done is to use a *preteritio*: he "will not enquire," but his syntax does, and as we read the period, the suspension of judgment on the gardener's art provides not only room for "gradations of attitude in the judging mind," but a kind of re-creation of the confusing process of going through Shenstone's garden. The prose here is as undulant as the groves themselves, and Johnson wants us to sense the absence of mind that accompanies such luxuriance of vegetation before he goes on to give, in a surprising turn, Shenstone praise as "him, who does best what such multitudes are contending to do well."

After another paragraph Johnson continues in a different style:

The pleasure of Shenstone was all in his eye; he valued what he valued merely for its looks; nothing raised his indignation more than to ask if there were any fishes in his water. [III, 352]

This is as close as Johnson ever gets to the exploded period of the curt style. The sentence is paratactic, punctuated only by semicolons. We may feel here the flashing of unpremeditated thought, of a single aspect of Shenstone's character viewed in several different lights. With its pointed conclusion, this is the kind of sentence that could have led a contemporary to find Johnson's *Lives* very like conversation before Boswell muddied the critical waters by presenting Johnson's actual conversation to a broad public that had never heard the great man in the drawing room. The only polysyllabic word, the abstract "indignation"—part of a laugh at Shenstone's expense—is opposed to the concrete factuality of the "fishes."

The description of Shenstone's house which follows is as flatly

28. Watt, "The Ironic Tradition," p. 43.

factual and simply coordinated as Defoe might have made it, but
it is also characteristic, and necessary for what is to come:

> His house was mean, and he did not improve it; his care was all of his
> grounds. When he came home from his walks he might find his floors
> flooded by a shower through the broken roof; but could spare no
> money for its reparation. [III, 352]

This is seen and delivered with an unclouded eye. The style is
admirable but hardly calls attention to itself and does not mean
to. As we read the very different style of the next sentence, we
should keep in mind that it is not only impressive in isolation but
gains force from its juxtaposition to the material and style which
come before it:

> In time his expences brought clamours about him, that overpowered the
> lamb's bleat and the linnet's song; and his groves were haunted by
> beings very different from fauns and fairies. [III, 352]

This is the Johnsonian antipastoral mode, and the unnecessary
doubling of terms ("lamb's bleat and linnet's song," "fauns and
fairies") is his way of dramatizing the excessive nature of the
imagination he attacks. R. T. Davies has referred to the "disci-
plined luxuriousness" of Johnson's prose. The phrase is a good
one, and worth a bit of expansion. When Johnson satirizes an
attitude or action his hyperbolic imaginative development
parodies the thinking or behavior, as he sees it, of the target.
Johnson's judgment is found in the formalization and contain-
ment of the syntax, as well as the diction. This strategy is the
Johnsonian version of giving a man enough rope to hang
himself—while he makes sure that the gallows is tidy and the
noose well-plaited—yet it rarely leads to impersonation of the
target, as in Swift. The voice we hear is Johnson's. The voice is
asking us to feel the seductiveness as well as the silliness of what
it describes, and, having felt it, to reject it. Johnson returns in
this paragraph to a plainer but still dignified prose:

> He spent his estate in adorning it, and his death was probably hastened
> by his anxieties. He was a lamp that spent its oil in blazing. It is said, that
> if he had lived a little longer he would have been assisted by a pension:
> such bounty could not have been ever more properly bestowed; but that
> it was ever asked is not certain; it is too certain that it was never enjoyed.
> [III, 252–53]

The first sentence is simply coordinated and lifted from plainness only by the slight paradox of "spent his estate in adorning
it" and the minor stiffening of "hastened by his anxieties." The
second is epigrammatic in form and strikingly metaphoric. The
next sentence is far more complex, though the separate members are not especially Rambleresque. It works toward a chiastic
conclusion (ever asked: not certain / too certain: never enjoyed),
which has a cross pattern of antithesis (not ever more properly
bestowed / ever asked not certain). The effect is a rather looser
version of the sort of thing that the eighteenth century admired
so much in Denham's famous lines from *Cooper's Hill*.

If we return to Johnson's criticism of Swift, we should observe
that Johnson objects not to the plain style itself but to the lack (as
he sees it) of any variety in the style: "His sentences are never too
much dilated or contracted. . . . His style was well suited to his
thoughts, which are never subtilised by nice disquisitions, decorated by sparkling conceits, elevated by ambitious sentences, or
variegated by far-sought learning. [The reader of Swift] is
neither required to mount elevations nor to explore profun-
dities; his passage is always on a level, along solid ground, without asperities, without obstruction" (III, 52). In short, Johnson
finds Swift, except in *A Tale of a Tub*, boring. By contrast, all the
things he finds lacking in Swift are among the glories of his own
prose, and we would do well in speaking of Johnson's style to
remember that it is valuable for its variety as well as its characteristic orotundities.[29] And it is nowhere so wonderfully varied
as in his biographies. To see that style in its larger manifestations, I shall turn in the next chapter to one of Johnson's major
achievements, arguably his best biography, the *Life of Savage*.

29. A study of Johnson's sermons—a genre Wimsatt does not consider—tends
to a great extent to support Wimsatt's position; but unlike biography, which
would "teach what is not known," the sermon, like the essay, would "recommend
known truths by [its] manner of adorning them" (*Rambler* No. 3). See James
Gray, *Johnson's Sermons: A Study* (Oxford: Clarendon Press, 1972), especially Ch.
IV, "The Form and Style of the Sermons." Donald J. Greene, however, argues
that "it is surely misleading to talk about 'Johnson's prose style'—he had at least
half-a-dozen at his disposal." See "Is There a 'Tory' Prose Style?" *BNYPL*, 66
(1962), 451.

CHAPTER 9

The *Life of Savage*

One could choose a number of biographies to illustrate Johnson working at his best and to show with some fullness the nature of Johnsonian biography: *Pope, Milton, Dryden, Addison*— even *Shenstone* for great biography on the smallest scale. Biography, however, is in some ways an impossible art, one contingent on the lucky findings of the biographer and not simply the intrinsic interest of the life. The best choice for my purpose is the one that fulfills uniquely Johnson's own requirement for good biography, that "nobody can write the life of a man, but those who have eat and drunk and lived in social intercourse with him." As the *Life of Pope* proves, Johnson's dictum is wrong, but by looking at the *Life of Savage* we can see what Johnson was capable of doing when he had the most firsthand information at his disposal and the fullest knowledge of his subject's personality. If this life, written in the middle of his career, may be looked at as something apart from the *Lives of the Poets,* that too is to the good, for it is not cramped by the requirements of collective biography. And in its favor, above all, is its excellence.

The popular voice and the critics are in agreement that the *Life of Savage* is one of the masterpieces of English biography, either the best Johnson wrote or among his generous handful of great biographies. Hesketh Pearson has called it the "best short biography in the English language," and Bertrand H. Bronson says that "it is godlike, irreplaceable."[1] There is not as much

1. Pearson, *Johnson and Boswell* (London: William Heinemann, 1958), pp. 33–34; Bronson, "A Note on *The Life of Savage,*" in *Samuel Johnson: Rasselas,*

agreement as to its nature. To take only some of the most recent critics, Paul Fussell speaks of it as "complicated comedy," and John A. Dussinger says its "basic structure . . . resembles a Greek tragedy or medieval morality play."[2] Perhaps the most striking comment on the genre of the work was Cyril Connolly's publication of *Savage* as part of a collection of *Great Short English Novels,* a decision which ironically runs counter to Johnson's proud assertion prior to the book's appearance:

> It may be reasonably imagined that others may have the same design, but as it is not credible that they can obtain the same Materials, it must be expected that they will supply from Invention the want of Intelligence, and that under the title of The Life of *Savage* they will publish only a Novel, filled with romantic Adventures and imaginary Amours. You may therefore perhaps, gratify the lovers of Truth and Wit, by giving me leave to inform them in your Magazine, that my Account will be published in 8vo by Mr. *Roberts* in *Warwick-lane.*[3]

Johnson's fears were justified, for the story of Richard Savage has been turned into at least three novels and several plays, apart from the dubious enlistment of his own work as fiction.[4]

There are reasons for this diversity. The form of the biography and its dominant rhetoric proceed from Johnson's conception of Savage's character as presented in the formal summary description which immediately follows the conclusion of the "life" section and precedes the "character": "Such were the Life and Death of Richard Savage, a Man equally distinguished by Virtues and Vices, and at once remarkable for his Weaknesses and Abilities" (p. 135).[5] "Virtues and Vices," the standard ethical

Poems, and Selected Prose (San Francisco: Holt, Rinehart, and Winston, 1971), p. xxi. My indebtedness to W. Jackson Bate's excellent general article, "Johnson and Satire Manqué," in *Eighteenth-Century Studies in Honor of Donald F. Hyde,* ed. W. H. Bond (New York: Grolier Club, 1970), pp. 145–160, will be readily apparent.

2. Fussell, *Samuel Johnson and the Life of Writing* (New York: Harcourt, Brace, Jovanovich, 1971), pp. 258–64; Dussinger, "Style and Intention in Johnson's *Life of Savage,*" *ELH,* 37 (1970), 564–80.

3. *Gentleman's Magazine,* 13 (August 1743), 416.

4. Novels about Savage have been written by Charles Whitehead (1842), Stanley V. Makower (1909), and Gwyn Jones (1935); plays, by Lucette Madeleine Ryley (1901) and by J. M. Barrie and H. B. Marriott Watson in collaboration (1891).

5. In this chapter all references to Tracy's edition of the *Life of Savage* (Oxford: Clarendon Press, 1971) will be by page in the text.

fare, do not lead to a simple account of assets and liabilities, but rather to a complex interrelationship where one may undercut or qualify the other; the whole drift of the biography is to show how much we have to take into account before making the necessary ethical judgments. The *Life of Savage* may be looked upon as a series of brilliant equilibrations of these central oppositions. For its like we should have to turn to eighteenth-century music.

In a sense we can say that given the circumstances of Savage's life, as perceived by Johnson, the *Life of Savage* could be at best tragic (he would be a bit like Hamlet: done out of his rightful title by an adulterous mother, the time out of joint), but because of the shortcomings of Savage's character Johnson's biography is tragedy *manqué,* and hence satiric. Indeed, the minute we try to think of Savage as tragic hero—and as I have argued earlier, Johnson does think him a hero of sorts—the closest parallel we can scrape up is not Hamlet but Coriolanus: proud, haughty, childish; unwillingly courting those who can do him good, dictating to his friends, contemptuous of his enemies and the mob. Yet the differences are every bit as striking. Thinking on Savage we can see him as the very parody of the *megalopsychos,* the great-minded or magnanimous man. The role may even be said to have been recommended to him. Early in the biography Johnson mentions that Savage "was once told by the Duke of *Dorset,* that it was just to consider him as an injured Nobleman" (p. 20). It was a lesson Savage never forgot. When Pope wrote a letter to Sir William Lemon in Savage's name in order to effect Savage's reconciliation with Lord Tyrconnel, Savage "very justly observed, that the Style was too supplicatory, and the Representation too abject, and that he ought at least to have made him complain with *the Dignity of a Gentleman in Distress*" (p. 113). Later, in a letter to a friend from the Bristol jail in which he was to die, Savage writes: "I murmur not, but am all Resignation to the *divine Will.* As to the World, I hope that I shall be endued by Heaven with that Presence of Mind, that serene Dignity in Misfortune, that constitutes the Character of a true Nobleman; a Dignity far beyond that of Coronets; a Nobility arising from the just Principles of Philosophy, refined and exalted, by those of Christianity" (p. 123). The terms here have shifted somewhat.

Savage seems to cast himself more in the mold of Steele's Christian Hero than in that of the magnanimous man. Nobility is no longer something to be fought for in courts of law, Parliament, or pamphlets. The Savage of this letter sounds quite unlike the man who attempted to harass an admission of his nobility from his putative mother. Perhaps at last renouncing the quest but not its goal, Savage was willing to find a nobility within him happier far, at least in his epistolary intercourse.

Johnson is usually very clear-eyed about the shortcomings of Savage's role as nobleman, though he does not think it simply a pose. In a letter to Cave (also from jail) Savage responds to a suggestion that he should not publish *London and Bristol Delineated:* "You doubt, my friend Mr S[trong] would not approve of it—And what is it to me whether he does or not? Do you imagine, that Mr S__ is to dictate to me? If any Man, who calls himself my Friend, should assume such an Air, I would spurn at his Friendship with Contempt" (p. 131). Johnson quotes this letter at length and comments:

Such was his Imprudence and such his obstinate Adherence to his own Resolutions, however absurd. A Prisoner! supported by Charity! and, whatever Insults he might have received during the latter Part of his Stay in *Bristol,* once caressed, esteemed, and presented with a liberal Collection, he could forget on a sudden his Danger, and his Obligations, to gratify the Petulance of his Wit, or the Eagerness of his Resentment, and publish a Satire by which he might reasonably expect, that he should alienate those who then supported him, and provoke those whom he could neither resist nor escape. [P. 132]

Those who "presume to dictate" to Savage, frequently enough well-meaning friends, soon feel his resentment (pp. 61, 113). And yet Savage suffers just such indignities. As we have seen, Pope almost literally "dictate[s] a letter to him" (p. 113).

Magnanimous men, according to Aristotle, "seem . . . to remember any service they have done but not those they have received (for he who receives a service is inferior to him who has done it, but the proud man wishes to be superior)."[6] Savage's variation on this theme combines the request the magnanimous

6. *Nichomachean Ethics,* in *The Basic Works of Aristotle,* ed. Richard McKeon (New York: Random House, 1970), p. 993.

man would never make with the attitude that he would strike
after having kindnesses forced upon him:

> It was observed that he always asked Favours of this kind without the
> least Submission or apparent Consciousness of Dependence, and that
> he did not seem to look upon a Compliance with his Request as an
> Obligation that deserved any extraordinary Acknowledgements, but a
> Refusal was resented by him as an Affront, or complained of as an
> Injury; nor did he readily reconcile himself to those who either denied
> to lend, or gave him afterwards any Intimation, that they expected to be
> repaid. [P. 98]

No wonder a twentieth-century psychoanalyst sees Savage as an
"injustice collector," a neurotic parasite whose life reads like a
case study.[7]

Again, Aristotle finds it "the mark of the magnanimous
man . . . to be dignified towards people who enjoy high position
and good fortune, but unassuming towards those of the middle
class; for it is a difficult and lofty thing to be superior to the
former, but easy to be so to the latter."[8] Savage, "in his lowest
State . . . wanted not Spirit to assert the natural Dignity of Wit,
and was always ready to repress that Insolence which Superiority
of Fortune incited, and to trample the Reputation which rose
upon any other Basis than that of Merit: he never admitted any
gross Familiarities, or submitted to be treated otherwise than as
an equal" (p. 99). When Savage was "without Lodging, Meat, or
Cloaths," a friend, intending to do him good, left word that they
should meet at nine the next morning. Savage "was very much
disgusted, that he should presume to prescribe the Hour of his
Attendance, and . . . refused to visit him, and rejected his Kindness." Johnson, whose own refusal at Oxford of a pair of shoes
charitably left him is one of the stories every schoolboy knows, is
not sure if this "invincible Temper" is "Firmness or Obstinacy."
The most ludicrous anecdote in this vein derives from the
scheme of friends who would help him but knew his imprudence: "he came to the Lodging of a Friend with the most violent
Agonies of Rage; and being asked what it could be that gave him

7. Edmund Bergler, "Samuel Johnson's 'Life of the Poet Richard Savage'—a
Paradigm for a Type," *American Imago*, 4 (December 1947), 42–63.
8. *Ethics*, p. 993.

such Disturbance, he replied with the utmost Vehemence of Indignation,'That they had sent for a Taylor to measure him' " (p. 112). Johnson also finds this "Firmness or Obstinacy" at work in Savage's demands for the continuation of his allowance from Lord Tyrconnel "with whom he never appeared to entertain for a Moment the Thought of soliciting a Reconciliation, and whom he treated at once with all the Haughtiness of Superiority, and all the Bitterness of Resentment" (pp. 99–100).

To see the relevance of the magnanimous man permits us also to place Frank Brady's suggestion that "there are some touches of Satan" in Savage. He quotes aptly:

> that fixt mind
> And high disdain, from sence of injur'd merit
> .   .   .   .   .
> And study of revenge, immortal hate,
> And courage never to submit or yield.[9]

Satan has been taken persuasively as part of Milton's critique of the magnanimous man of earlier epics.[10] Brady instances Savage's "independence, resentment, insolence, and self-delusion." To these we may add—and the words occur frequently in Johnson's biography—pride, contempt, and haughtiness. Along with consciousness of merit and concern with honor and shame, these are the commonplaces of magnanimity. Once the biography is well-launched, almost any page is apt to produce a congeries of such traits: "he could not bear to conceive himself in a State of Dependence, his Pride being equally powerful with his other Passions, and appearing in the Form of Insolence at one time and of Vanity at another" (p. 138).

Even Savage's appearance and deportment, apart from a "tremulous and mournful voice," fit the stereotype. Aristotle claims that "a slow step is thought proper to the magnanimous man, a deep voice, and a level utterance; for the man who takes few things seriously is not likely to be hurried, nor the man who

9. *Paradise Lost*, I, 97–98, 107–8; quoted by Brady, "The Strategies of Biography and Some Eighteenth-Century Examples," in *Literary Theory and Structure: Essays in Honor of William K. Wimsatt*, ed. Frank Brady, John Palmer, and Martin Price (New Haven: Yale University Press, 1973), p. 254.

10. For example, by John M. Steadman, *Milton and the Renaissance Hero* (Oxford: Clarendon Press, 1967), Ch. vi.

thinks nothing great to be excited."[11] Savage, according to Johnson, was "of a grave and manly Deportment, a solemn Dignity of Mien, but which upon a nearer Acquaintance softened into an engaging Easiness of Manners. His Walk was slow.... He was easily excited to Smiles, but very seldom provoked to Laughter" (p. 136). Not to cut things too fine—and Chesterfield on laughter is probably appropriate here as well—this portrait, whether of nature or second nature, is of a piece with Savage's behavior. Sir John Hawkins claims that Savage's manners probably first won over Johnson when they met, for Savage was "very courteous in the modes of salutation." Hawkins adds, "I have been told, that in the taking off his hat and disposing it under his arm, and in his bow, he displayed as much grace as those actions were capable of."[12]

Johnson's final judgment on Savage's social attitude is uncompromising: "he appeared to think himself born to be supported by others" (p. 137). This is certainly a negative version of Savage's role as nobleman. (Indeed, it sounds rather like a Marxist definition of the nobleman.) Savage, as presented by Johnson, has a great deal in common with the subject of a minor masterpiece of twentieth-century biography, Frederick Rolfe, alias Baron Corvo. Corvo was like Savage in his claims to nobility, his enchanging conversation and minor but decided literary talents, his facility at acquiring both friends and enemies—and at making enemies of his friends—his haughtiness and litigiousness, his poverty and his pathos. They share enough traits to suggest that the two men are examples of a type rather than coincidentally alike.

Although the magnanimous man is apt to be the protagonist of tragedy or epic, the standard heroic literature, Savage's manifestations of magnanimity are, with some striking exceptions, such as his gift of half of his only guinea to the woman who bore witness him at his murder trial, not seen as tragic, but as part of the more risible ironies of his life. His genuine heroism is not based for Johnson on his putative nobility but on his intellectual gifts, and in writing this biography Johnson gives us an

11. *Ethics*, p. 994.
12. *The Life of Samuel Johnson, LL.D.*, 2d ed. (London, 1787), p. 52.

early example of a figure who was to become significant in the later eighteenth and the nineteenth centuries, the poet as hero.

If the discrepancy between Savage's role of distressed nobleman–poet and the actual terms of his existence often provides the material for satire, it is also the source of the most authentically tragic passage in the biography:

He lodged as much by Accident as he dined and passed the Night, sometimes in mean Houses, which are set open at Night to any casual Wanderers, sometimes in Cellars among the Riot and Filth of the meanest and most profligate of the Rabble; and sometimes, when he had no Money to support even the Expences of these Receptacles, walked about the Streets till he was weary, and lay down in the Summer upon a Bulk, or in the Winter with his Associates in Poverty, among the Ashes of a Glass-house.

In this Manner were passed those Days and those Nights, which Nature had enabled him to have employed in elevated Speculations, useful Studies, or pleasing Conversation. On a Bulk, in a Cellar, or in a Glass-house among Thieves and Beggars, was to be found the Author of the *Wanderer*, the Man of exalted Sentiments, extensive Views and curious Observations, the Man whose Remarks on Life might have assisted the Statesman, whose Ideas of Virtue might have enlightened the Moralist, whose Eloquence might have influenced Senates, and whose Delicacy might have polished Courts. [P. 97]

Richard Savage, bastard and wanderer (to use the titles of his best-known works), surely an alienated man if ever there was one, remains essentially alone in the midst of this social world. "Among Thieves and Beggars," he is hardly, I hasten to add, a Christ figure. But the pathos of his existence is conveyed by the almost Sisyphean nature of his endless rounds—day and night, summer and winter. Johnson does not give us the voluminous details of the novelist, but the bulk and ashes are no less concrete for not being described.

So, too, while Savage was writing his tragedy *Sir Thomas Over-bury*, "he was without Lodging, and often without Meat; nor had he any other Conveniences for Study than the Fields or the Streets allowed him, there he used to walk and form his Speeches, and afterwards step into a Shop, beg for a few Moments the Use of the Pen and Ink, and write down what he had composed upon Paper which he had picked up by Accident" (p. 21). The nouns in this generalized anecdote—lodging, meat, fields, streets, shop, pen, ink, paper—give us the blunt realities of Savage's daily existence.

Savage is a tragic hero *manqué* not because he fails to fulfill his full promise (this is, of course, the very condition of tragedy), but because he never becomes aware enough of the meaning of his own actions. Anagnorisis or recognition is not absolutely necessary to the tragic effect, even for Aristotle, who prefers it, but Savage's self-knowledge is at too low a level to elicit anything from readers at certain points in his career but derisive laughter. Although he quests incessantly for his name, he never establishes an unequivocal identity. Commenting on Savage's apprenticeship to a shoemaker, Johnson says, "It is generally reported . . . that *Savage* was employed at the Awl longer than he was willing to confess; nor was it perhaps any great Advantage to him, that an unexpected Discovery determined him to quit his Occupation" (p. 10). Johnson suggests that Savage would be better off sticking to his last. Savage's lack of awareness is somewhat extenuated by Johnson, for in some ways he never had a chance to grow up: "He may be considered as a Child *exposed* to all the Temptations of Indigence, at an Age when Resolution was not yet strengthened by Conviction, nor Virtue confirmed by Habit" (p. 75). And here is yet another way to perceive the man who thought himself "born to be supported by others."

Savage's delusions walked their narrow round, all too often within the confines of the mint or a cell: "He proceeded throughout his Life to tread the same steps on the same Circle; always applauding his past Conduct, or at least forgetting it, to amuse himself with Phantoms of Happiness, which were dancing before him; and willingly turned his Eyes from the Light of Reason, when it would have discovered the Illusion, and shewn him, what he never wished to see, his real State" (p. 74). Savage is like a minor denizen of Dante's Inferno, compelled by his own lack of light to continue round and round through his night-lit life. Elsewhere, too, an unobtrusive metaphor will give us a sense of felt life as the narrator recognizes what his subject fails to see at all, Savage's inability to profit in any way from the passage of time: "While he was thus wearing out his Life in Expectation . . ." (p. 102); "While he was thus spending the Day in contriving a

scheme for the Morrow, Distress stole upon him by impercepti-
ble Degrees" (p. 119). Savage's relationship to time is complex
and Johnson's registration of his behavior is at once lucid and
subtle. Nevertheless, some of the patterns of Savage's actions, as
Johnson presents them, may give rise to suspicions that go beyond Johnson's own judgments. After writing his first poem,
against the controversial Bishop of Bangor, "Mr. *Savage* was
himself in a little time ashamed of it, and endeavoured to suppress it, by destroying all the Copies that he could collect" (p.
12). When we later see him blotting out his name from the list of
actors in *Sir Thomas Overbury* (p. 24) or blotting out Lord Tyrconnel's name from the effusive dedication to *The Wanderer* after
they had quarreled (p. 61), we should realize that Savage is not
only ashamed of his past but wants to change it by fiat, and we
may perhaps suspect that this is precisely what he has done in
billing himself as the bastard son of the Earl Rivers. In any case
we may see such behavior as part of the main theme, the magnanimous man's refusal to consider his debasement as part of his
real existence. Savage, as Johnson puts it, is "too easily reconciled to himself."

Savage treads "the same steps on the same Circle" because he
fails to learn from his experience. His death, which I discussed
earlier while considering deathbed scenes as a *topos* of biography,[13] is thus in context suggestive of his relationship to his
whole life. Savage's lack of awareness is exposed by Johnson's
social presentation of him. In defining the "literature of worldliness" Peter Brooks calls it "a literature directed to man's self-
conscious social existence—to know, assess, celebrate, master
and give meaning to man's words and gestures as they are
formed by his consciousness of society." It exploits "the drama
inherent in man's social existence, the encounters of personal
styles within the framework and code provided by society."[14]
Although Johnson's world has little to do with *le monde*, society in
the sense of a small self-conscious elite, his belief that man is a
social animal—and the role that being in society plays in his own

13. See Ch. 5, p. 111.
14. *The Novel of Worldliness: Crébillon, Marivaux, Laclos, Stendhal* (Princeton:
Princeton University Press, 1969), p. 4.

life—makes his *Life of Savage* depend to a large extent on the significance of gestures, looks, and words upon some observer. This is why the role of the narrator, who only appears once *in propria persona*, though we sense his presence at other times, is so important. Frequently, as in Savage's scheme of "flowery felicity," we are given Johnson's rendering, and therefore socializing, of Savage's remarks. And we should also notice that part of the pleasure·we take in Johnson's third-person observation that Savage could never "read his Verses without stealing his Eyes from the Page, to discover in the Faces of his Audience, how they were affected with any favourite Passage" comes from the way a sly observer is himself observed (p. 138).

If Savage is unaware of the meaning of his behavior, the same cannot be said of Johnson's readers, and one aspect of the social presentation of Savage is our growing awareness of what kind of man he is, of our complicity in the superior knowledge of the narrator, whose voice we continually hear. Johnson makes the knowledge he obtained eating and drinking with Savage count, not only in terms of specific information and interpretation, but in making us know Savage as well. Instancing Lord Tyrconnel's charges that Savage gave the best wine in Tyrconnel's cellar to Savage's rowdy company and that Savage pawned "a Collection of valuable Books, stamped with his own Arms," Johnson adds, "Whoever was acquainted with Mr. *Savage*, easily credited both these Accusations." After Savage is "banished from the Table of Lord *Tyrconnel*, and turned again adrift upon the World ... ," Johnson comments, "though it was undoubtedly the Consequence of accumulated Provocations on both Sides, yet every one that knew *Savage* will readily believe, that to him it was sudden as a Stroke of Thunder; that though he might have transiently suspected it, he had never suffered any Thought so unpleasing to sink into his Mind, but that he had driven it away by Amusements, or Dreams of future Felicity and Affluence" (pp. 65–66).

As he moves to the last years of Savage's life, Johnson can present without comment Savage's satisfaction with the subscription of less than fifty pounds a year to enable him to retire to the country, "being now determined to commence a rigid

Oeconomist, and to live according to the exactest Rules of Fru-
gality; for nothing was in his Opinion more contemptible than a
Man, who, when he knew his income, exceeded it, and yet he
confessed that Instances of such Folly, were too common, and
lamented, that some Men were not to be trusted with their own
Money" (p. 114). Like the friends who sent a tailor, we know
Savage and can take his measure. He is not an Oeconomist yet
(and a "rigid Oeconomist" at that) but "determined to commence" one—hyperbolic modes of expression which make his
claims all the funnier. This surely is a confession in which nothing is confessed. Through Johnson's eyes and our own experience of Savage's actions we participate in an amused conspiracy
of silence as we hear his confession and lamentation. And yet the
very next paragraph marks the only direct appearance of the
author in his biography: "Full of these salutary Resolutions, he
left *London*, in *July* 1739, having taken Leave with great Tenderness of his Friends, and parted from the Author of this Narrative with Tears in his Eyes" (p. 114). Johnson can move from
satire to this sentimental parting because he is not writing satire
but something better.

The appearance of the tearful author should serve to remind
us that there is much in this life which we have not yet considered. I have been emphasizing Savage's failure and the way in
which his behavior leaves him open to Johnson's satiric treatment, and yet the other side needs examination before the two
can be set in context together. Indeed, some critics have seen
Johnson's sympathies so firmly engaged that one of them can
speak of his "preposterous partiality."[15] Johnson is in some ways
a defense attorney, and a very skillful one. His intention to serve
as Savage's defender was first declared in an advertisement in
the *Gentleman's Magazine* recalling Savage's contributions to
Cave's periodical and assuming that Mr. Urban's faithful readers
will support any work with a "tendency to the preservation of
[Savage's memory] from Insults or Calumnies."[16] Johnson's very

15. Joseph Wood Krutch, *Samuel Johnson* (New York: Harcourt, Brace, and
World, 1963), p. 82.
16. *Gentleman's Magazine,* 13 (1743), 416.

title, *An Account of the Life of Mr Richard Savage, Son of the Earl
Rivers*, is polemic. It puts forward with dignity what Savage constantly asserted, sometimes with a sense of what others must
have thought of this practice. In his preface to *Miscellaneous
Poems* Savage says, "My Readers, I am afraid, when they observe
Richard Savage join'd so close, and so constantly, to *Son of the late
Earl Rivers*, will impute to a ridiculous Vanity, what is the Effect
of an unhappy Necessity, which my hard Fortune has thrown me
under" (p. 27).

The sentimental and melodramatic sides of the biography
need to be weighed before we can understand the whole. Benjamin Boyce has suggested interestingly that the account may be
colored by Defoe's melodramatic *Roxana,* the printed sources
tinted by Aaron Hill before Johnson reached them.[17] As in *The
Vanity of Human Wishes* and *Rasselas*, both of which followed this
first great work by Johnson, we know from the outset what the
conclusion will be. This will be one more "mournful Narrative"
of "the Miseries of the Learned." The biography begins with a
generalization of the kind that Johnson was later to employ in
the *Rambler*: "It has been observed in all Ages, that the Advantages of Nature or of Fortune have contributed very little to the
Promotion of Happiness; and that those whom the Splendor of
their Rank, or the Extent of their Capacity, have placed upon the
Summits of human Life, have not often given any just Occasion
to Envy in those who look up to them from a lower Station" (p.
3). Johnson goes on to consider the possible reasons for such
failures in the pursuit of happiness and the rationality of expect-
ing a better outcome.

But this Expectation, however plausible, has been very frequently disappointed. The Heroes of literary as well as civil History have been very
often no less remarkable for what they have suffered, than for what
they have atchieved; and Volumes have been written only to enumerate
the Miseries of the Learned, and relate their unhappy Lives, and un-
timely Deaths.

To these mournful Narratives, I am about to add the Life of *Richard
Savage*, a Man whose Writings entitle him to an eminent Rank in the

17. "Johnson's *Life of Savage* and Its Literary Background," *SP*, 53 (1956),
576–98.

Classes of Learning, and whose Misfortunes claim a Degree of Compassion, not always due to the unhappy, as they were often the Consequences of the Crimes of others, rather than his own. [Pp. 3–4]

Fallen from the aristocracy at birth, Savage attempts to scamper back into it but winds up leading the life of the lowliest hack; a sensational life which begins with noble illegitimacy passes through murder and royal pardon and ends in a debtors' prison.

Johnson's sympathetic view of Savage develops through sentimental scenes, such as that of his attempt to catch a glimpse of his mother: "*Savage* was at the same Time so touched with the Discovery of his real Mother, that it was his frequent Practice to walk in the dark Evenings for several Hours before her Door, in Hopes of seeing her as she might come by Accident to the Window, or cross her Apartment with a candle in her Hand." One critic wants to see in this passage a late-blooming Family Romance, "imagery hinting at the Oedipus complex."[18] Yet before turning our attention to phallic candles, it would be better to observe the oppositions closer to the surface, the contrast between the purposive hours Savage spends in order to see her fleeting by, accidentally; Savage outside in the cold and dark, his mother enjoying her light, warmth, and shelter unconcerned about him and unaware of his presence. Dickens was the nineteenth-century master of this sort of scene, and perhaps in Magwitch's grotesquely touching account of his childhood, when a tinker "took the fire with him, and left me wery cold," we can perceive a similar pathos.

Johnson's biography, then, blends the distanced, witty, and evaluative "literature of worldliness" and the involved, emotional, and sympathetic sentimental literature which came into its own in the eighteenth century and is associated at its best with such figures as Richardson and Rousseau. At the outset we are made to sympathize with Savage and identify with him as he becomes the victim of a series of melodramatic actions beginning before his birth. Undoubtedly, this side of Johnson's biography

18. Dussinger, "Style and Intention," p. 571. Despite the work of Dussinger and Bergler, I think that Johnson's *Savage* would yield more to an Eriksonian than a straight Freudian approach. Neither Dussinger's Freudian nor myth criticism seems very helpful, but there is a good deal of value in his article.

kept Joshua Reynolds reading the book while leaning on his mantle, unaware that his arm had fallen asleep. And it led the author of "To the Memory of Mr. Richard Savage upon reading the extraordinary and most affecting series of events contained in the Account of his Life," a forgotten early response to Johnson's *Savage*, to claim that "Late times shall know thy birth, thy lays, thy woes. / Shall read, admire, compassionate and praise, / And while they give, with tears bedew, the bays."[19] While this poem will never compete with "On First Looking into Chapman's Homer," it does give us an idea of how Johnson's contemporaries may have taken the biography. James Ralph's comment in *The Champion* that Johnson's "reflections open to all the recesses of the human heart" also evidences an interest in the emotional and psychological.[20]

Throughout the biography Johnson's style, whether he is summing up for the defense or deciding points as judge, remains balanced. His style earns him the right to say what he says. At one point he comments that he is trying to be "impartial"; yet if we feel that even at his most judicious he is not by any means impartial, we may still perceive that he is presenting complicated truth. The difference can be observed in Johnson's defense of Savage's veracity: "his Accounts, tho' not indeed always the same, were generally consistent. When he loved any Man, he suppress'd all his Faults, and when he had been offended by him, concealed all his Virtues, but his Characters were generally true, so far as he proceeded; tho' it cannot be denied that his Partiality might have sometimes the Effect of Falsehood" (p. 139). Johnson loved Savage but never suppresses his faults, and in this sense his life is both impartial and true, just as in a later biography he does not attempt to conceal the virtues of the loathed Puritan clergyman, Francis Cheynel (1751). Johnson's shifts from lawyer for the defense to judge keep us from feeling too greatly the lack of a prosecuting attorney.

A good example of Johnson's method is observable in his account of the quarrel of Steele and Savage:

19. *Gentleman's Magazine*, 15 (1745), 633. I discuss some aspects of this poem in "Pope and Johnson's *Life of Savage*," *N & Q*, n.s. 20 (June 1973), 211–12.
20. Quoted by Boswell, *Life*, I, 169 and n. 2.

It is not indeed unlikely that *Savage* might by his Imprudence expose himself to the Malice of a Tale-bearer; for his Patron had many Follies, which as his Discernment easily discovered, his Imagination might sometimes incite him to mention too ludicrously. A little Knowledge of the World is sufficient to discover that such Weakness is very common, and that there are few who do not sometimes in the Wantonness of thoughtless Mirth, or the Heat of transient Resentment, speak of their Friends and Benefactors with Levity and Contempt, though in their cooler Moments, they want neither Sense of their Kindness, nor Reverence for their Virtue. The fault therefore of Mr. *Savage* was rather Negligence than Ingratitude; but Sir *Richard* must likewise be acquitted of Severity, for who is there that can patiently bear Contempt from one whom he has relieved and supported, whose Establishment he has laboured, and whose Interest he has promoted? [P. 16]

The qualities are abstracted and summarized. This is the language which Mary Lascelles in her study of Jane Austen finely compares to the inheritance of "a prosperous and well-ordered estate—the heritage of a prose style in which neither generalization nor abstraction need signify vagueness, because there was close enough agreement as to the scope and significance of such terms."[21] Johnson's consideration of this series of events leads him to find that in some ways both are culpable, and yet in others both should be "acquitted" (though his skill in attributing Savage's troubles in part to his "Discernment" and "Imagination" should not go unnoticed). The word "acquitted," as William Vesterman has noted, "makes explicit the legal metaphor which has organized the paragraph."[22] Johnson frequently uses legal metaphors in his biographies, and his quotation of the great seventeenth-century jurist Matthew Hale at the conclusion of *Rambler* No. 60 suggests the stance is apt. Yet there is something especially appropriate in his use of them in a biography that begins with a divorce trial, moves through a trial for murder, and ends in a debtors' prison. The biography is full of such language. The later quarrel between Savage and Tyrconnel results in "mutual accusations" and still later Savage's detractors "alledge" that he treated his subscribers with contempt. Johnson himself is sometimes forced to use the phrase "it must be con-

21. *Jane Austen and Her Art* (Oxford: Oxford University Press, 1939), p. 107.
22. "Johnson and the *Life of Savage*," *ELH*, 36 (1969), 659–78.

fessed" and its variants (pp. 45, 96). Although not all are actionable, "charges" are lodged against Savage throughout his life.

In this judicial atmosphere the rhetoric that conveys Johnson's balanced judgments frequently contains a sting. In the following chiastic sentence, the first half is high enough praise to stand as a man's epitaph: "It was his peculiar Happiness, that he scarcely ever found a Stranger, whom he did not leave a Friend"; yet the reversal turns this seeming panegyric into the deadliest satire: "but it must likewise be added, that he had not often a Friend long, without obliging him to become a Stranger" (p. 60). This is the way Johnson solves the problem of portraying a man of such marked strengths and weaknesses. In an excellent essay on eighteenth-century biography Frank Brady speaks of the two sides of the life as the "heroic" and the "prudential" (which correspond in a rough way to the Johnsonian "Virtues and Vices"). He suggests that "the unresolved tension between these two main structural patterns accounts ... for much of the interest generated by the *Life of Savage*."[23] Unresolved perhaps; yet they are not separate themes or views, but the expression of separate traits of character in the same man, and by holding them in perilous balance through his rhetoric, Johnson shows us what becomes of Savage's life after all extenuation. Such oppositions sometimes lead to a series of pointed contrasts:

For the Acquisition of Knowledge he was indeed far better qualified than for that of Riches; for he was naturally inquisitive and desirous of the Conversation of those from whom any Information was to be obtained, but by no Means solicitous to improve those Opportunities that were sometimes offered of raising his Fortune; and was remarkably retentive of his Ideas, which, when once he was in Possession of them, rarely forsook him; a Quality which could never be communicated to his Money. [P. 102]

The careful ethical comparison ends with a sly zeugma.

Johnson's depiction of a man of great capabilities and low actions makes his biography seem now tragic, now satiric, but after all qualifications are entered and no reader is permitted an easy sneer, he emphasizes the prudential and exemplary nature of his biography in lines which oxymoronically yoke the opposed

23. "The Strategies of Biography," pp. 245–65.

qualities considered throughout the work: "Negligence and Irregularity, long continued, will make Knowledge useless, Wit ridiculous, and Genius Contemptible" (p. 140). This conclusion has behind it the awesome couplet art of Pope:

> A Fop their Passion, but their Prize a Sot,
> Alive, ridiculous, and dead forgot!

Like *The Dunciad*, this is tragic satire, but in a different key. If we have been given much to sympathize with in Johnson's *Savage*, the final judgment is social and coercive. Characteristically, the reader cannot exempt himself from the ethical conclusions. Although we have accompanied Johnson through the narrative, sharing his moral superiority and his heightened awareness, we are reminded that Savage was actually an extraordinary man and that we are not likely to have his knowledge, wit, or genius, and that even if our actual "Capacities or Attainments" are as superior as those we take to ourselves while we read, we are still subject to follies analogous to those of Savage.

Anyone who thinks that Johnson's biography is hopelessly bifurcated or simply goes up and down roller-coaster fashion, a breathtaking but essentially mindless trip, has not sufficiently pondered this last sentence, which at once celebrates and judges Savage while reminding us, as it turns a baleful glance our way, that all the dead can do is point a moral or adorn a tale. The pattern is precisely that of Johnson's great essay on biography, *Rambler* No. 60. There he asserts that "all joy or sorrow for the happiness or calamities of others is produced by an act of the imagination, that realizes the event, however fictitious, or approximates it however remote, by placing us, for a time, in the condition of him whose fortune we contemplate; so that we feel, while the deception lasts, whatever motions would be excited by the same good or evil happening to ourselves" (*Yale*, III, 318–19). We begin, then, with sympathy, "a Degree of Compassion," as Johnson carefully puts it, but we will end, as the conclusion of the essay, invoking the words of Matthew Hale, also informs us, with judgment: "'Let me remember,' says Hale, 'when I find myself inclined to pity a criminal, that there is likewise a pity due to the country.' If we owe regard to the memory of the dead, there is yet more respect to be paid to knowledge, to virtue, and to truth" (*Yale*, III, 323).

"This world is a comedy to those who think, a tragedy to those who feel." Johnson knew this even better than Walpole, and his biographies insist that one must perceive both sides. Is the death of Savage, or for that matter his life, comic or tragic? Johnson distrusts the reductiveness of genre criticism, and despite some triumphs of his method his attitude has been perceived as disabling him from understanding some of the intensities of Shakespearian tragedy. Yet as an artist in his own right he embodies the vagaries of life in a vision which draws its strength from its breadth, and the *Life of Savage* is finer and richer than a merely tragic or satiric interpretation of Savage would be for its refusal to reduce Savage's life to either. If the *Life of Savage* is tragedy *manqué*, the failure is Savage's, not Johnson's.

CHAPTER 10

Conclusion

The literary form most congenial to Johnson's assumptions about art and nature was not the drama, novel, or essay but biography. It presented what really happened in the world and was therefore of its very nature both true and valuable. "Of the various kinds of narrative writing," he thought it "that which is most eagerly read, and most easily applied to the purposes of life." On his own joy in reading biographies, all his biographers, for once, are in agreement.

When Johnson came on the scene he found, to use his own words, a "penury of English biography." Though he admired earlier English biographers such as Walton, and had at least read some of those we think well of today, such as Roper and Aubrey, relatively few good biographies existed, and, according to Boswell, Johnson "did not think that the life of any literary man in England had been well written." Despite the many problems Johnson faced, he did not have to face what Walter Jackson Bate has called "the burden of the past." He could be, and was, the greatest biographer England had seen.

What is the legacy of Johnsonian biography? The answer would seem to be obvious for most critics: Boswell's *Life of Johnson*. Here is how one highly respected eighteenth-century scholar and student of biography provides a transition from Johnson to Boswell: "This afternoon I have been examining the work of a biographer who was not always able to reconcile his practice, admirable as it was, with his theory. Tomorrow I shall

214

examine the work of his disciple, who accepted the teaching of his master to a very large extent, and was more consistent in putting those theories into practice."[1]

This opinion has been maintained so often, and so frequently as if it were self-evident, that the time to refute it has come. Such an opinion implies that Johnson's biographies are a flawed attempt to put Johnson's theories into practice and that Boswell's biography is a successful attempt to put Johnson's theories into practice. Johnson's "theory," of course, begins formally, apart from passing hints, only in 1751, seven years after the publication of the *Life of Savage*, and all his writings on biography together with his comments in conversation add up to a useful and suggestive body of statements, but they do not bulk very large or account very fully for his practice. More importantly, what is best in Johnson's biographies themselves is not to be found in Boswell's *Life of Johnson* (and conversely, what is best in Boswellian biography is not to be found in the *Lives of the Poets*), but this is not to the discredit of either writer.

How this state of affairs came about is another story. Apart from the significant but minor truth such a conception of the relationship of Johnson to Boswell contains (we can easily imagine the *Life of Johnson* being essentially what it is if Johnson had not written biographies or written about biography), this emphasis comes directly from the skillful rhetoric of James Boswell.

The first sentence of the *Life of Johnson* claims that "to write the life of him who excelled all mankind in writing the lives of others . . . is an arduous, and may be reckoned in me a presumptuous task," yet I think even here Boswell is not greatly worried about the burden of his subject's preeminence as biographer, for he knew that where his work diverged from Johnson's it was original and compelling on its own terms; and where they agreed, he could take the agreement as authenticating and endorsing his work. And he seems to have been keenly aware, as not enough of his critics have been since, just where Johnson and he differed.

1. John Butt, *Biography in the Hands of Walton, Johnson, and Boswell* (Los Angeles: University of California Press, 1966), p. 32.

What Boswell does, then, is to gain acceptance for his book by insisting insofar as he can that "when I delineate him without reserve, I do what he himself recommended by both his precept and his example," and that one cannot complain of a book which its subject would have heartily endorsed. (Froude was to employ the same strategy in his great *Life of Carlyle*.) Thus Boswell makes his book the culmination of the Johnson tradition, and the general judgment that Boswell's is the greatest of English biographies serves to relegate Johnson to a minor position.

In saying this Boswell was being honest; he was also defending himself in advance against the adverse criticism which was leveled against him in any case. The effect upon the criticism of Johnson, however, of a book that ostensibly employed Johnson's principles and at the same time incorporated the man himself within the work is traced in Bertrand Bronson's classic "The Double Tradition of Dr. Johnson."[2] To many critics of the nineteenth century the logic was inescapable: who needs the works of Johnson when we have Boswell?

And yet if we think for a moment about the most significant features of their books, large and small, they will surely be found to be different. Boswell is tolerant; his style, which is apt to go off in two directions in a given sentence, is the fit instrument of that embracing inclusiveness we find in the *Life of Johnson*. Johnson's varied style is ironic, thumpingly blunt or mordantly elevated, though capable of a wide range of other tones. The authoritative voice we hear in the *Lives of the Poets* is one of the triumphs of eighteenth-century narrative literature. It does not give us the characteristic tone of Boswell's *Life of Johnson*, for in that book we have the drama of different voices, notably Johnson's and Boswell's, played off one against the other. As Richard D. Altick has said, "There is no need to decide who excelled whom. . . . The two books are not rivals but complements."[3]

What is ultimately most impressive about Johnson's achieve-

2. First published in *ELH* (1951), this essay is easily available in Bronson's *Johnson Agonistes and Other Essays* (Berkeley: University of California Press, 1965), pp. 156–76.

3. *Lives and Letters: A History of Literary Biography in England and America* (New York: Alfred A. Knopf, 1965), p. 58.

ment as a biographer is the unity of form and purpose, the correspondence between his conception of man and the biographical style in which he conveys it. The sinewy strength of his biographies is provided by Johnson's skepticism. Skepticism links his unwillingness to let his subjects appear "magnified like the ancient actors in their tragic dress," his treatment of historical evidence, his typical need for reflective commentary, his separation of book and life so that each can be judged and analyzed, the caution with which he draws inferences from the poet's works, the pervasive irony to which he exposes his subjects' words and deeds.

Johnson himself shows an awareness of the relation of his biographical method to his skeptical cast of mind in a short prefatory note to his second biography, the "Life of Boerhaave": "We could have made it much larger by adopting flying Reports and inserting unattested Facts; a close Adherence to certainty has contracted our Narrative, and hindered it from swelling to that Bulk, at which modern Histories generally arrive" (*Works*, VI, 270). The suggestion is strong that the life-and-times tradition lends itself to reverence and the concise tradition to skepticism, wit, and even satire. This emphasis on conciseness and skepticism remains constant and appears, to take a few instances, as a "succinct narration" in the "Life of Blake" or "little Lives and little Prefaces" when he comes to write the *Live of the Poets*. "To reduce this narrative to credibility," he says of an account of Burman's seemingly remarkable attainments as a student, "it is necessary that admiration should give place to inquiry" (*Works*, VI, 398). Not to admire is hardly all the art Johnson knows, but his skeptical attitude makes his admiration more convincing when it comes.

In his "Review of the *Account of the Conduct of the Dutchess of Marlborough*" he sums up the attitude that serves so often as the starting point for his work: "distrust is a necessary qualification of a student in history" (*Works*, VI, 5). Johnson's intention to "promote piety" in the *Lives of the Poets* most often involves pulling down vanity. His distrust is usually exercised in reducing reported actions to credibility. Throughout his works we find shrewd appraisals of evidence and a consistently skeptical attitude toward appearances. This is part and parcel of his whole conception of man, for if the Romantic biographer is apt to overrate his subject, to sympathize with him at every turn, to accommodate himself to the ineffable genius of the poet, to dwell lovingly on his every action, he is also likely to take his subject's words at face value and to put the most favorable construction upon whatever comes his way.

Johnson's particular brand of skepticism remains valuable, especially since Stracheyan liberties with evidence have brought Strachey's brand of skepticism into disrepute. Indeed, we can draw an arsenal of skeptical aphorisms from the *Lives of the Poets*: "Seldom any splendid story is wholly true" (*Dorset*; I, 305); "Pointed axioms and acute replies fly loose about the world and are assigned to those whom it may be the fashion to celebrate" (*Waller*; I, 275); "Large offers and sturdy rejections are among the most common topics of falsehood" (*Milton*; I, 132). As one might guess from such an emphasis on truth, Johnson's inaccuracies are failures of the flesh, not the spirit. Accuracy, as A. E. Housman put it, "is a duty, not a virtue," and Johnson was always scrupulous about letting his readers know where he had failed in his duties, but we often have to search out his virtues for ourselves. Writing to Charles Burney about the historian of music's forthcoming *Commemoration of Handel*, Johnson says, "That your book has been delayed, I am glad, since you have gained an opportunity of being more exact.—Of the caution necessary in adjusting narratives there is no end. Some tell what they do not know, that they may not seem ignorant, and others from mere indifference about truth. All truth is not, indeed, of equal importance; but if little violations are allowed, every violation will in time be thought little" (*Letters*, III, 243). This is Johnson's settled conviction and deserves to be pasted on the wall in front of the scholar's desk. It is the proper antidote for those who want to take too seriously the complaints in the *Life of Dryden*.

And this belief also explains why Strachey, who is the foremost twentieth-century inheritor of the tradition of critical biography, the Johnson tradition, is such an equivocal legatee. Although Strachey's preface to *Eminent Victorians* is the only defense of biography in English worthy to stand alongside *Rambler* No. 60, to write as Johnson did one needs to be skeptical of oneself, and Strachey, who had distrust aplenty for unexamined assumptions and paradoxes of personality, was not ready to apply such sharp weapons to his own position. I do not mean to denigrate Strachey, for I think that his too frequent crudity and irresponsibility have masked for many the real seriousness of which his humor is a part. To find the tradition of critical biography at its best, however, we must return to Johnson, whose work is unique and indispensable.

Bibliography

Note

Those who wish to look farther into the subject can consult my annotated bibliography in "Samuel Johnson as Biographer" (Ph.D. diss., Cornell University, 1968), pp. 158–75; Lawrence Lipking's "Bibliographical Sketch," Part IV, in *The Ordering of the Arts* (Princeton: Princeton University Press, 1970), pp. 484–87; and James L. Clifford and Donald J. Greene's *Samuel Johnson: A Survey and Bibliography of Critical Studies* (Minneapolis: University of Minnesota Press, 1970), especially the sections "The *Life of Savage* and other Early Biographies" and "The *Lives of the Poets*." The standard bibliography is William Prideaux Courtney and David Nichol Smith, *A Bibliography of Samuel Johnson* (Oxford: Clarendon Press, 1925) along with R. W. Chapman and Allen T. Hazen, "Johnsonian Bibliography: A Supplement to Courtney," *Proceedings of the Oxford Bibliographical Society*, 5 (1939), 119–66. See also Studies of Johnson's Biographies, below, for articles devoted to the sources. A good rule of thumb in reading Johnson criticism is that the value of the work varies inversely with the number of references to "the Great Cham," "Ursa Major," etc.

First Editions of Johnson's Biographies, Related Writings, and Attributions

The First Editions of Johnson's Biographies.

The editions are listed below in order of publication. For more information about these and subsequent editions, see Clifford-Greene, Courtney-Smith, and Chapman-Hazen. Courtney-Smith, long the standard, sometimes omits significant terms from the titles of the biographies. Throughout this list the *Gentleman's Magazine* appears as *GM*. J. D. Fleeman brings together almost all of the early biographies in *Early Biographical Writings of Dr Johnson* (Westmead: Gregg International, 1973). I call attention to some of his choices of edition below.

"The Life of Father Paul Sarpi, Author of the History of the Council of Trent." *GM*, 8 (1738), 581–83.

"The Life of Dr Herman Boerhaave, late Professor of Physick in the University of Leyden in Holland." *GM*, 9 (1739), 37–38, 72–73, 114–16, 172–76.

"The Life of Admiral Blake." *GM*, 10 (1740), 301–7.

The Supplement to the *GM* this year includes a map with inset portrait of Blake opposite p. 660.

"The Life of Sir Francis Drake."*GM*, 10 (1740), 389–96, 443–47, 509–15, 600–603; 11 (1741), 38–44.

"Some Account of the Life of John Philip Barretier." *GM*, 10 (1740), 612; 11 (1741), 87–88, 93. "Additional Account of the Life of Mr John Philip Barretier." *GM*, 12 (1742), 242–45.

Johnson brought the accounts of Barretier—actually Baratier—together coherently in a pamphlet of 1744, "An Account of the Life of John Philip Barretier." Fleeman reprints this pamphlet.

"A Panegyric on Dr Morin, by Mr Fontenelle." *GM*, 11 (1741), 375–77.

Although presented as straight translation of an *éloge*, this is a characteristic adaptation.

"An Account of the Life of Peter Burman." *GM*, 12 (1742), 206–10.

"The Life of Dr Sydenham." In *The Entire Works of Thomas Sydenham*, ed. John Swann, pp. v–x. London, 1742. And *GM*, 12 (1742), 633–36.

Various lives in *Medicinal Dictionary*, ed. Robert James. London, 1743–45. Johnson's contributions remain uncertain.

See Allen Hazen's articles in the *Bulletin of the Institute of the History of Medicine*: "Samuel Johnson and Robert James," 4 (1936), 455–65, and "Johnson's Life of Frederic Ruysch," 7 (1939), 324–34. Fleeman reprints the lives of Actuarius, Aegineta, Aesculapius, Aetius, Alexander, Archagathus, Aretaeus, Asclepiades, Oribasius, Tournefort, and Ruysch.

An Account of the Life of Mr Richard Savage, Son of the Earl Rivers. London, 1744.

Revised for the *Lives of the Poets*. Fleeman reprints the second edition of 1748, which Tracy takes as copy text for his *Savage*..

"Life of the Earl of Roscommon." *GM*, 18 (1748), 214-17.
Revised for the *Lives of the Poets*.
"The Life of Dr. Francis Cheynel." *The Student*, 2 (1751), 260-69, 290-94, 331-34.
Actually Cheynell; Johnson also characteristically wrote "Boswel."
"An Account of the Life of the late Mr Edward Cave." *GM*, 24 (1754), 55-58.
Fleeman reprints the little-known revision of this life for the *Biographia Britannica* (1784).
"The Life of Sir Thomas Browne." In Thomas Browne, *Christian Morals*, pp. i-lxi. 2d ed. London, 1756.
"Memoirs of the King of Prussia." *Literary Magazine*, 1 (1756), 327-33, 389-90, 439-42. With portraits, 326.
Charles Frederick, better known today as Frederick the Great.
"The Life of Roger Ascham." In *The English Works of Roger Ascham*, ed. James Bennet, pp. i-xvi. London, 1761.
The whole book may have been edited by Johnson.
"The Life of the Author." In Zachary Pearce, *A Commentary with Notes on the Four Evangelists and the Acts of the Apostles . . . to the Whole is Prefixed some Account of his Lordship's Life and Character, Written by Himself*, ed. John Derby, I, i-xlv. 2 vols. London, 1777.
I accept this biography, which incorporates Pearce's autobiography, as fully Johnson's. See also R. W. Chapman, "Johnson's Works: A Lost Piece and a Forgotten Piece," *London Mercury*, 21 (1930), 438-44. Not included or discussed by Fleeman.
Prefaces, Biographical and Critical, to the Works of the English Poets, 10 vols., I-IV (London, 1779), v-x (1781). Revised 1781, 1783.
Vol. I. Cowley, 1-165; Waller, 1-128.
Vol. II. Milton, 1-223; Butler, 1-39.
Vol. III. Dryden, 1-349.
Vol. IV. Denham, 1-31; Sprat, 1-15; Roscommon, 1-27; Rochester, 1-20; Yalden, 1-12; Otway, 1-12; Duke, 1-4; Dorset, 1-9; Halifax, 1-12; Stepney, 1-6; Walsh, 1-5; Garth, 1-13; King, 1-11; J. Philips, 1-42; Smith, 1-64; Pomfret, 1-4; Hughes, 1-13.
Vol. V. Addison, 1-162; Blackmore, 1-53; Sheffield, 1-20.
Vol. VI. Granville, 1-56; Rowe, 1-30; Tickell, 1-43; Congreve, 1-38; Fenton, 1-19; Prior, 1-63.
Vol. VII. Pope, 1-373.
Vol. VIII. Swift, 1-112; Gay, 1-30; Broome, 1-12; Pitt, 1-7; Parnell, 1-11; A. Philips, 1-23; Watts, 1-24.
Vol. IX. Savage, 1-147 (small type); Somervile, 1-7; Thomson, 1-40; Hammond, 1-11; Collins, 1-14.

Vol. X. Young, 1–113 (biographical section by Herbert Croft); Dyer, 1–8; Mallet, 1–16; Shenstone, 1–20; Akenside, 1–18; Lyttelton, 1–22; West, 1–15; Gray, 1–56.

Related Writings

Here I list a few pieces by Johnson which, while not simply or solely biographies, deserve mention. I include also a piece by John Nichols to which Johnson contributed.

"Essay on the Description of China in two Volumes Folio. From the French of Jean Baptiste Du Halde." *GM*, 12 (1742), 320–23, 354–57, 484–86.

Jacob Leed suggests that Johnson's extensive reworking of the materials on Confucius in this review warrants our attention as a biographical sketch. See "Johnson, Du Halde, and 'The Life of Confucius,'" *BNYPL*, 70 (1966), 189–99. Fleeman reprints pp. 354–57.

["Some Account of the Admirable Crichton"], *The Adventurer*, No. 81, August 14, 1953. Not in Fleeman.

The title appears in the table of contents to the first collected edition (1753–54) and is probably not Johnson's.

[Character of William Collins]. In Francis Fawkes and William Woty, "Some Account of Mr. William Collins," *Poetical Calendar*, 12 (1763), 110–12.

Johnson used this character, slightly revised, in the *Lives*. Fleeman reprints the whole "Account."

[Death Notice of Zachariah Mudge]. *London Chronicle*, April 29–May 2 1769, p. 410.

Fleeman reprints.

"Biographical Notice of ... Dr. Thirlby." *GM*, 54 (1784), 260–262.

By John Nichols, incorporating manuscript anecdotes by Johnson which amount to nearly half of the material on Thirlby. Fleeman reprints.

Attributions

This list includes some attributions which I consider false and a few probationers for admission to the canon.

The History of Tahmas Kuli Khan, Shah, or Sophi of Persia. Extracted from the French. London, 1740.

Attributed by Frederick V. Bernard, "The History of Nadir Shah: A New Attribution to Johnson," *British Museum Quarterly*, 34 (1973), 92–104. An interesting argument on the basis of external and inter-

nal evidence that Johnson translated this work for Wilcox, an early
publisher-friend for whom he undertook no known work. Stylisti-
cally, the piece is at times even more like Johnson's work than Bernard indicates.

"The Life of Nicholas Rienzy." *GM*, 16 (1746), 1-6, 65-67.

Attributed in the *European Magazine* (1785) as a piece which "has been
pointed out, but with no degree of certainty" as Johnson's. I find this
highly conjectural attribution very unlikely.

"Sir Thomas de Veil's Life." *GM*, 17 (1757), 562.

Attributed by C[arl] Lennart Carlson, *The First Magazine: A History of
the Gentleman's Magazine* (Providence: Brown University Press, 1938),
p. 132. He claims "a part" for Johnson, but I find no part Johnsonian.

"Supplement to the Life of M. Burman." *GM*, 18 (1748), 405-07.

Convincing attribution by Donald Greene in his manuscript list of
Johnson attributions, which he kindly lent me. He says it seems to be
"a continuation" and translation of remarks in the *Bibliothèque Raison-
née* by J. Wetstein on Burman's edition of Virgil.

"Some Account of the Life and Writings of Chaucer." *Universal Visiter
and Monthly Memorialist*, 1 (1756), 9-15.

Signed ** and attributed in the *European Magazine*, rejected by Boswell and by Edward A. Bloom; supported by Roland B. Botting
(1939). Although signed the same way as three of Johnson's authentic
pieces in this periodical, it is, as Donald D. Eddy informs me, an
abridgment of Thomas Birch's biography in George Vertue's *Heads of
Illustrious Persons of Great Britain* (1743).

"Some Account of the Life and Writings of the late Dr Richard Mead."
GM, 24 (1756), 510-15.

Attributed by John Lawrence Abbott, "Samuel Johnson and 'The Life
of Dr. Richard Mead,' " *Bulletin of the John Rylands Library*, 54 (1971),
12-27. The piece is a translation from the *Journal Britannique*. Abbott,
who has studied the sources of Johnson's translations from the
French in a series of careful articles, is certainly well qualified to make
such an attribution, but despite Johnson's interest in Mead and other
work for the *GM* at this time, I find the attribution unconvincing.
Abbott has usefully ruled out Hawkesworth as a candidate.

"Memoirs of the late Dr Berkeley, Bishop of Cloyne." *Annual Register*, 6
(1763), 2-5.

Attributed in *Works* (1788), XIV, 427. Rejected in *Works* (1789). Although Monk Berkeley told a fuzzy story of Johnson's seeking family
permission to write a life of the great philosopher, there is no reason
for thinking that this is it.

"Memoirs of Oliver Goldsmith, M.B." In *The Vicar of Wakefield with the Life of the Author by Dr Johnson*. New York: E. Gee, 1826.
This work has been exposed by E. L. McAdam, Jr., as essentially based on Malone, "PseudoJohnsoniana," *MP*, 41 (1944), 186–87.

Studies of Johnson's Biographies

The list below cites the most important studies of individual lives following the order of publication of the lives as established above. Modern study of Johnson's sources must properly begin with Bergen Evans' unpublished (and difficult to obtain) doctoral dissertation, "Dr. Johnson as a Biographer" (Harvard, 1932). This work, which is too little known, tracks down most of the sources for all the lives except *Shenstone* (q.v.). Hill's notes to his edition of the *Lives* (Oxford: Clarendon Press, 1905) contain much information, often textually inaccurate. Sir Walter Raleigh's *Six Essays on Johnson* (Oxford: Clarendon Press, 1910) has something to say of the collections preceding Johnson's, and Edward A. Bloom discusses the sources of a number of early lives briefly in *Samuel Johnson in Grub Street* (Providence: Brown University Press, 1957). Studies of particular sources include W. R. Keast, "Johnson and 'Cibber's' *Lives of the Poets*, 1753," *Restoration and Eighteenth-Century English Literature: Essays in Honor of Alan Dugald McKillop*, ed. Carroll Camden (Chicago: University of Chicago Press, 1963) on Johnson's contribution to the work, nominally by Cibber but chiefly by Shiels (a double deception, for the Cibber was not Colley but Theophilus). The materials for a study of Johnson's use of Spence are to be found in James M. Osborn's edition of *Observations, Anecdotes, and Characters of Books and Men* (Oxford: Clarendon Press, 1966). In addition to articles devoted to the sources of the individual biographies listed below, John Lawrence Abbott considers the sources of "Sarpi," "Morin," and *A Medicinal Dictionary* in the context of Johnson's ideas about translation in "No 'Dialect of France': Samuel Johnson's Translations from the French," *UTQ*, 36 (1967), 129–40.

"Sarpi": J. L. Abbott, "Dr Johnson and the Making of the Life of Father Paul Sarpi," *Bulletin of the John Rylands Library*, 48 (1966), 255–67. And see McAdam below (s.v. "Blake").

"Blake": E. L. McAdam considers this biography in "Johnson's Lives of Sarpi, Blake and Drake," *PMLA* 58 (1943), 466–76, but he does not realize that Johnson is working from the *General Dictionary* rather than from *Lives English and Forrein*, as Bergen Evans had pointed out eleven years earlier.

"Drake": See McAdam above (s.v. "Blake").

"Morin": John L. Abbott, "Samuel Johnson's 'A Panegyric on Dr. Morin,'" *Romance Notes*, 8 (1966), 55–57.

Medicinal Dictionary: See the entries under this listing in First Editions of Johnson's Biographies, above, and J. L. Abbott, "Dr. Johnson, Fontenelle, LeClerc, and Six French Lives," *MP*, 63 (1965), 121–27.

Savage: Richard E. Lyon, introduction to "The Life of Richard Savage: An Edition" (Ph.D. diss., University of Chicago, 1958); Benjamin Boyce, "Johnson's *Life of Savage* and Its Literary Background," *SP*, 53 (1956), 576–98; Clarence Tracy, ed., *Life of Savage* (Oxford: Clarendon Press, 1971); J. D. Fleeman, "The Making of Johnson's *Life of Savage*, 1744," *The Library*, 5th ser., 22 (1967), 346–52. This last is a bibliographical essay which clears up some source problems as well.

"Roscommon": Charles L. Batten, Jr., "Samuel Johnson's Sources for 'The Life of Roscommon,'" *MP*, 72 (1974), 185–89.

"King of Prussia": F. V. Bernard, "A Possible Source for Johnson's *Life of the King of Prussia*," *PQ*, 47 (1968), 206–15.

Prefaces (*Lives of the Poets*):

    Cowley: George Lorent Lam, "Johnson's *Lives of the Poets*: Their Origin, Text and History, with Remarks on Sources and Comment on his *Life of Cowley*" (Ph.D. diss., Cornell, 1938). Repeats, unknowingly it would seem, a good deal of Evans' work on the *Lives*.

    Dryden: James M. Osborn, *John Dryden: Some Biographical Facts and Problems* (New York: Columbia University Press, 1940).

    Roscommon: See listing above.

    King: "Some New Sources of Johnson's *Lives*," *PMLA*, 65 (1950), 1088–1111. This article comments on John Nichols' aid to Johnson in the *Lives*.

    Addison: James Lyons Battersby, Jr., "Samuel Johnson's *Life of Addison*: Sources, Composition, and Structure" (Ph.D. diss., Cornell, 1965); James L. Battersby, "Johnson and Shiels: Biographers of Addison," *SEL*, 9 (1969), 522–37.

    Pope: Frederick W. Hilles, "The Making of *The Life of Pope*," in *New Light on Johnson*, ed. Frederick W. Hilles (New Haven: Yale University Press, 1959), pp. 257–84.

    Swift: Harold Williams, "Swift's Early Biographers," in *Pope and His Contemporaries: Essays Presented to George Sherburn*, ed. James L. Clifford and Louis Landa (Oxford: Clarendon Press, 1949), pp. 114–28; Wayne Warncke, "Samuel Johnson on Swift: The *Life of Swift* and Johnson's Predecessors in Swiftian Biography," *JBS* 7 (1968), 56–64.

Savage: See listing above.

Thomson: Hilbert H. Campbell, "Shiels and Johnson: Biographers of Thomson," *SEL*, 12 (1972), 535–44.

Young: Henry Pettit, "The Making of Croft's Life of Young for Johnson's *Lives of the Poets*," *PQ*, 54 (1974), 333–41.

Shenstone: James H. Leicester, "Johnson's Life of Shenstone: Some Observations on the Sources," in *Johnsonian Studies*, ed. Magdi Wahba (Cairo: Privately printed, 1962), pp. 189–222.

Index

Entries for Johnson's biographies are listed individually under Johnson, *Works*. References to Johnson's subjects independent of the biographies will be found under their own names.

Library of Congress Cataloging in Publication Data
(For library cataloging purposes only)

Folkenflik, Robert, 1939–
  Samuel Johnson, biographer.

  Bibliography: p.
  Includes index.
  1. Johnson, Samuel, 1709–1784—Criticism and
interpretation.   2.   Biography (as a literary form)
I. Title.
PR3537.B54F64   828'.6'09   78-58050
  ISBN 0-8014-0968-3

237